Lee, R Alton.

Truman and Taft-Hartley

TRUMAN AND TAFT-HARTLEY

Truman and Taft-Hartley

a question of mandate

R Alton Lee

GREENWOOD PRESS, PUBLISHERS
WESTPORT, CONNECTICUT

Library of Congress Cataloging in Publication Data

Lee, R Alton.
Truman and Taft-Hartley.

Reprint of the ed. published by the University of Kentucky Press, Lexington.
Bibliography: p.
Includes index.
1. Labor policy--United States--History.
2. Truman, Harry S., Pres. U.S., 1884-1972.
3. United States. Laws, statutes, etc. Labor management relations act, 1947. 4. United States--Politics and government--1945--1953. I. Title.
[HD8072.L33 1980] 331'.0973 80-17251
ISBN 0-313-22618-0 (lib. bdg.)

FOR MY MOTHER AND FATHER

Reprinted in 1980 by Greenwood Press,
A division of Congressional Information Service, Inc.
88 Post Road West, Westport, Connecticut 06881

Printed in the United States of America

10 9 8 7 6 5 4 3 2 1

PREFACE

ONE OF THE important characteristics of contemporary American politics is a dichotomy in the national constituency. In recent years the President of the United States has increasingly owed his election to, and tends to represent the interests of, the urban laborer. The United States Congress, on the other hand, tends to be dominated by members who are elected by, and reflect the interests of, the business, middle-class, and agricultural segments of American society. The result is a fundamental cleavage between the executive and legislative branches beyond that intended in the constitutional system of checks and balances—a situation which practically makes for a deadlock for liberal legislation. This is accentuated when the two branches are controlled by different parties and is distinguished by an increasing use of the presidential veto.

Thus, since the Great Depression, a President seeking legislation to assist the lower socio-economic urban groups has been frustrated by a majority coalition of conservative Republicans and Southern Democrats in Congress that functions regardless of which party has control of the legislature. Since the beginning of the New Deal, which brought about an increase in government activities for social welfare, these congressmen have cooperated closely in trying to bring about a termination of this so-called paternalism. This has been particularly true in the period since 1945 and the executive branch has been hard-pressed to defeat the assaults of this conservative opposition upon the progressive legislative achievements of the 1930s and upon any efforts to enlarge upon these foundations, as has been the liberals' desire.

The New Deal, which had begun a program of profound reform in social and economic melioration, had been stimulated by the most severe depression in history and was interrupted by the most devastating war the world had yet endured. In the chaos of the "reconversion" era, the period of transition from war to peace, the American public suffered from extreme frustration and confusion over the postwar world they faced and a political reaction ensued. The elections of 1946 resulted in a Congress controlled by a combination of conservatives representing agrarian and business interests. This Eightieth Congress passed the Taft-Hartley Act over President Harry S. Truman's veto in an attempt to curtail the growing power of their opposition, organized labor. Truman subsequently fought for its repeal in an effort to assist a major segment of his constituency, the urban workers.

This volume traces the early political history of the Taft-Hartley law, using the national labor policy issue as an illustration of the functioning of this political phenomenon. It is not intended to be a complete history of the act from either the political or administrative viewpoint. Rather, it is a case study of the struggle between the agricultural and industrial groups that dominated Congress and the laboring elements that, through the President, controlled the executive branch of the government. Emphasis has been placed upon the influence of public opinion and the effect that this labor issue had in continuing the Democratic-labor alliance created during the New Deal.

The decision of the United States Supreme Court in *Reynolds v. Sims,* rendered June 15, 1964, enhances the historical value of this study. In this decision, the court used the phrase "one man, one vote" to describe its application of the equal-protection clause of the Fourteenth Amendment in ordering the state legislatures involved to redistrict their states on the basis of population. One possible result of this precedent could be, eventually, a Congress based upon actual representation of population and thus a revision of the present dichotomy in national politics. However, urban voters undoubtedly still face a prolonged struggle to achieve completely an equal representation in the House of Representatives.

I am deeply indebted to Professor Gilbert C. Fite of the University of Oklahoma for his encouragement, counsel, and criticism of this book. I also owe a debt of gratitude to his colleagues Dean John S. Ezell and Professors William E. Livezey of the Department of History and John H. Leek of the Department of Government for their penetrating comments. And I would be remiss if I neglected to thank William R. Johnson of Texas Technological College, Robert L. Branyan, and Jesse Clardy of the University of Missouri at Kansas City, Theodore H. Brown of the University of Wisconsin, Milwaukee, Gerlof Homan of Kansas State College, and Herman Fullgraf and Edmund R. Whitson of Central State College, Edmond, Oklahoma, who offered numerous observations and suggestions on parts of the manuscript. However, I alone am responsible for any errors in fact or interpretation that remain.

I must also express my appreciation to the Harry S. Truman Library Institute for a grant that provided financial assistance for the research. Dr. Philip C. Brooks, Philip D. Lagerquist, and the staff at the Harry S. Truman Library deserve special recognition for their services, which greatly facilitated the research. I would also like to thank Dr. Kenneth LaBudde's library staff at the University of Missouri at Kansas City, Mr. Morris Rieger of the National Archives, and Mr. Tom Baker of the Central State College Library for their assistance. Finally, I should commend my wife, not only for her excellent job of typing the manuscript, but also for her patience and understanding during the throes of authorship, and Michael, for being "quiet" while Daddy was working.

Vermillion, South Dakota R. ALTON LEE

CONTENTS

1

THE DICHOTOMY IN POSTWAR AMERICAN POLITICS

THE TAFT-HARTLEY ACT of 1947 aroused as much controversy and political contention as any domestic policy formulated by Congress in the decade after World War II. This legislation was conceived in a period of particularly bitter labor-management strife arising from the struggle to convert from a wartime to a peacetime economy. As Harry S. Truman declared, this labor unrest presented his administration with "one of the most difficult and persistent of all the domestic problems" he encountered as President.[1] And for several years after its passage, politicians as well as labor and management were stimulated to zealous denunciation or praise at the very mention of the Taft-Hartley Act in their appeals for public support.

In the ensuing controversy over this law, which altered the basic labor policy of the United States, it soon became familiar to every American, at least by name although not necessarily by content. In fact, this was one of the many curious features of the Taft-Hartley Act—in legal terms it was one of the most complicated laws that Congress ever passed and yet its name became almost a household word for a period of time. The average citizen regarded the act as all black or all white, depending upon his background and experience or more particularly upon his exposure to the pro or the con propaganda that flooded the country.

Public opinion concerning this law is highly significant, for popular pressure played an important part not only in its formulation but also in the various attempts to repeal or amend it. Public opinion in a democracy, for good or ill, plays a vital role in the creation of congressional policy and in its administration; thus, in a democracy, public opinion must be courted and won before a national policy can be effected. The Taft-Hartley Act provides an excellent example of this fact of national political life. The act was conceived and adopted in the heat of appeals for popular support and was subsequently used to influence voters in political campaigns that followed its passage. However, in spite of this, only a few citizens who expressed an opinion about the law actually comprehended the various ramifications of its far-reaching provisions.

The political history of the Taft-Hartley Act during the administrations of President Harry S. Truman graphically illustrates that the Congress and the President of the United States are elected by different constituencies. Contemporary American political society is a dichotomy of two basic interests, a rural faction and an urban faction. Although these in turn splinter into various groups, some of whose interests coincide and others conflict, the fundamental cleavage remains intact and is solidifying even more as the progression from an agrarian to a highly industrialized

[1] Harry S. Truman, *Memoirs* (Garden City, N.Y.: Doubleday, 1955), I, 495.

nation becomes more pronounced. The agrarian tradition of the United States is reflected and maintained in the composition of Congress, especially the House of Representatives. The legislative branch of the national government has remained the stronghold of the farm element throughout most of the nation's history and represents the middle-class and business interests of the nation as well. Congress has always been, and remains today, the citadel for these inherently conservative elements. This is illustrated by the fact that well over a majority of the members of the House of Representatives come from districts which have no city larger than 50,000 population. When Truman became President there were 248 nonindustrial districts represented in Congress and only 187 industrial districts.[2] Thus, on domestic policies, Congress tends to reflect the interests and desires of the farm, middle-class, and business segments of the nation and, in regard to labor policy, its actions incline toward antiunionism. This does not hold true for the Senate as much as for the House of Representatives. Senators, elected on a statewide basis rather than by districts, tend to have broader interests and influences than Representatives that compel them to consider their urban labor constituents as well as their rural and business supporters. The Senate, therefore, tends to be more liberal than the House since its constituencies are more heterogeneous and have more of the characteristics associated with liberalism than the constituencies of Representatives.

The President, on the other hand, represents a different constituency. As election to this office is determined by the electoral majority of each state, the urban vote is decisive, particularly in the highly industrialized states. With the tremendous growth of labor unions during and since the

[2] Stephen K. Bailey and Howard D. Samuel, *Congress at Work* (New York: Holt, 1952), p. 414; Wilfred E. Binkley, *President and Congress* (New York: Vintage, 1962), p. 342.

New Deal, organized labor has become increasingly important in national politics. In 1947 there were approximately 15,000,000 union members, with the AFL (American Federation of Labor) accounting for about 7,000,000, the CIO (Congress of Industrial Organizations) some 6,000,000, and the unaffiliated unions 2,000,000. These numbers, representing roughly a potential 30,000,000 votes, counting the workers' wives, can be a tremendously decisive factor in a national election, if cohesively organized. Thus by contrast with the constituencies of Congress, the industrialized centers of the nation where organized labor is strongest make their political power felt by dominating the electoral vote of their state and, to a lesser degree, the election of Senators. In recent years, the President of the United States has increasingly relied upon the city worker for his election and subsequently, in domestic policies, tends to reflect and sympathize with the interests of labor.

This phenomenon of dual constituency is illustrated on the state level by the fact that many state legislatures are controlled by the agricultural interests which predominated when states were first districted perhaps a century or more ago. Industrialization and the laborer have since come to predominate but urban voters are denied their full potential political power by the agricultural interests, which refuse to redistrict and thus preserve their unjustified power. These state legislatures in turn affect the composition of the national Congress by dividing their states into districts for the election of members to the House of Representatives in such a manner as to permit agrarian interests to be overrepresented.

This underrepresentation of the urban population in Congress is not a result of mere chance. When Congress established the membership of the House of Representatives at 435 in 1929, it significantly omitted the traditional restriction upon state legislatures that congressional districts be compact, contiguous, and contain "as nearly as practicable an equal number of inhabitants." The original bill contained this stipulation when first introduced[3] but during the course of debate[4] it was deleted from the final measure that the President signed into law June 18, 1929.[5] This lack of federal restraint then permitted rural-dominated state legislatures to gerrymander their states so as to overrepresent grossly the agricultural, business, and middle-class interests in the House of Representatives. Urban populations seemed powerless in their attempts to achieve redress until 1962, when the Supreme Court ruled in *Baker v. Carr* that state apportionment laws are subject to federal judicial review under the equal-protection clause of the Fourteenth Amendment.[6] Two years later the Supreme Court broadened this interpretation in *Reynolds v. Sims* by interpreting the equal protection clause to mean "one person, one vote" and ordered certain state legislatures to redistrict their congressional districts on this basis of equal representation.[7] But during the period between the 1929 apportionment law and these decisions, there was no federal control over gerrymandering with its resulting dichotomy in national politics.

This dual constituency has been exemplified in national politics, since the advent of the New Deal in particular, by the increasing use of the presidential veto in the field of domestic affairs. Samuel Lubell, the noted political analyst, has pointed out that the current "President-Congress conflict" which began in 1938 is the longest such "duel" in American history and that it stems from the development of pro-New Deal elements that are concentrated in the cities where New Deal reforms had the greatest impact, whereas anti-New Dealers are "rooted largely in agricultural con-

3 *Congressional Record,* 70 Cong., 2 Sess., 1928, LXX, 1490.
4 *Ibid.,* p. 1604.
5 *Ibid.,* 71 Cong., 1 Sess., 1929, LXXI, 3023.
6 *Baker v. Carr,* 369 U.S. 186 (1962).
7 *Reynolds v. Sims,* 377 U.S. 533 (1964).

stituencies" where the American myths and traditions of "free enterprise" and "rugged individualism" have remained more strongly rooted. These opposing coalitions have "entrenched" themselves in the executive and legislative branches of the national government, respectively.[8]

One of the major aspects of the New Deal was the entrance of the federal government into the sphere of labor-management relations where it began, for the first time, to play an active, positive role. This initial effort of the national government was made on behalf of unions to assist them in organizing members.

Labor was slow to match the organization and growth established by American industry. As the industrial giants arose, organized, and expanded, laboring men in turn were forced to coordinate their actions and bargain collectively with these colossi to maintain and better their working conditions. Also, as machine technology increased, the worker began to lose his identity as an individual part of the productive process and this stimulated the need for organization to promote and protect his interests. But the concepts of "free enterprise" and "rugged individualism" had become ingrained American traditions that retarded this labor regimentation. Thus, the early labor movement was restrained by the use of government injunction to curtail labor activities, with the organization of labor being looked upon as a type of conspiracy in restraint of trade, and certain union practices were restricted through court interpretation of the antitrust laws. Congress then passed the Norris-LaGuardia Act in 1932—"Labor's Magna Carta"—which restricted the use of the injunction in labor disputes, thus more or less neutralizing the role of government in labor-management strife.

With the advent of the Great Depression and the New

[8] Samuel Lubell, *The Future of American Politics* (New York: Harper, 1956), p. 250.

Deal, the attitude of the nation and the federal government underwent a marked change. The Democratic party, under the leadership of Franklin D. Roosevelt, revised the national labor policy so as to stimulate the organization of labor. This positive role of government in labor matters had its inception in Section 7(a) of the National Industrial Recovery Act of 1933 when, for the first time, workers were given a guarantee of the basic right to organize and bargain collectively under the "Blue Eagle" codes. When the Supreme Court declared the NIRA unconstitutional in *Schechter v. United States*,[9] Section 7(a) was revived and enlarged, serving as the basis for the National Labor Relations Act, or Wagner Act, of 1935. This statute placed the national government in the role of encouraging the organization of labor. It placed restrictions upon employers in the form of prohibiting unfair labor practices which had been used in the past to discourage such organization. A three-man National Labor Relations Board was established to administer the law. The purpose of the Wagner Act, as declared in its statement of policy, was "to eliminate the causes of certain substantial obstructions to the free flow of commerce . . . by encouraging the practice and procedure of collective bargaining and by protecting the exercise of workers of full freedom of association, self-organization, and designation of representatives of their own choosing, for the purpose of negotiating the terms and conditions of their employment or other mutual aid or protection."[10]

This law, one of the cornerstones of the New Deal program, was designed to assist American workers in their efforts to organize and bargain collectively. This change in policy soon created a political alliance between labor unions and the Democratic party. Democratic administrations worked for the interests of organized labor, interpreting

[9] 295 U.S. 495 (1935).
[10] U.S., *Statutes at Large*, XLIX, Part I, 449-50.

and administering the Wagner Act in such a way as to favor unions. The workers of the nation reciprocated by becoming an important segment of this party's political constituency.

In the period between the creation of the Wagner Act policy and the end of World War II unionism was characterized by optimism and exuberance. Membership doubled in these years, with the CIO breaking away from the AFL and taking the lead in organizing the mass-production industries. Although the AFL and other craft unions had been developing for years, the mass-production workers had been neglected and therefore offered a fruitful field for unionization. But the period of incubation and growth in industrial unions was also typified by aggressiveness. Under the Wagner Act labor began to realize its potential power, and actions were committed which the public regarded as excesses. The tactics used to organize these new unions included such innovations as the sitdown strike, which appeared to be quite extreme when contrasted with traditional labor techniques. Also, the activities of a few union leaders whose delinquency was caused by lack of public responsibility and desire for personal power and aggrandizement damaged organized labor's public relations.

The climax of union aggression came after World War II. In the unstable economic conditions of the reconversion interim, organized labor sought to consolidate its wartime gains in a series of strikes, as had occurred in the era following World War I. And, as had happened after World War I, public opinion turned against unions in this later phase of industrial strife. In a postwar reaction, the American people regarded these waves of strikes as union abuses of power; a climate of opinion developed that was receptive to the idea of circumscribing the seemingly unfettered activities of organized labor.

This nationwide hostility toward unions was exploited

in a sustained drive by conservatives in Congress and American industry. Industrial organizations had opposed the Wagner Act from its inception and conducted a continuous campaign to convince the American public that labor's power should be restricted. Republicans and Southern Democrats, whose constituencies were basically the agrarian, middle-class, and business groups of the nation, agreed that union activities should be curtailed; each session of Congress saw the introduction of an increasing number of bills which would carry out this conviction. This campaign was reinforced by the presentation of labor news in the nation's mass media. Union activities, such as the series of postwar nationwide strikes, were presented to the public in the form of sensationalism, and the actions of the few extremely assertive labor leaders made front-page headlines in the reconversion period. All these factors coalesced to convince the American public, which was becoming increasingly frustrated over other postwar problems, that the national labor policy needed revision.

In the elections of 1946 the Republican party gained control of both houses of Congress for the first time since 1930. The increased strength of the anti-New Deal coalition, combined with the postwar reaction against labor, enabled the Republican Eightieth Congress to revise the labor policy by passing the Taft-Hartley Act over the forceful veto of President Truman, heir to the Roosevelt, New Deal tradition. This act, which was supposed to equalize the power between management and the ever-increasing power of labor unions, fundamentally modified the national labor policy. Now, instead of playing an active role in stimulating union growth, the federal government was to play the impartial role of umpiring the struggle between labor and management in order to protect the paramount public interest. The new policy contained the premise that labor unions were now strong enough—even too strong—and that henceforth the public interest was to take precedence over the interests of both labor and management. The Taft-Hartley Act, which amended the Wagner Act, significantly inserted the following addition to the Wagner Act's statement of policy: "Experience has further demonstrated that certain practices by some labor organizations, their officers, and members, have the intent or the necessary effect of burdening or obstructing commerce by preventing the free flow of goods in such commerce through strikes and other forms of industrial unrest or through concerted activities which impair the interest of the public in the free flow of such commerce. The elimination of such practices is a necessary condition to the assurance of the rights herein guaranteed."[11] The agricultural, business, and middle-class interests, having won control of Congress in 1946, were able to reverse one of the basic New Deal tenets over the protest of the executive branch, which reflected the concern of working men in the urban areas.

The passage of the Taft-Hartley Act in 1947 was the culmination of a long and sustained propaganda drive sponsored by the NAM (The National Association of Manufacturers) and the United States Chamber of Commerce, the two most powerful business organizations in the country. These two associations and their satellite institutions had always opposed, not necessarily the interests of the working man as such, but the growing economic and political power of labor unions. In fact, the common interest of industry "in opposing organized labor has served to hold the membership together" in the NAM "and to provide a never-failing bond of opposition to liberal-social legislation of the New Deal variety."[12] Led by the NAM, these groups began their campaign to destroy the Wagner Act as soon as it was enacted. This concerted move was effected with typical

[11] *Ibid.*, LXI, Part I, 137.

[12] Robert A. Brady, *Business as a System of Power* (New York: Columbia, 1943), p. 213.

propaganda methods of appealing slogans, half-truths and misinterpretation in the attempt to discredit unions and remove the paternalistic protection of the national government. The NAM frankly admitted that its targets in this drive were "The great, unorganized, inarticulate, so-called middle class; The younger generation; and The opinion-makers of the nation."[13] Senator George Aiken, a liberal Republican from Vermont, estimated in May of 1947 that the total spent by the NAM in this program of education amounted to at least $100,000,000. At the same time he referred to his statement delivered in the Senate a year previously that the NAM had spent $2,000,000 in March of 1946 in an advertising campaign in newspapers against labor, declaring that this charge had "not been contradicted as yet."[14]

That this operation succeeded so well was due in part to the presentation of the news by much of the mass media. The press tended to present labor news, although usually unintentionally, in the worst possible light, thus helping to mold public opinion against unions. That this could easily be unintentional and yet very effective stems from the nature of the press. Newspapers tend to print what will appeal to their readers and the reading public prefers sensationalism. The actions of a few extremely aggressive labor leaders in this period were emphasized by the press, as they should have been, but the result was that all union leaders were painted with the same brush as these atypical few. When the actions of immoderate leaders made the news but the much more common activities of the run-of-the-mill labor officials were omitted, the average reader soon pictured the more rash union leader as typical. Thus many critics regarded John L. Lewis, whom President Truman referred

[13] National Association of Manufacturers, *The Challenge and the Answer* (New York, Sept., 1947), as quoted in Harry A. Millis and Emily Clark Brown, *From the Wagner Act to Taft-Hartley* (Chicago: Chicago, 1950), pp. 290-91.

[14] *Congressional Record,* 80 Cong., 1 Sess., 1947, XCIII, 5015.

to as a "headline hunter,"[15] as having damaged the cause of labor unions during this difficult period. His actions invariably made flashy newspaper headlines. Although Lewis sincerely acted in what he considered to be the best interests of his miners and has even been labeled "conservative" by Arthur J. Goldberg,[16] his activities, as presented by the press, did much to convince the public that labor "bosses" needed to be controlled.

On the other hand, legitimate claims were made that the press in general was unfriendly to labor. Most of the nation's newspapers opposed legislation favorable to labor during and after the New Deal and strongly supported the Taft-Hartley Act. In addition, labor spokesmen claimed that they did not have access to the avenues of public opinion through which to state their views in the labor-management conflict. This one-sided news coverage by the country's mass media kept organized labor constantly on the defensive in an attempt to gain, or even to neutralize, public opinion.

Labor emerged from World War II with a good record and high in public esteem. Except for occasional wildcat strikes and minor disturbances, labor faithfully remained on the job with man-days idle due to strikes accounting for "only one-ninth of one per cent of available working time."[17] The maintenance of stable labor relations during the war was based on two factors: the no-strike, no-lockout policy mutually agreed to by labor and management in the labor-management conference called by President Roosevelt in December 1941, and the wage stabilization policy announced by President Roosevelt on April 27, 1942, and given statutory confirmation by Congress in the Economic Stabilization Act on October 2 of the same year. The War Labor Board, set

[15] Press Conference, June 9, 1949, Truman Papers, OR 22, Harry S. Truman Library, Independence, Missouri (hereafter cited as HSTL).

[16] Arthur J. Goldberg, *AFL-CIO: Labor United* (New York: McGraw-Hill, 1964), p. 8.

[17] Joel Seidman, *American Labor From Defense to Reconversion* (Chicago: Chicago, 1953), p. 134.

up by Roosevelt on January 12, 1942, administered this stabilization program. The WLB had its powers broadened when a coal strike, called by John L. Lewis, threatened the war effort. An enraged Congress enacted the War Labor Disputes or Smith-Connally Act, passed over President Roosevelt's veto on June 25, 1943. This act provided for a thirty-day "cooling off" period and an ensuing worker vote before striking in a war plant. But the WLB, rooted in presidential war powers, ceased to exist with the conclusion of the war.

With the termination of hostilities the nation entered into an era of reconversion. This transition from a wartime to a peacetime economy, *Newsweek* warned, would not "be a quick, easy trip over a well-paved, well-lighted superhighway,"[18] and this admonition proved to be well calculated. The Truman program for the postwar economy embodied the wonderful objectives of full employment and full production, but few concrete proposals were offered to implement such a program. Less than a month after the Japanese surrender President Truman reported to Congress that during the reconversion period production of civilian goods must proceed "without interruption" and that labor and management should "cooperate to keep strikes and lockouts at a minimum" during the transition. He then admonished: "Those who have the responsibility of labor relations must recognize that responsibility. This is not the time for shortsighted management to seize upon the chance to reduce wages and try to injure labor unions. Equally it is not the time for labor leaders to shirk their responsibility and permit widespread industrial strife."[19]

This ringing call to duty simply amounted to a request

18 "Relations With Labor will be Key to Truman's Economic Program," *Newsweek*, XXV (April 23, 1945), 72.

19 Message to Congress, Sept. 6, 1945, *Public Papers of the Presidents of the United States: Harry S. Truman, 1945* (Washington, D.C.: U.S. Government Printing Office, 1961), p. 282; hereafter cited as *Truman Papers* with appropriate year.

for labor and industry to resume peacefully the art of collective bargaining when wartime controls were lifted. But Truman seemed to overlook the fact that during the war period collective bargaining had fallen into disuse. During the war many of the disputes handled by the War Labor Board, especially in defense industries, were resolved by board decrees with little or no mediation. Following the war, true collective bargaining had to be revived and, in many cases, had to be relearned by labor and management. However, while both sides were oiling up collective bargaining machinery, the country was swept by an inundation of strikes which in turn led to antilabor legislation culminating in the Taft-Hartley Act.

There is a very close parallel in the reconversion periods following World War I and World War II in the field of labor relations. Basically the same pattern was followed in both eras—nationwide strikes succeeded by a public reaction and a crackdown on labor. The movement against labor after World War I took the form of the open-shop drive during which the AFL, the largest federation of unions, lost about one-quarter of its members. Total union membership was reduced from 5,000,000 in 1920 to 2,850,000 by 1933.[20] The NAM led this drive, sometimes called the American Plan, for the open shop and Welfare Capitalism, with company unions being instituted when necessary for the maintenance of good employer-employee relations. The reaction following World War II molded the Taft-Hartley Act, an attempt to curb and, in the opinion of many, eventually to destroy the power of organized labor.

One of the major differences between the two periods was that labor unrest after World War II was more moderate than in the preceding era. Secretary of Labor Maurice J. Tobin emphasized this distinction during an attempt to

[20] Maurice J. Tobin, "Town Meeting of the Air," March 15, 1949, Secretary Tobin File (Speeches), R.G. 174, National Archives.

repeal the Taft-Hartley Act. Comparing the percentage of workers on strike in relation to the total labor force for the first two years following the end of both wars, Tobin pointed out that the percentage in 1919 was 20.8 and 7.2 in 1920. But in 1946 the percentage was 14.5 and in 1947 only 6.5. This, he felt, constituted a considerable difference, particularly in comparing the 1919 and 1946 figures.[21] Nonetheless, in the minds of many people the outbreak of strikes in 1946, particularly those in the basic industries of coal, steel, automobiles, and transportation, which directly and indirectly involved millions of workers, presented a serious threat to reconversion and economic progress. Liberals and moderates did their best to discourage antiunion feeling, but the move to "put labor in its place" continued. In fact Truman later told William Green, president of the AFL, there was "little doubt" in his mind "that a definite plot was hatched at the close of the war to smash, or at least to cripple, our trade union movement in a period of postwar reaction. The conspiracy was developed by a little group of politicians, working with the representatives of our most reactionary employers. These men thought that history would repeat itself and that they could do after World War II what had been done after the First World War when our trade unions were set upon by the so-called 'open-shop movement' using the anti-labor devices of spies, finks, blacklists, and yellow dog contracts."[22]

An underlying factor in the nationwide wave of strikes during the reconversion period was labor's apprehension that mass unemployment was imminent. At the end of the war there were about twelve million people serving in the armed forces and another eight million directly engaged in war production. With the return to a peacetime economy

[21] U.S. Senate, Committee on Labor and Public Welfare, *Hearings on S. 249, Labor Relations,* 81 Cong., 1 Sess., 1949, p. 216.

[22] Harry S. Truman to William Green, Sept. 13, 1952, Truman Papers, PPF 85, HSTL.

this would mean, as at the end of every war, a tremendous displacement of labor and at least temporary economic uncertainty until reconversion was completed. For example, between V-E and V-J days, unemployment jumped from one-half million to one million. After the Japanese surrender, war contracts were cancelled and unemployment immediately tripled. In the last four and one-half months of 1945 strikes created over 28,400,000 man-days of idleness compared to the war-year high of 13,500,000 in 1943.[23] More man-days were lost due to strikes during the first two months of 1946 than the total lost during the war.[24] The natural reaction of labor was to strike before mass unemployment curtailed its bargaining power.

Coinciding with this fear of unemployment and magnifying the desperate situation of labor was the fact that during reconversion American workers found themselves in a wage-price squeeze. Wartime controls, which had stabilized wages and prices, were due to expire June 30, 1946. When the administration requested continuation of these controls, Congress replied with a bill so impotent that President Truman vetoed it and the country was without means of controlling prices. Immediate inflation occurred and the price of some basic commodities rose as much as 25 percent in two weeks. Frightened by this development Congress passed a price-control law, but with higher ceilings on many manufactured items than were maintained during the war, and the administration had to accept it as better than nothing.

In addition to higher prices, real wages were lowered when wartime bonuses and overtime were reduced or abolished. So, although wages were not actually cut, the net effect was less take-home pay for the average worker.

[23] Seidman, *American Labor From Defense to Reconversion*, p. 221.

[24] Barton J. Bernstein, "Walter Reuther and the General Motors Strike of 1945-1946," *Michigan History*, XLIX (Sept. 1965), 260.

This wage-price squeeze triggered the postwar strikes. These strikes were unique in that they were more moderate than many people expected at the time. In this strife both labor and management appealed to the public with pamphlets and press releases; statistical evidence of industry's ability to pay higher wages was the focus of argument in all the controversies.

The War Labor Board, which had administered the Wage Stabilization Act, was abolished January 1, 1946, and was replaced on the same date with the National Wage Stabilization Board. This board, functioning during the reconversion period, ruled only upon voluntary wage increases and compensatory price increases. The first round of postwar strikes began to dissipate in February 1946 when the National Wage Stabilization Board granted United States Steel permission to increase the price of steel $5 per ton. In turn, the company signed an agreement with its workers for an increase of 18½ cents per hour. At the same time President Truman issued an executive order permitting other industrial price increases to compensate for wage increases and this pattern of 18½ cents was adopted by most industries.

When President Truman signed the new price-control bill in June 1946 he warned of its inadequacy, correctly predicting that inflation would not be checked. And in the last half of 1946 consumer prices rose 15 percent, with food prices rising almost 30 percent, which more than cancelled the wage increases won by the 1945-1946 strikes. The 1946 elections reflected a sharp political swing to the right, and it thus seemed futile to attempt to control prices in the face of this public disgust and frustration over wartime controls. On November 9, 1946, President Truman proclaimed the end of all controls on wages and prices. With no controls inflation increased and price squeezes in turn brought on the second round of strikes in 1946-1947.

To a population eager to shake off wartime restrictions

and responsibilities, these waves of strikes irritated public nerves and helped to create increasing hostility toward labor. Labor's public relations were further damaged by the constant reiteration of the press that wage increases were responsible for high prices and inflation. Secretary of Labor Lewis Schwellenbach attempted to correct this idea by pointing out that for a two-year period "representatives of business, in the press and magazines, have dinned into the ears of the American people the claim that advances in prices were exclusively caused by advances in wages."[25] While he admitted wage raises were a factor, that did "not justify any effort . . . to place the whole blame" for rising prices upon labor alone. And he had previously referred to the "phenomenal increases in profits during the last year," saying that corporation profits for the first quarter of 1947 were $875,000,000 as compared to $323,000,000 for the same period in the previous year, pointedly suggesting this was a basic contribution to inflation.[26]

But the campaign to place the blame for higher prices upon labor succeeded. Letters and telegrams poured into the White House referring to "union tyrants" and demanding that labor power be restricted the same as any other monopoly. A Gallup Poll illustrated labor's decline in public esteem during this period. In August 1945, 79 percent of the people approved of the "law guaranteeing collective bargaining" and 75 percent thought unions were "a good thing for the country." But by June 1946, 95 percent approved of a compulsory prestrike vote and 90 percent thought there should be a requirement for regular elections of union officials, giving some indication of a drop in union popularity and a growing desire to control union activities.[27]

[25] L. B. Schwellenbach, Address to the CIO National Convention, Boston, Oct. 14, 1947, Schwellenbach Papers, Library of Congress.

[26] Radio Address on NBC, Aug. 31, 1947, *ibid.*

[27] Gallup Poll, Public Opinion on Case Bill, Truman Papers, OF 407-B, HSTL.

While President Truman agreed that reduction in take-home pay was a factor in the strike situation, he had earlier blamed the strikes on "reaction . . . from the tremendous war effort" similar to that following "every war we ever fought" when everyone felt like "letting down."[28] His answer to the strike problem was to appoint fact-finding boards. And like Secretary Schwellenbach, Truman realized that labor was being unjustly blamed for inflation. On December 20, 1945, he issued a statement in which he said these fact-finding boards "should be empowered by Congress to examine employer's books if necessary to determine ability to pay, where ability to pay was in question, provided that the detailed information so obtained should not be made public."[29]

Harry S. Truman assumed the presidency with a good senatorial record in labor legislation. He voted for the Wagner Act, the Social Security Act, the Guffey-Snyder Act, and the Fair Labor Standards Act in his first term as Senator. During the war, in his second term, he also voted for the Senate version of the Smith-Connally War Labor Disputes Act. However, he did not vote for the House version of this act, which was more antilabor, and he voted to sustain President Roosevelt's veto of the final act. In addition, he opposed the attempt in 1944 to liquidate the Fair Employment Practices Committee and the proposal to place unemployment insurance benefits under state control.[30] Thus, as far as labor was concerned, his record was clean. Truman was a staunch party man, which helps account for this consistent prolabor attitude. Since the Democratic party sponsored legislation favorable to labor,

28 Press Conference, Tiptonville, Tenn., Oct. 8, 1945, Truman Papers, OR 20, HSTL.

29 Press Release, Summary of Report to the President by Fact-Finding Board, General Motors Dispute, Jan. 10, 1946, Truman Papers, OF 407-B, HSTL.

30 See Eugene Francis Schmidtlein, "Truman the Senator" (unpublished Ph.D. dissertation, University of Missouri, 1962), p. 131.

he followed the party line, few politicians having more party loyalty. The best indication of Truman's good labor record and the attitude of unions toward him was the support he received from them for the vice-presidential nomination in 1944. When organized labor was thwarted in getting Henry A. Wallace renominated for this position, both the AFL and CIO backed Truman's candidacy.

Although labor was certain he would be their friend as President, many union officials were also aware of his temper: he could not be pushed too far. Daniel J. Tobin, president of the Teamsters union, wrote an editorial for the *International Teamster* soon after Truman became President, saying that Truman was "for the working man in every way possible within justice and reason, but even to get the Presidency in 1948 he would not sacrifice his principles or make false promises to the workers of the nation. President Truman is going to make history, and labor, in my judgment, will have no better friend than Truman, even though he will have the courage and honesty sometimes to disagree with labor."[31]

President Truman proved particularly adamant on one issue regarding labor relations. He did not believe that strikes against the government were legal, and he said if they ever came to be legal the government "would cease to exist."[32] Also, he felt that in a contest of power between labor and industry it would be necessary for the government to "assert the fact that *it* is the power of the people."[33] Whenever labor leaders were completely in the wrong he would be one of the first to indicate such, as he did when John L. Lewis violated the Lewis-Krug Agreement in 1946 and led his miners out on strike while the national government was operating the coal mines. In this instance the

31 Daniel J. Tobin, copy of Tobin editorial to be published, to Matthew J. Connelly, May 21, 1945, Truman Papers, OF 407, HSTL.

32 Press Conference, May 2, 1946, Truman Papers, OF 20, HSTL.

33 Press Conference, Jan. 24, 1946, *ibid.*

government brought suit and Judge Alan Goldsborough found the UMW (United Mine Workers) and Lewis guilty of civil and criminal contempt, fining them $3,500,000 and $10,000 respectively. This sensational fine against the union was lowered to $700,000 in March 1947 by the Supreme Court.[34]

But as President and as titular head of the Democratic party, it was necessary for Harry S. Truman to continue the prolabor policies of his predecessor. At times he agreed that certain labor leaders were abusing their power, especially when they thwarted the desires of Harry S. Truman, and he then admitted that corrective legislation was necessary. But in general, the President found it imperative to promote labor's interest so as to continue to receive its support, which composed a major segment of the political coalition of the Democratic party formed during the New Deal. This became progressively more apparent with the approach of the presidential election of 1948 when the urban vote would be vital to his reelection. But also as President he opposed the growing postwar conservative reaction that was sweeping the nation, a reaction that culminated in a Republican-controlled Eightieth Congress determined to reverse certain aspects of the New Deal. With the combination of circumstances resulting from the various manifestations of postwar reconversion difficulties, the scene was set for a political struggle. This would be the result of the simultaneous presence of a Democratic President who would want to protect the interests of the urban masses and a Republican Congress, long out of power, that would try to promote the interests of the less numerous but powerful and well-organized rural and business groups of the nation.

[34] *United States v. United Mine Workers of America,* 330 U.S. 258 (1947).

2

THE SEARCH FOR A RECONVERSION LABOR PROGRAM

At the end of the war, President Truman was determined that the nation should convert to a peacetime economy as quickly as possible. To achieve this end he was resolved to rebuild the Department of Labor, which had lost so many of its functions to special wartime agencies such as the War Labor Board, the War Manpower Commission, and the U. S. Employment Service. Frances Perkins, the New Deal secretary of labor, had indicated her desire to resign, so Truman searched for a replacement. Her successor's primary job of rebuilding would be complicated by the current labor unrest. Lewis Schwellenbach, an old Senate crony and currently a federal judge in Washington, was chosen for this task; he was a man who Truman said, "saw right down the same alley on public policy" with him.[1]

Coinciding with his desire to strengthen the Department of Labor was Truman's conviction that true collective bargaining with a minimum of governmental intervention should be restored as soon as feasible. So Truman summoned a National Labor-Management Conference to convene in Washington, D. C., on November 5, 1945, to discuss possible means of achieving this goal. Meanwhile, until the conference met, the President called upon labor and management to continue adherence to the no-strike, no-lockout pledge. Any labor dispute that threatened "a substantial interference with the transition to a peacetime economy should be submitted to the War Labor Board" and both parties would be expected "to comply voluntarily with the determination" of that board.[2] It has been noted that the administration's failure to secure renewal of this wartime pledge provided the "root of later difficulties" in controlling inflation and labor-management conflict.[3] The idea of such a national labor-management meeting had been under serious consideration by the administration and was given impetus when Senator Arthur H. Vandenberg sent a letter to Secretary Schwellenbach on July 30, 1945. Vandenberg suggested such an assembly to "lay the groundwork for peace with justice on the *home* front," as the United Nations conference in San Francisco had been successful "in laying the groundwork for *external* peace with justice." This letter "crystallized" the administration's decision to go ahead with its plans.[4]

William Green of the AFL, Philip Murray of the CIO, Ira Mosher of the NAM, and Eric Johnson of the United States Chamber of Commerce were designated as a committee to plan the agenda and nominate thirty-six delegates, eighteen

[1] Truman, *Memoirs,* I, 325.

[2] Message to Congress, Sept. 6, 1945, *Truman Papers, 1945,* pp. 127-28.

[3] See Barton Bernstein, "The Truman Administration and its Reconversion Wage Policy," *Labor History,* VI (Fall 1965), 214-31, for an excellent account of the administration's confused attempts to formulate a wage policy prior to the national conference.

[4] Report, National Labor-Management Conference to the President, Dec. 31, 1945, Appendix B, Truman Papers, OF 407-C, HSTL.

from labor and eighteen from industry.[5] President Truman telegraphed invitations to the nominees and they assembled on schedule. Truman opened the assembly by reminding the delegates that it was a labor-management, not a government, conference. It was time, he said, for labor and management to handle their own affairs "in the traditional American, democratic way." He expressed the hope that he could soon give up his wartime powers and then it would be their responsibility to provide the necessary production "to safeguard our domestic economy and our leadership in international affairs." He reminded the delegates that for four years they had "performed a miracle of production" with a minimum of control, but that as soon as some of those controls were removed, industrial conflict had appeared. He did not ascribe any blame for this development, because he believed both sides were at fault. Labor was the cause for much strife through jurisdictional disputes, he said, but management had to share the blame because too often it used delaying tactics to the point where collective bargaining became a farce. The President concluded his message with the warning that "if the people do not find the answers here, they will find them someplace else. For these answers must and will be found. The whole system of private enterprise and individual opportunity depends on finding them."[6]

Despite high expectations of success, the conference produced few results and conferees reached agreement only on some nebulous generalities. In a similar period of industrial strife, Woodrow Wilson had called the National Industrial Conference in 1919 which had not even been able to agree upon establishing the principle of collective bargaining in industrial conflict. At this 1945 meeting it was agreed that grievances should be settled by arbitration, not by the use

[5] William Green, Philip Murray, Ira Mosher, and Eric Johnson to the President, Oct. 23, 1945, Truman Papers, OR, HSTL.

[6] Opening the Labor-Management Conference in Washington, Nov. 5, 1945, Truman Papers, OR, HSTL.

of economic power, and that such meetings should be continued. While this harmony indicated an acceptance of the basic principle of collective bargaining, nothing was achieved in regard to machinery for settling the immediate labor-relations problems of the country. The United States Conciliation Service was praised for the part it played in labor disputes and the meeting adjourned with no concrete proposals.[7] Although the President emphasized that the government had absolutely nothing to do with the conference beyond calling it, administration officials were afraid that Truman would be censured for its collapse and failure. The publicity director of the conference pointed out that the delegates were not going to admit they had spent a fruitless three weeks and that the press was planning to pitch the blame to the President.[8]

Immediately after the conference President Truman took a weekend cruise down the Potomac during which he "spent several hours" with Samuel I. Rosenman and George E. Allen. The outcome of their discussions was a special message to Congress.[9] In this message the President informed the congressmen that the purpose in calling the conference had been to work out a program by which wartime controls could be removed and thus "labor relations would be turned back to those involved." He emphasized that the responsibility for failure lay with the delegates and that government representatives participated only as observers. The government had made no suggestion to the delegates as to machinery but had only pointed out "the objective which the American people expected it to attain" —industrial peace. "Now that the conference has adjourned

7 Report, National Labor-Management Conference to the President, Dec. 31, 1945, Truman Papers, OF 407-C, HSTL.

8 Fred Smith to Matthew J. Connelly, Nov. 27, 1945, Truman Papers, OF 407-C, HSTL.

9 "Historic Truman Labor Curbs Aimed at Strikes Against Peace," *Newsweek*, XXVI (Dec. 10, 1945), 31.

without any recommendation on the subject," he continued, "it becomes the duty of the Government to act on its own initiative." He then recommended that Congress enact labor legislation covering nationwide industries based on the principles of the Railway Labor Act.

Specifically, he requested that Congress set up a program of fact-finding boards. These would be appointed by the President upon certification by the secretary of labor that a labor dispute required such action. The board would be appointed within five days of such certification and during this period and the time of the panel's deliberations, plus five days thereafter, it would "be unlawful to call a strike or lockout, or to make any changes in rates of pay, hours, or working conditions . . . in effect prior to the time the dispute arose." A report should be made within twenty days, but the parties to the dispute would not be bound by the fact-finding board's recommendations. How would the dispute be settled? Settlement would follow similar to railway labor disputes, Truman assured Congress, because the public would then "know all the facts" and the resulting public pressure would force the two parties to accept the board's suggestions. He then cautioned Congress not to adopt "repressive or coercive measures against either side" that would "stifle full freedom of collective bargaining" because this "would be a backward step which the American people would not tolerate."[10]

Seen in the light of subsequent events, this plan was an ineffectual, halfhearted gesture. Apparently the administration was groping for a policy and suggested this approach as better than nothing. At a time when the country needed vigorous leadership to work out an effective program for peacetime labor relations in anticipation of repressive antilabor legislation, the administration appears to have fumbled the ball. To call for voluntary cooperation when the country

[10] Message to Congress, Dec. 3, 1945, *Truman Papers, 1945*, pp. 516-21.

was being convulsed by labor strife seems ingenuous to say the least. This complete misreading of the attitude of labor and management and the temper of a Congress preparing to utilize public restiveness to enact legislation curbing union power can be explained only in terms of Truman's awkward position in his early months as President.

Always a strong party man, Harry Truman felt obligated to continue the New Deal and yet at the same time was faced with the problem of trying to secure cooperation from a Congress controlled by an anti-New Deal coalition of Southern Democrats and Republicans, also inherited from Franklin D. Roosevelt. Less than a month after V-J Day Truman had sent a message to Congress on September 6, 1945, with a 21-point program that was definitely designed to continue and expand the New Deal. Among other items, he requested an increase in the minimum wage, expansion of Social Security to cover a health program, low-cost housing and slum clearance, and a permanent fair employment practices act.[11] But when Congress balked on these requests and the postwar national mood indicated little enthusiasm for such proposals, he reiterated these suggestions from time to time but never really pressed for their enactment. In a period of increasing partisanship, Truman was attempting to continue the bipartisanship spawned by the patriotism engendered by the war. From 1945 to 1947 Truman was "reacting to the strongest pressures of the moment,"[12] and at the same time trying to carry out his predecessor's policies. In this instance Truman's call for voluntary cooperation from labor and management failed and the country became increasingly impatient with what was considered the arrogant attitude of labor. Congress was already moving toward "putting labor in its place" and was utilizing this public sentiment to advantage.

[11] *Ibid.*, pp. 263-309.

[12] Eric Goldman, *The Crucial Decade—And After* (New York: Vintage, 1961), p. 21.

Even before the end of the war Congress seriously considered revision of the national labor law. The Wagner Act, the basis of the national labor policy, had been created as a result of public reaction to the treatment of labor during the depression of the thirties and as the culmination of a long drive by labor and liberals to place unions in a legal position to bargain on an equal basis with management. The Wagner Act thus imposed restrictions upon employers by curtailing certain practices they had been utilizing in checking union organization. With this governmental assistance unions increased rapidly in membership and strength, with the result that labor could meet management at the bargaining table on a basis of equality. But along with this growth in union power came a corresponding increase in what the public viewed as union irresponsibility. The general public therefore believed that it needed protection from labor abuses that were reaching dangerous proportions, and, as the President of General Electric said, it was also necessary "to save labor from its own excesses—excesses which if unrestrained will in the long run be injurious to labor itself."[13]

The so-called labor abuses that drew criticism were to a large degree the result of growing pains. In the years following the passage of the Wagner Act, organized labor was in the process of maturing, and both management and labor were learning to accept the principle of collective bargaining. But in learning these lessons by experience, unions were criticized at times for not bargaining in good faith. Although management was also reproved for stalling, by President Truman and others, labor received a greater share of public censure. Another criticism leveled at unions centered on the closed shop, which made it necessary for a worker to belong to a union before he could take a job. To many people this union-security device seemed contrary to

[13] Charles E. Wilson to Harry S. Truman, June 5, 1945, Truman Papers, OF 407-B, HSTL.

the American tradition of equality of opportunity; the result was a successful drive in many states to outlaw the closed shop by statute or constitutional amendment. Coinciding with this abuse, or what many considered an abuse, were the excessive initiation fees charged by some unions and the checkoff clause in contracts which many unions forced management to accept, whereby the employer withheld the employee's membership dues and remitted the sum to the union. Undemocratic union practices such as not holding regular elections, allowing union officials to determine whether or not to strike, denying membership to Negroes in some cases, and refusing to report finances, also drew their share of criticism. And as the Cold War unfolded in the postwar years, many unions, particularly those affiliated with the CIO, were accused of being dominated by communists.

Another source of friction came from jurisdictional disputes and raiding between unions. When the CIO withdrew from the AFL to organize the industrial and noncraft workers, this in turn stimulated the older craft unions to greater activity, resulting in more numerous organizational campaigns. Union rivalry in membership and jurisdictional drives was intensified by the use of secondary boycotts and picketing in attempts to persuade workers to change their affiliation or to force an employer to extend recognition. Secondary boycotts were unusually effective for certain types of unions such as the Teamsters who could thus tie up many subsidiary industries, and of course the more successful the boycott, the more the public raged against union "tyrants" and demanded legislation to regulate them.

Labor made little apparent effort to clean house, only intensifying the impression of union irresponsibility. Indeed, instead of giving some indication of reforming offensive behavior, union leaders attacked all legislative reformatory measures with vehemence. And just as the callous and brutal treatment of employees created a public sentiment for the Wagner Act, in turn union indifference to the public helped to create a climate of public opinion in which the Taft-Hartley Act was possible. But this antiunion drive must also be considered in the light of the postwar wave of strikes.

One of the most serious setbacks to labor resulting from antiunion sentiment in this period came in the field of state labor laws. After Congress passed the Wagner Act, many states imitated the federal action by setting up "baby Wagner Act" programs. Some of these states soon reversed themselves and set the new pattern of restricting union activities, a policy later followed by Congress. The crusade against unions in state legislatures reached a climax during the postwar period. One authority maintains that in 1947 state legislatures passed more antiunion laws than at any time since the Haymarket Riot. Twenty-one states provided for strike notices and cooling-off periods, sixteen outlawed the closed shop or other union-security provisions, twelve prohibited secondary boycotts, eleven restricted picketing, ten forced unions to file financial statements, and six permitted a restricted use of injunctions in labor disputes.[14]

Harry A. Millis and Emily Clark Brown point out that there were three main arguments used for changing both federal and state labor laws after 1939: (1) unions had become too powerful and a new balance had to be struck; (2) many unions lacked the necessary sense of responsibility to industry, the public, and individual union members; and (3) unions should have the equivalent limitations and responsibilities of employers.[15] These writers also state that in the ten-year period from 1937 to 1947 a total of 169 amendments to the national labor policy were proposed in Con-

[14] Joseph G. Rayback, *A History of American Labor* (New York: Macmillan, 1959), pp. 395-96.

[15] Millis and Brown, *From the Wagner Act to Taft-Hartley*, p. 272.

gress. The changes were concerned only with national labor policy and did not include other labor proposals dealing with wages, hours, social security, and similar matters.[16] These various proposals generally fell into one of four groups: (1) regulation of internal union affairs in the areas of elections and finance reporting; (2) strike limitations such as cooling-off periods; (3) union activities such as picketing and boycotting; and (4) union security arrangements such as the closed shop and maintenance of membership.

Philip Murray presented a study to President Truman which showed that in this same ten-year period 109 bills in Congress dealt with these four subjects. It is interesting to note that the second category, dealing with strike limitations, had the largest number with 31 proposed bills, closely followed by the fourth category with 28, and yet union security did not become an issue in Congress until 1941. The fact that 50 of the 109 bills were proposed in the Seventy-seventh Congress is indicative of the activities of the Smith Committee of 1939-1940 which made the first major attempt to rewrite the Wagner Act. Murray complained in this letter that whenever the country faced a serious problem, such as war production, new bills were proposed which "mechanically repeat the same chant of hate, 'Regulate labor, curb labor, destroy labor,'" the basic aim of which was a means of smearing "labor and of artificially stimulating resentment against trade unions."[17]

When Congress convened in January 1946, President Truman renewed his appeal for new labor legislation based on the Railway Labor Act. In a message from the White House he again requested the program he had asked for on December 3, 1945. There was nothing harmful to labor or management in his proposal, he said, because "there is no reason

16 *Ibid.*, p. 333.

17 Philip Murray to the President, May 31, 1946, Truman Papers, OF 407-B, HSTL.

why a strike cannot be postponed for thirty days," nor was the detailed information he sought from company books to be revealed. He then reiterated his opposition to the anti-labor bills pending in Congress which were aimed at depriving "labor of the right to bargain collectively" or of "its ultimate right to strike."[18] But the temper of Congress supported this more drastic legislation as reflected in a bill introduced by Representative Francis Case, Republican from South Dakota.

The liberal *New Republic* termed the Case bill, H.R. 4908, "an unashamed and hateful attempt to emasculate organized labor."[19] In its final form the bill proposed setting up a tripartite Federal Mediation Board to assume jurisdiction of labor disputes involving interstate commerce with provisions quite similar to the Railway Labor Act. In addition, the bill had an antiracketeering clause and an antitrust section. It also would have restricted employers in making payments to unions, as in the form of welfare funds, and would have made unions suable for breach of contract. Among its miscellaneous provisions was the one excluding supervisors from the Wagner Act. Finally, the major feature of the Case bill was a cooling-off provision. This required a five-day strike or lockout notice and maintenance of the status quo for thirty days after such notice if the board assumed jurisdiction.

No one had an opportunity to testify before the House Labor Committee on the Case bill because no public hearings were held. This was a highly unusual congressional procedure. The *Nation* stated that no hearings were called because the bill had the "secret blessing of the Republican high command." According to the writer for this magazine, Indiana Republican Charles Halleck was "a prime mover"

18 Address from the White House, Jan. 3, 1946, Truman Papers, OR, HSTL.

19 "Congress and Strikes," *New Republic*, CXIV (Feb. 11, 1946), 174.

in that committee's decision to rush the bill to the House floor without benefit of public hearings.[20] That Halleck was chairman of the Republican Congressional Campaign Committee at this time contributes to an explanation of this irregular procedure. The House approved the Case bill 258 to 155 on February 7 and sent it to the Senate for consideration.[21]

Secretary of Labor Schwellenbach testified before the Senate Labor Committee on February 25 in opposition to the bill, maintaining that it would reverse the progress of fifteen years and flood the courts with litigation.[22] The bill came up for final action in the Senate during a prolonged coal strike and at the height of a railroad strike. To say the least, these strikes did not help the cause of labor at this inopportune time. As the conservative *United States News and World Report* charged, "Once again John L. Lewis has inspired a stampede in Congress to do something about strikes," drawing a parallel between this and his strike in 1943 which had helped bring about the Smith-Connally Act.[23]

John L. Lewis had begun negotiations early in 1946 for a new contract which would provide for a welfare fund to come from royalties on coal mined and to be administered by himself. The usual breakdown in negotiations came and Lewis called a strike of the bituminous coal miners for April 1, 1946. The nation went into a "brown-out" to conserve coal and industry began to slow down for lack of fuel. From March to May Truman held six conferences with Lewis and the operators' representatives and finally seized the mines in May. On May 29 Lewis accepted the Lewis-Krug Agreement, a plan devised by himself and Secretary of Interior

20 "Labor in Wanderland," *Nation,* CLXII (Feb. 16, 1946), 184.

21 *Congressional Record,* 79 Cong., 2 Sess., 1946, XCII, 1069-70.

22 L. B. Schwellenbach to the President, March 8, 1946, Truman Papers, OF 419-B, HSTL.

23 *United States News and World Report,* XX (May 17, 1946), 43.

Julius Krug, whereby a welfare fund and a retirement fund were established to be jointly administered by the union and the operators. However, this coal strike was not finally settled for several months. In October 1946, Lewis announced another strike to begin the following month because of an alleged violation by the government of the Lewis-Krug Agreement. This call resulted in the famous injunction against the strike and the eventual fining of Lewis and the UMW in December 1946 by Judge Alan Goldsborough. It was the crisis of the strike in May that helped convince Truman of the need for emergency legislation "to safeguard the nation against precipitous strikes" and that contributed to his request to draft workers striking against the government.[24]

But it was the railroad strike that brought unforeseen political consequences and that illustrated the lengths to which President Truman might go when opposed by recalcitrant labor leaders. Negotiations over wages had been in progress for some time between railroad operators and twenty railroad unions. President Truman had invoked the Railway Labor Disputes Act under which the parties were attempting, unsuccessfully, to arbitrate their differences. Truman had begun conferring with the union officials in February 1946 and when negotiations under the Emergency Board deadlocked, he submitted a compromise. The board had recommended a 16-cents-per-hour wage increase but the unions also wanted certain rules changed. Truman proposed that they accept the 16 cents, which the operators were willing to give, plus 2½ cents per hour in lieu of the rules changes, which the owners also were willing to concede.

Eighteen of the unions accepted the compromise. However, Alvanley Johnston, president of the Locomotive Engineers, and Alexander F. Whitney, president of the Trainmen, refused to arbitrate the rules changes for their unions.

[24] Truman, *Memoirs,* I, 502.

Instead they asked for a strike vote and a strike of some 300,000 union members from most of the major lines was ultimately called for May 23, 1946. A strike had previously been announced for May 18, but at Truman's request it had been postponed for five days while a compromise was sought. In the meantime, on May 17, 1946, President Truman seized the railroads. Truman had held three conferences with Johnston and Whitney and when they proved obdurate he decided that this was "no contest between labor and management but one between a small group of men and their government." He informed Johnston and Whitney that they were "not going to tie up the country. . . . If this is the way you want it," he declared, "we'll stop you."[25]

On May 24 Truman took the issue to the people in a nationwide radio address. He summarized the dispute and the negotiations, describing the compromise as "eminently fair" since it would raise the take-home pay above the highest war year and yet stay within the wage stabilization formula. He felt it "inconceivable" that the rank-and-file members of these two unions realized "the terrifying situation created by the action of these two men." He reviewed his labor record in the Senate, pointing out that he had always been and always would be a friend of labor and would continue to oppose restrictive labor legislation. He reminded the nation that since the railroads were under government operation as a result of the strike, the men were striking against their government. He issued a call to the men to return to work as a "duty" to their country. If they did not return he would have no alternative but to call in the army to assist in operating the trains to overcome the "acute" emergency.[26]

On May 25 Truman appeared before a joint session of Congress requesting "strong emergency legislation" which

25 *Ibid.*, pp. 500-501.
26 Radio Address, May 24, 1946, Truman Papers, OR, HSTL.

would permit drafting the strikers. In a memorandum of the previous day Secretary of War Robert Patterson suggested that the President ask Congress to amend the Selective Service Act so as to broaden the current age bracket of twenty through thirty to new limits of twenty through forty-five years of age. This would "enable the military forces to get the men with railroad experiences" necessary to operate the trains,[27] and from this came Truman's strike draft proposal. At the same time government representatives, headed by Dr. John R. Steelman, Truman's trouble-shooter in labor disputes, were conferring with union officials in an attempt to reach a settlement. Truman was interrupted in his speech when a message was handed him by Leslie Biffle, secretary of the Senate, stating that the obstinate unions had accepted the offer and the strike was called off. The President then continued his speech in apparent disregard of the note. Republican Senator Wayne Morse of Oregon accused Truman of "ham acting"; Truman, he charged, already knew what the railroaders' position was when he began his address.[28] However, as Professor Seidman points out, Steelman, the President's negotiator, reached the agreement with the unions only three minutes before Truman began his message.[29] Truman said Morse later apologized to him when he knew the facts.[30]

That he continued his message even after the strike was called off indicated Truman's deep disgust with what he considered the unreasonable actions of union officials. He fully appreciated the resentful attitude of Congress and the country in this situation, he said. Therefore, he wanted to "urge speedy action to meet the immediate crisis," as well

[27] Robert Patterson to the President, May 24, 1946, Truman Papers, OF 407-B, HSTL.

[28] *Congressional Record,* 79 Cong., 2 Sess., 1946, XCII, 5801.

[29] Seidman, *American Labor From Defense to Reconversion,* p. 236.

[30] Truman, *Memoirs,* I, 501.

as deliberate and weighty consideration on legislation affecting the basic rights of labor. He drew this distinction by pointing out that the benefits labor had gained in the past thirteen years had to be preserved, but that in this case a "handful of men" had the power "to cripple the entire economy of the Nation," necessitating emergency legislation to circumvent the immediate crisis. This temporary legislation should be in effect for six months after cessation of hostilities and would affect only those industries that had been or would be taken over by the government. His proposal would: authorize injunctive proceedings against union officials if they encouraged or incited a strike in a government-operated industry, deprive workers of seniority rights if they persisted "without good cause" in striking against the government, provide for criminal penalties for violation of this strike clause, and subject such workers to be drafted into the armed forces. When President Truman requested the drafting of strikers, he received "prolonged cheers and applause." He was then handed the note and announced the end of the strike, an announcement which was followed by "great and prolonged cheers and applause."

Truman admitted that his proposal was "drastic" and that was why he wanted it to be temporary. He then went on to say that the right to strike against private employers had to be preserved but that it was time to adopt "a comprehensive labor policy" to reduce strikes. This permanent long-range policy, however, should be studied "afresh." He recommended the creation of a committee to make such a study and to propose recommendations within six months for a program which would be fair to labor, industry, and the public.[31]

This speech evoked an immediate outburst from labor that one magazine lavishly described as more unified than

31 Message to Congress, May 25, 1946, *Truman Papers, 1946*, pp. 277-80.

any since Cleveland had intervened in the Pullman Strike of 1894.[32] The most outspoken, A. F. Whitney, pledged his union's entire treasury of $47,000,000 to defeat Truman in 1948 if he should be a candidate.

The House of Representatives immediately approved the bill drawn up by Attorney General Tom Clark, embodying Truman's proposals, by vote of 306 to 13. But this same bill was blocked in the Senate by Robert A. Taft, who insisted that Truman's draft-labor request went "farther toward Hitlerism, Stalinism, totalitarianism than I have ever seen proposed in any strike."[33]

The Case bill, which had passed the House on February 7, was being amended and rewritten in the Senate. The Senate had been debating this bill for some time prior to Truman's message and, in spite of the delaying tactics of Claude Pepper of Florida and James Murray of Montana, was ready to take action on it. Taft insisted that the revised labor policy in this legislation would meet the needs requested by Truman and, answering the President's clarion call for immediate action, the Senate passed the Case bill a few hours after he spoke by vote of 49 to 29.[34] The measure, owing to Taft's action then, did not include the labor draft proposal and, in addition, was to be permanent legislation. On May 29 the House accepted the Senate version 320 to 106,[35] and the Federal Mediation bill of 1946 was presented to President Truman on May 31. The antiunion feeling of many congressmen, combined with public indignation over the two current major strikes, enabled Congress to pass the first postwar restrictive labor legislation.

United States News and World Report, in reviewing this fast legislative action, pointed out that "public reaction to

[32] *Newsweek,* XXVII (June 10, 1946), 23.
[33] *Ibid.,* p. 26.
[34] *Congressional Record,* 79 Cong., 2 Sess., 1946, XCII, 5739.
[35] *Ibid.,* p. 5946.

strikes" was great enough to cause a majority in the Senate to impose restrictions on union leaders in spite of the fact that the Senate was "normally responsive to the slightest wish of labor leaders." Truman's reversal of his prolabor attitude, this magazine explained, was "politically necessary" in order to end the paralyzing strikes.[36] *Newsweek* described the week as a "trial by fire for Harry S. Truman," because he was "faced with anger that burned across the nation" on the one hand and had to ask labor for its "cooperation" in ending the strike on the other. But, this magazine pointed out, President Truman got more than he asked for because the "temporary" legislation was also the long-range program for which he had requested a comprehensive study of six months by a committee preceding any congressional action.[37]

Reaction to the Case bill was immediate and vociferous. Representatives of industry flooded the White House with mail in an attempt to influence the President's decision. The president of General Electric urged Truman to continue his record of "friend and champion" of organized labor by signing the bill and thus "save labor from its own excesses."[38] The chairman of the board of the National Association of Manufacturers pointed out that the American people were "demanding action" and that Truman should take the "courageous and constructive action" of signing the bill thus saving the nation from "economic disaster." The bill was not antilabor as charged, the chairman said, but was pro-public because it would protect millions of laborers from the "ill-advised and misguided acts" of their leaders. The president of the United States Chamber of Commerce urged Truman's approval because the bill was in the public

[36] "What's Ahead for Labor—Era of Limiting Strikers," *United States News and World Report,* XX (May 31, 1946), 12.

[37] "Strikes: Mr. Truman Cries 'Halt!' to Labor at Zero Hour of Nation's Creeping Paralysis," *Newsweek,* XXVII (June 3, 1946), 19-22.

[38] The following public opinion mail can be found in the files on the Case bill, Truman Papers, OF 407-B, HSTL.

interest and reflected "a strong public demand" for such legislation. The president of the Southern States Industrial Council, a stronghold of antiunionism, declared that the large majorities in Congress for the bill reflected the "overwhelming favoritism" that the national government had shown toward unions and that led to "dictatorial powers" of labor leaders. Most of the pro-Case bill mail referred to the need of protecting the public from "monopolistic excesses" of labor and management.

Even the agricultural groups voiced strong opinions. The heads of two of the three leading farm organizations, the National Grange and the American Farm Bureau, sent telegrams urging Truman's signature. The bill "would protect the public from labor abuses" and the "overwhelming majority of the American people" favored it, they said. But the third leading agricultural organization, the liberal National Farmers Union, urged a veto on the grounds that if this or "similar throttling legislation" was passed, in the future no group, including farmers, would be safe from comparable "legislative encirclement."

Labor leaders sent frantic appeals to President Truman to save them with a veto. Philip Murray wrote a nine-page letter analyzing proposed antilabor legislation since the enactment of the Wagner Act. He said that the Case bill was "not merely ill-considered and injurious to labor," but it also posed an "exceeding grave danger" to the public because it would increase rather than diminish labor disputes. Sidney Hillman told Truman that Murray's analysis and prediction of resulting "evils," if the bill became law, needed no elaboration from him. The mail opposing the Case bill included letters and telegrams not only from local unions but from individuals who requested a veto of the "antilabor" measure which was a "vicious shackle" leading to "Fascism" and eventual "enslavement" of American labor.

Urgent appeals also came from congressmen. Case called

the President's attention to the fact that his bill sought "to achieve many of the objectives" which the President himself had requested. Another Representative thought it would be "a wise policy" to let the bill become law and then the President could again request his "careful study" of national labor policy. One Democratic congressman expressed the fear that a veto would cause the Democrats to lose the House in the 1946 elections. He pointedly added that no administration ever lost the House in midterm elections and won the Presidency two years later. When questioned by the press about the unusual amount of lobbying on the Case bill, the President replied that it was "the usual amount on a piece of legislation of that kind" and that it did not have any effect on him because he was "used to it."[39]

In the meantime Truman was consulting and gathering opinions from department heads and advisers on what he should do. He had asked William R. Thom, Democratic congressman from Ohio, to summarize his views in written form concerning the provision for suability of unions. Thom replied that unions were already suable in most states for breach of contract. The reason for erroneous public opinion to the contrary, he said, was that editors of "the foremost papers" continually told their readers that unions were immune from such suits.[40] Of the administration reports received by the President on the Case bill, only one approved of it. John Snyder, former director of War Mobilization and Reconversion who became Secretary of the Treasury in July 1946, stated that the bill was "in the public interest" and "most emphatically" did not deprive labor unions or employees of any basic rights. These amendments to the national labor law, the probusiness Snyder said, were limited

39 Press Conference, June 6, 1946, Truman Papers, OR 20, HSTL.

40 William R. Thom to Harry S. Truman, June 7, 1946, Truman Papers, OF 407-B, HSTL.

to "demonstrated abuses," many of which labor itself thought would be "desirable and fair" to correct.[41]

Secretary of Interior Julius Krug urged a veto on the grounds that the bill had been "drastically revised" on the floor of the Senate during a time when it was difficult to give it "the mature and deliberate judgment" which the provisions demanded.[42] The chairman of the Labor Policy Committee of the Department of Commerce wrote Secretary of Commerce Henry Wallace that the bill was a good start in limiting abuses and urged approval.[43] Despite this recommendation, Wallace submitted a four-page proposed veto message based on the idea that "upon calm, deliberate and analytical consideration" the bill was basically antilabor and would foment "additional labor unrest."[44] Attorney General Tom Clark also offered a proposed veto message. He objected to the provision extending the criminal penalties, to the treble damages provisions, and to the application of injunctive sanctions of the antitrust laws to union activities. He also repeated President Truman's May 25 request for a study committee before enacting permanent labor legislation.[45]

Secretary of Labor Lewis Schwellenbach was the most specific in his objections. He disliked the provision for replacing the United States Conciliation Service with the new Federal Mediation Board, which would be outside of his jurisdiction. He felt that the problem of excluding supervisors as employees in the national labor law was "complicated" and needed more study. Schwellenbach ob-

41 John Snyder, Analysis of Case Bill, n.d., Truman Papers, Rosenman File, OF 407-B, HSTL.

42 Julius Krug to the President, Memorandum, June 4, 1946, Truman Papers, OF 407-B, HSTL.

43 Charles R. Hook to Henry A. Wallace, June 3, 1946, Truman Papers, OF 407-B, HSTL.

44 Henry A. Wallace to the President, June 5, 1946, Truman Papers, OF 407-B, HSTL.

45 Tom Clark to the President, June 7, 1946, Truman Papers, OF 407-B, HSTL.

jected to the indefiniteness of the language in the clause covering damage suits against labor unions. He also felt that such permanent legislation needed more detailed study before Congress acted. Then, in an interesting sidelight, he mentioned the current complaint that the Senate and House labor committees were "loaded in favor of organized labor." He doubted if this charge were true, but was certain that both committees had "some of the most ardent anti-labor members" in Congress.[46]

After "careful consideration" Truman decided against the bill and sent his veto message to Congress on June 11. In his message Truman said his primary consideration had been whether the bill would benefit the public by reducing industrial strife and he had concluded that it would not. He reiterated his May 25 appeal for temporary emergency legislation, pointing out that the request dealt with strikes against the government and not against private employers, which were covered in the Case bill. His specific objections to the bill included the formation of a new Mediation Board. He believed that the Conciliation Service had done a good job since its creation in 1913 and the new Mediation Board would not have affected the outcome of any of the recent major disputes if it had then been in existence.

Truman then went on to point out that the Case bill itself confirmed the need for careful study from a long-range viewpoint; it demonstrated the necessity of "painstaking and exhaustive consideration" before drafting permanent legislation. "H.R. 4908 strikes at symptoms and ignores underlying causes," he said. The issues must be considered against the broad background "of inflationary pressures, of problems of full employment, of economic security" and only then would such legislation be workable.[47] That same

[46] L. B. Schwellenbach to the President, June 4, 1946, Truman Papers, OF 407-B, HSTL.

[47] Veto Message to House of Representatives, June 11, 1946, *Truman Papers, 1946*, pp. 289-97.

day the House of Representatives sustained his veto by a vote of 255 to 135, only five votes less than the two-thirds necessary to override.[48]

While Congress was unsuccessful in this major drive of 1946 to check union power by amending the national labor policy, it was successful in halting some of the specific abuses. In April of 1946 Congress passed, and Truman signed, the Lea Act or "Anti-Petrillo Act," aimed at curbing featherbedding practices in the musicians' union. The law set up criminal penalties for compelling or coercing radio broadcasters to hire more employees than needed or to pay for services not actually rendered, such as rebroadcasting a tape recording. And in July of 1946, Congress passed the Hobbs Anti-Racketeering Act, which had been a clause in the vanquished Case bill. This measure amended the 1934 racketeering law, making it a criminal offense to delay or interfere with the flow of interstate commerce by extortion. It was directed at the Teamsters union practice of compelling the hiring of union drivers or paying to the union the equivalent of a union driver's wage in addition to the regular operator's pay if a nonunion driver was employed. President Truman signed the Hobbs bill, stating that when he vetoed the Case proposal on June 11 he was in "full accord with the objectives of . . . [that provision] the Case bill."[49] At the same time during 1946 the drive to curb unions was gathering momentum in the state governments.

The congressional elections of 1946 resulted in a sharp swing to the right and the election of several conservatives. In the fall of 1946 John L. Lewis again stepped into the national spotlight by threatening a new coal strike because the government, he maintained, had violated the welfare fund agreement reached the previous May. This new threat came just before the elections of 1946 were held and, in

[48] *Congressional Record,* 79 Cong., 2 Sess., 1946, XCII, 6678.
[49] Message to Congress, July 3, 1946, *Truman Papers, 1946,* pp. 336-37.

Truman's opinion, helped produce the conservative results of those elections. President Truman believed that Lewis deliberately threatened a strike at this inopportune time in order to bring about a "turnover" in Congress, but his plan backfired. Instead of a sympathetic Congress, Lewis faced a "reactionary-controlled group" which passed the Taft-Hartley Act.[50]

When the miners struck on November 21 in defiance of Judge Goldsborough's injunction, it was suggested that a special session of Congress be called to deal with the situation. But the administration decided to fight it out in the courts. In an editorial survey of 225 newspapers on this question, the Government Information Service evaluated public opinion as being against the special session. The service concluded that editors felt that any change in labor laws should be made by the newly elected Congress because the electorate failed to give the Seventy-ninth Congress a vote of confidence "mainly for its lack of foresightedness in labor matters and its willingness to allow labor unions to escape responsibility on a par with management."[51] A December survey made by the Government Information Service indicated an increasing desire among editors for the next Congress not only to restrict the miners' power to "paralyze our economy again, but also to prevent the excessive use of power by any labor group." The new Congress, these editors felt, would take away labor's "unwarranted gains" made under the New Deal, and most of them blamed the "despotic ambitions" of John L. Lewis for this threat to organized labor.[52] One commentator wrote that "a veritable typhoon of public opinion" was removing control of the situation from the moderates. "Senators and Congressmen are hearing

50 Truman, *Memoirs,* I, 505.

51 "Editorial Reaction to Current Issues; Bituminous Coal Crisis," Division of Press Intelligence, Government Information Service, Nov. 25, 1946, Truman Papers, OF 407-B, HSTL.

52 *Ibid.,* December 7, 1946.

from the country," he warned, and what they heard was an "upsurge of public feeling" sweeping across the country against unions. "The stampede is on," he concluded, "and there is little that labor, either the AF of L or CIO, can do to halt it."[53]

When the new Congress met in January 1947, President Truman presented it with a labor legislation program in his State of the Union message. He asked Congress to work on five major domestic policies and first on his list was labor-management relations. In this passage he dealt at length with the issue of labor disputes, emphasizing that much of the problem consisted of price increases which had swept away the value of wage increases. Although the past year had been marred by industrial strife, he did not want Congress to pass "punitive legislation" in order to punish a few obstinate labor leaders "under the stress of emotion." Rather, the nation should continue the national policy established by the Wagner Act and provide additional legislation to correct certain abuses.

Truman's attempt to circumvent drastic legislation consisted of a four-point program to reduce industrial strife. Point one called for curtailing improper union practices such as jurisdictional disputes involving both representation and work tasks, secondary boycotts in pursuit of unjustifiable objectives, and the use of economic force to decide interpretation of existing contracts. The second point asked for expansion of the Department of Labor to provide additional facilities in assisting collective bargaining, facilities consisting of integrated governmental machinery for mediation and voluntary arbitration. Point three requested social legislation to alleviate the causes of labor insecurity, such as broader social security coverage, better housing, a higher minimum wage, and a comprehensive national health pro-

[53] "Interpreting the Labor News," Robert Maisil Associates, New York, Bulletin No. 10, Dec. 11, 1946, Truman Papers, OF 407, HSTL.

gram. Finally, he called for his often-requested study committee. He proposed a joint committee consisting of twenty members, twelve of whom Congress would choose from both Democrats and Republicans in the House and Senate, and eight representing labor, management, and the public to be chosen by the President. This commission should study and make recommendations not later than March 15, 1947, upon three major problems: nationwide strikes in vital industries, the best procedures for carrying out collective bargaining, and the underlying causes of labor-management disputes.[54]

But this program proved much too moderate for the Eightieth Congress. As a result of the 1946 elections in which industrial strife was a key issue, the Republicans gained control of both houses of Congress for the first time since 1930. Utilizing the public frustration over inflation and the dearth of consumer goods, Republicans campaigned for office in 1946 principally on the issue of curbing union power. As early as July 1946, the Republican candidate for governor in Oklahoma, Olney F. Flynn, plastered the highway billboards in his state with signs reading, "Haven't You Had Enough?" This caption was shortened in the East to "Had Enough?" and Republicans throughout the nation then had their campaign slogan.[55] In an attempt to counterattack, the CIO-PAC (Political Action Committee) announced a campaign to solicit one-dollar contributions and thus raise $1,000,000 to be used to defeat antilabor candidates. But in late October Jack Kroll, PAC director following the death of Sidney Hillman on July 10, 1946, stated that only $170,000 had been raised at that time.[56]

The Republicans successfully captured the public mood with "Had Enough?" The voters apparently had because the

[54] State of the Union Message to Congress, Jan. 6, 1947, *Truman Papers, 1947*, pp. 1-12.
[55] *Newsweek*, XXVIII (Nov. 4, 1946), 28.
[56] *Ibid.* (Oct. 28, 1946), p. 28.

elections gave Republicans a 246-to-189 majority in the House and a 51-to-45 majority in the Senate. In addition, 109 of the Democrats in the House were Southerners. So overwhelming was this Republican trend that voters in Atlantic City, New Jersey, elected a Republican as justice of the peace who had died a week before election day.[57] Only 34,000,000 people voted in these elections and a light vote is believed to favor the Republican party in recent years. Truman later told labor that it got what it deserved by staying away from the polls in 1946. The thinking of some of the national political leaders after this landslide was reflected in a proposal by Senator William Fulbright of Arkansas. Since the national mood and Congress was so overwhelmingly Republican, he suggested that Truman appoint a prominent Republican as secretary of state and then resign immediately so that person could succeed to the presidency. This proposal touched off an uproar from both Republicans and Democrats with Truman refusing to "dignify the suggestion with a public rejection." Despite this, Fulbright persisted with his proposal, maintaining that this would eliminate a serious weakness in our governmental system caused by the fact that opposing parties can control the White House and Congress, but few took him seriously.[58]

[57] *Ibid.* (Nov. 18, 1946), p. 35.

[58] See *Ibid.*, p. 36; *Time*, XLVIII (Nov. 18, 1946), 22; New York *Times*, Nov. 7, 8, 10, 1946.

3

THE EIGHTIETH CONGRESS REVERSES A NEW DEAL POLICY

When the Eightieth Congress met in January 1947, Representative George Bender of Ohio presented his fellow Republicans with new brooms and the caption, "Here's yours. Let's do the job," saying it was time "to sweep away the cobwebs which have cluttered up our thinking."[1] Many Republicans viewed their 1946 victory as an opportunity to reverse much of the New Deal social legislation and there was little doubt that they would use these brooms to help enact some sort of legislation dealing with the national labor policy.

A campaign to amend the Wagner Act had been building in intensity since the activities of the Smith committee in 1939. In addition, the big majorities given to the Case bill by the previous Congress and the "mandate from the people" received in the 1946 elections assured action in this area. Then, too, the antilabor drive in the states reached its peak in 1947 when, under the lobbying pressure of state and local employer associations and the backing of the NAM and the United States Chamber of Commerce, some thirty states restricted the rights of organized labor. This antiunion legislation in the states went hand-in-hand with the legislative drive in Washington by the Eightieth Congress. Also, the fact that President Truman gave primary consideration to labor legislation in his State of the Union message further emphasized its importance to Congress.

That the administration was expecting changes that would be more drastic than Truman's proposals was indicated in an intradepartmental memorandum. Before the Eightieth Congress met, Paul Herzog, chairman of the NLRB, drew up a list of probable changes that Congress would make in its attempt to "equalize" labor-management relations under the Wagner Act. The changes Herzog predicted were: to separate the judicial and prosecutory functions of the NLRB; to deprive supervisors of NLRB rights; to confer the right on employers to petition for an election in some "one-union" cases; to expand employers' right to "free speech"; to list unfair practices of unions; to increase the reviewability of NLRB decisions in the courts; and to penalize employees for "illegal" strikes[2]—a prediction that was amazingly accurate, inadequate only in its scope.

Professor Henry Steele Commager forecast that this first session of the Eightieth Congress would, almost without doubt, pass some bill to curb labor's power.[3] Raymond Moley, in contemplating the situation, could not see any hope for real cooperation between the administration and Congress. Although the administration seemed unaware

1 New York *Times*, Jan. 3, 1947.

2 David A. Morse to Secretary Schwellenbach, Memorandum, Nov. 14, 1946, Secretary Schwellenbach File (Legislation, 1946), R.G. 174, National Archives.

3 Henry Steele Commager, "A Turning Point for Labor," *Senior Scholastic*, L (May 12, 1947), 7.

that the country faced a labor problem, the conservative Moley observed, the public was aware of it and did not want "to go through another year like 1946." The country expected Congress to provide effective reforms, he said, and unless the administration woke up to this fact the remedies might be "overdrastic."[4] The *Congressional Digest* reported early in 1947 that labor-management relations were providing the "most lively domestic drama of the day" and that the labor question made front-page news almost daily in the nation's newspapers. This report added that among congressional committees, the two labor committees were drawing the largest public crowds for their hearings.[5] Throughout the country the atmosphere was charged with an air of expectancy that at last Congress would "put labor in its place."

This public reaction intensified a similar feeling in Congress. When describing the congressional atmosphere later, Representative John McCormack, Democrat from Massachusetts, claimed that it was so "intense" that labor legislation could not receive rational consideration.[6] Senator Wayne Morse, Republican from Oregon, echoed this sentiment, saying that in 1947 Congress "yielded to public heat, not to public reason." The country was mad at labor's "excesses" and as a result, was not thinking clearly on labor legislation, Morse claimed.[7] When Secretary of Labor Tobin charged, during Senate Labor Committee hearings in the Eighty-first Congress, that the Taft-Hartley Act was passed in "a period of great emotional stress," Senator Robert A. Taft, Republican from Ohio and coauthor of the bill, denied it. Compared to the emotion aroused by the Case bill and the President's labor draft proposal, Taft countered, the Taft-Hartley Act

4 Raymond Moley, "Suggestions for a Labor Program," *Newsweek*, XXIX (Feb. 10, 1947), 100.

5 *Congressional Digest*, XXVI (March 1947), 69.

6 *Congressional Record*, 81 Cong., 1 Sess., 1949, XCV, 5134.

7 *Ibid.*, p. 7430.

was passed "with the greatest care and consideration" of any legislation of a Congress he had ever served in.[8] Despite this protest, all evidence indicates that the Taft-Hartley Act was passed at a time when the nation was fully aroused against organized labor. A Gallup Poll conducted after the elections on the question "Should the Congress elected in November pass new laws to control labor unions?" indicated 66 percent affirmative, 22 percent negative, and 12 percent undecided.[9] Only with an overwhelming public demand could a Republican Congress carry a majority of Democrats against a Democratic administration and drastically amend, for the first and to date only time, an established New Deal policy.

In the first day's session of the Eightieth Congress seventeen bills dealing with national labor policy were introduced in the House of Representatives. By mid-March there were over sixty-five such bills introduced in Congress and they were still coming in.[10] Altogether the two congressional labor committees had over one hundred bills to consider. These two committees were chaired by Fred A. Hartley, Jr., Republican from New Jersey, and Senator Robert A. Taft. Taft had first been elected to the United States Senate in 1938. The son of a former President, Taft personified the Republican party of the postwar period, capping his political career by being designated "Mr. Republican" by the nation. He became the national symbol for conservatism and isolationism whose "following included those old-stock Americans who had not taken well to the new power of the unions and the minorities in the big cities."[11] When a Republican

[8] U.S. Senate, Committee on Labor and Public Welfare, *Hearings on S. 249, Labor Relations,* 81 Cong., 1 Sess., 1949, p. 259.

[9] *Public Opinion Quarterly,* XI (Spring 1947), 151.

[10] John A. Fitch, "The New Congress and the Unions," *Survey Graphic,* XXXVI (1947), 231.

[11] Walter Johnson, *1600 Pennsylvania Avenue* (Boston: Little Brown, 1963), p. 227.

majority was returned to the United States Congress in 1946 he was convinced that "the popular mandate was to cast out a great many chapters of the New Deal, if not the whole book."[12] As chairman of the Republican Policy Committee he was now in a position to do just that. Expanding and cultivating the already growing alliance of rightwing Republicans and conservative Southern Democrats who opposed many of the New Deal policies, he was able to create the "masterwork of his life," the Taft-Hartley Act.[13]

His sympathetic biographer, William S. White, was a reporter who covered the congressional debates on the Taft-Hartley Act and thus saw Taft "nearly every day." White is convinced that Taft's purpose in fashioning the law which bears his name was not to hurt labor, but that it stemmed from the sincere conviction that the rank and file of laboring men were in the grip of labor "bosses." "He never to my knowledge said a word or took an action that indicated any contempt or underappreciation for labor," reports White.[14] Taft's views on labor legislation were his own, gathered without any "apparent deep bias," White insists, and any employer was very mistaken if he "thought that in Taft he was dealing with a captive."[15]

When the Republicans organized Congress in 1947, Taft had a choice of being the chairman of either the Finance Committee or the Labor and Public Welfare Committee, as he was the ranking Republican member on both. He chose the Labor Committee assignment to the disappointment of Senator George Aiken, Republican from Vermont, who wanted the position but "was considered much too liberal by the G.O.P. leadership."[16] Taft's right-hand man on this committee was Joseph Ball, Republican from Minnesota,

12 William S. White, *The Taft Story* (New York: Harper, 1954), p. 57.
13 *Ibid.*, p. 65.
14 *Ibid.*, p. 102.
15 *Ibid.*, p. 70.
16 Bailey and Samuels, *Congress at Work*, p. 417.

who "made no secret of his antipathy for many of the leaders and practices of organized labor."[17] There were thirteen Senators on this committee, eight of whom were Republicans. Other outstanding Republicans, besides Taft, Aiken, and Ball, were Wayne Morse and Irving Ives of New York. Morse and Ives had accumulated considerable labor relations experience in their states before coming to the Senate. These Republican Senators had served a total of twenty-five years on the Labor Committee, Taft himself contributing seven of these years. The Democratic members included Elbert D. Thomas, Democrat from Utah, the ranking Democrat who was to lead the fight to repeal the Taft-Hartley Act in 1949. The five Democratic members had served a total of forty-nine years on this committee.[18] The amount of experience of the Senators on this committee contrasts markedly with the lack of such experience on the part of the members of the House Committee on Education and Labor.

On the other side of the Capitol, Taft's counterpart was Fred A. Hartley, Jr., chairman of the House Committee on Education and Labor. Hartley had first been elected to the House of Representatives in 1928, prior to the advent of the New Deal. It is paradoxical that Hartley sponsored one of the strictest antiunion bills in United States history and yet at one time was heartily endorsed by a labor union in an election. One of the aims of the Smith committee of 1939-1940 had been to protect the craft unions against the overwhelming numerical superiority of the horizontal or industrial union. It was felt by critics that the NLRB was pro-CIO during this period, so Hartley fought for amendments to the Wagner Act in 1939, the Smith Act, which would have revamped the NLRB. Hartley was the first congressman to testify before the Smith committee in favor of these AFL

17 *Ibid.*, p. 419.

18 These figures are from Millis and Brown, *From the Wagner Act to Taft-Hartley*, p. 374.

amendments.[19] As a reward, William Green issued a letter to the union locals in the Tenth Congressional District of New Jersey prior to the 1940 elections, stating that by his votes and general attitude Hartley had "proven himself to be an outstanding friend of labor." Green requested that AFL members therefore support him in this election.[20] The CIO on the other hand opposed Hartley and in the 1946 election fought him bitterly but he was elected by a comfortable margin. Hartley was to serve in Congress only through the creation of his "masterpiece," having decided before the sessions of the Eightieth Congress to retire from Congress.[21]

When the House of Representatives was organized, Richard Welch, Republican from California and ranking Republican member of the Labor Committee, was persuaded to take the chairmanship of the Committee on Public Lands since he was considered prolabor and "had seldom seen eye to eye with his fellow party members."[22] This gave Hartley the chairmanship. Hartley's appointment induced Mary Norton from New Jersey, the ranking Democrat and former chairman, to resign from the committee. Mrs. Norton resigned because she had "no respect for the present chairman" and thus could not serve with him. In the ten years she had served as chairman of the House Education and Labor Committee, Hartley had attended "exactly six meetings" and yet talked "about labor as if he knew something about it."[23] Hartley did not refute this charge, but concluded that Mrs. Norton resigned because she was "a bad loser."[24]

19 Fred A. Hartley, Jr., *Our New National Labor Policy* (New York: Funk and Wagnalls, 1948), pp. 13-15.

20 William Green to City Central Bodies and Local Labor Union of the Tenth Congressional District of New Jersey, April 26, 1940, *Congressional Record,* 80 Cong., 1 Sess., 1947, XCIII, 3432.

21 Hartley, *Our New National Labor Policy,* p. 171.

22 Bailey and Samuel, *Congress at Work,* p. 417.

23 *Congressional Record,* 80 Cong., 1 Sess., 1947, XCIII, 3432.

24 Hartley, *Our New National Labor Policy,* p. 26.

The House committee was composed of fifteen Republicans and ten Democrats. Included were two newcomers to Congress, Richard M. Nixon, Republican from California, and John F. Kennedy, Democrat from Massachusetts. The House committee had much less experience in labor matters than its Senate counterpart. Ten of the fifteen Republicans had no prior service, and the remaining five had a total of only twenty years since the enactment of the Wagner Act. Hartley accounted for over ten of these years but, according to Mrs. Norton, did not pick up too much experience in that time. Four of the Democrats had not seen prior service on the Labor Committee but the other six had acquired thirty years' experience since 1935.[25]

Beginning February 5 and ending March 13, the House Committee on Education and Labor held hearings for six weeks on various bills to amend the Wagner Act. During this period the committee accumulated five volumes of testimony, including letters and statements, from over 130 witnesses. Both the majority and minority members agreed that this aspect of the committee's work was conducted fairly; a good representation of public and private viewpoints was made. The hearings of the Senate Committee on Labor and Public Welfare on the labor bills introduced in the upper house were even more ably conducted, lasting from January 29 to March 8. This committee accumulated four volumes of testimony, including letters and statements, from almost one hundred witnesses. Even the prolabor Senator Morse complimented the Senate committee on its fine work, saying he was "deeply moved" by the "fine spirit that characterized all of the deliberations."[26]

Much of the testimony of witnesses who favored amending the Wagner Act was directed toward criticisms of the NLRB in regard to its administration and interpretation of the act.

[25] Millis and Brown, *From the Wagner Act to Taft-Hartley*, pp. 365-66.
[26] *Congressional Record*, 80 Cong., 1 Sess., 1947, XCIII, 3614.

Chairman Paul Herzog attempted to answer these charges on behalf of the board before both the Senate and House committees. In testifying before the Senate committee on March 6, Herzog declared that the policy the board had been administering for twelve years was a "wise one" and any changes in that fundamental policy would bring "unhappy consequences." The critics of the law or its administration were in many cases those who had lost power under the Wagner Act because of the resulting growth of collective bargaining and thus, Herzog claimed, their testimony should be assessed accordingly. Emphasizing the prodigious growth of union membership under the act from 4,000,000 to 15,000,000, he said that while it was not the function of the board to help union organization, one of the act's purposes was to make it "less hazardous" for workers to join unions. He pithily added that the board assumed that Congress looked upon the resulting growth as a desirable trend. He pointed out that under the Wagner Act work stoppages caused by organizational strikes had dropped from about 60 percent in 1937 to around 8 percent in 1946. The postwar waves of strikes were caused by wage disputes fought between "strong unions and strong employers." The present need, Herzog declared, was not to "turn the clock back" by amending the basic policy, but to encourage industry and labor "to sit down and reason together." And he pointedly called attention to the fact that the efficacy of the law had never been tried in normal times; the creation of the act was followed by the five years of "heated litigation" and then the abnormal six years of war and reconversion.

Herzog then explained why the board opposed certain changes under consideration by the committee. The board opposed excluding supervisors from the act because under a broad interpretation an employer could convert almost all employees into "supervisors." The NLRB doubted the value of making it an unfair labor practice for unions to refuse to bargain because this would merely impose an obligation "to perform the very function they were created to perform." The board also opposed the amendment providing penalties for violation of a no-strike, no-lockout pledge during a cooling-off period because it realized from experience how difficult it could be to interpret this since employers frequently locked out employees and claimed a strike was in progress, and vice versa. Splitting up the board's administrative powers by creating an "Assistant Attorney General" was opposed because good administration could be accomplished best by a single agency; and it did not favor changes in the board's proceedings by requiring board findings to be supported "by the weight of evidence," since this would be contrary to the basic principle of administrative law which allows the specialist to appraise evidence and determine facts with discretion. He concluded the board's testimony by saying that if these substantive and procedural changes were made, the result, at best, would be years of court litigation and uncertainty and, at worst, workers would be so resentful that "work stoppages would sweep the country."[27] Herzog gave the same testimony before the House committee, but added that the board would not resist "attempts to eliminate abuses." The problem with the House proposals, he said, was that "their impact falls alike upon the just and the unjust."[28]

The only other major administrative official who testified before these committees was Secretary of Labor Lewis Schwellenbach. In reviewing the industrial strife of the

[27] U.S. Senate, Committee on Labor and Public Welfare, *Hearings on S. 55 and S.J. Res. 22, Labor Relations,* 80 Cong., 1 Sess., 1947, pp. 1847-936. A minute examination of these committee hearings is beyond the scope of this book. Instead, only that testimony of leading administrative officials that has been considered pertinent to the theme of this study, i.e., administration efforts to protect its labor constituents against a rural-dominated Congress, has been included.

[28] U.S. House of Representatives, Committee on Education and Labor, *Hearings on Bills to Amend and Repeal the National Labor Relations Act,* 80 Cong., 1 Sess., 1947, pp. 3086-196.

reconversion period, Schwellenbach emphasized that conditions had changed since V-J Day. He maintained that the postwar strife was caused by the fear of workers in regard to loss of jobs and pay cuts and that they were tired of long work weeks of the war period. On the other side, employers wanted price relief and also some employers were utilizing the reconversion conditions to try to destroy the effectiveness of unions. When these two forces met, strife resulted. Both sides, he argued, had forgotten the art of collective bargaining during the war, intensifying the problem. But there was a different attitude on the part of both labor and management now, and to prove this, 1946 saw American production reach the highest point of any peacetime year.

In regard to specific proposals under consideration, Schwellenbach had slightly mixed views. The Secretary explained the uselessness of making unions subject to suit. Since the adoption of the Federal Rules of Civil Procedure, there were only thirteen states in which an unincorporated association could not be sued and enacting such a provision would be futile. Schwellenbach also opposed the amendments which would restrict union-security provisions. The checkoff system had been in existence for a long time and he could see nothing "immoral" about it. He reminded the committee members that as of April 1947, 77 percent of all organized workers had contracts which contained union-security provisions. The figures he gave were: closed shop, 30 percent; maintenance of membership, 29 percent; union shop, 15 percent; and preferential hiring, 3 percent. If Congress were to outlaw such provisions, he warned, the result would be "industrial chaos." He insisted that many employers, as well as employees, would object to this move as they had discovered that when they granted such concessions "the industrial stability which resulted was to their advantage." He said that with respect to secondary boycotts, Congress was going "far beyond the President's recommendation."

But in regard to banning industrywide bargaining, Schwellenbach had reservations. His experience had shown that this type of bargaining was desirable in some cases and undesirable in others. He pointed out that this problem was complicated by the fact that many local union committees were untrained and sometimes dominated by radicals, in contrast to their international organizations, and thus were less able and less willing to bargain, so the answer to this had to be taken from each situation.[29]

Schwellenbach later referred to the bans on union-security provisions as opening "a veritable Pandora's box of labor troubles" when taken in connection with the other restrictive measures proposed.[30] Also, he later reiterated his views against making labor unions subject to suit in federal courts. Since they were already liable for violation of contract in most state courts, this would set them apart from all other organizations as there was no limit to the amount in controversy or no diversity of citizenship in such private suits as proposed by Congress.[31] Since Schwellenbach was a federal judge from 1940 to 1945 before becoming secretary of labor, his opinion in regard to judicial interpretation should have carried weight.

Although the House committee finished its hearings last, it was the first to produce a bill in Congress. Hartley had maintained that he was not in a race with the Senate committee to see who could devise the first measure and that he had talked the situation over with Taft. But soon after the House hearings began, Hartley decided that the final proposal would have to be written in conference. Therefore it would strengthen Taft's hand at that time if he had

[29] *Ibid.*, pp. 2994-3086.

[30] L. B. Schwellenbach, Address to the National Textile Seminar, Shawnee-on-Delaware, Pa., May 15, 1947, Schwellenbach Papers, Library of Congress.

[31] L. B. Schwellenbach, Address at the University of California, March, 1947, Schwellenbach Papers, Library of Congress.

available a House bill with sterner provisions. Taft himself admitted that the two houses worked together "to some extent" but that the connection was "a loose one."[32] Hartley's first major decision in regard to producing labor legislation was to work out an omnibus bill and then "put the entire weight of the Republican Party and the Southern Democrats behind it." In contrast, the Senate committee was considering a series of bills at this time. When the House thus forced the onmibus approach, Hartley felt it "made its greatest single contribution to the rapidly developing labor legislation."[33]

Hartley's committee used a unique method of writing his bill, H.R. 3020. The bill was being written before hearings were concluded, strongly suggesting that the ideas were already germinated and that he felt the usual collection of evidence was unnecessary. This serious charge was brought by Representative Arthur G. Klein, Democrat from New York, who stated that the bill was being written before the hearings began.[34] Some support for this accusation could be found from Hartley himself. Although this is inconclusive proof, on January 29, a week before the House hearings commenced, Hartley was reported to have said that his committee would have an omnibus bill ready by March 15 and the issues he predicted the committee would handle were contained in his bill.[35]

The House minority report complained that H.R. 3020 was not a committee bill since no general committee meetings were held to consider it. It was introduced on the floor of the House on April 10, the same day the minority members were first given a copy of it with a request to

32 Robert A. Taft, Foreword to Hartley, *Our New National Labor Policy*, p. xi.

33 Hartley, *Our New National Labor Policy*, p. 35.

34 *Congressional Record*, 80 Cong., 1 Sess., 1947, XCIII, 3420.

35 New York *Times*, Jan. 30, 1947.

have their report ready April 12.[36] John Lesinski, the ranking minority member, said the bill was presented to the minority members on Thursday morning, April 10. The full committee convened Thursday and Friday afternoons to sit through the reading of the bill and met on Saturday afternoon to vote to report out the measure. The minority then had to file its report that night.[37] Representative John Kennedy later charged that the committee spent one day to cover a 67-page, extremely complicated bill, to which Graham A. Barden, Democrat from North Carolina, replied "If you can do a job in one day why work the second?"[38]

In the House debates, the reproach was also made that the committee itself did not write the bill. While committees and individual congressmen have services available for writing their bills and seldom personally draw up their own legislation, this assistance usually takes the form of putting into technical and legal language the ideas that the congressman wishes to enact. Philip Philbin, Democrat from Massachusetts, stated that it had been "conclusively shown that this punitive legislation" was the brainchild of the National Association of Manufacturers and big business.[39] Adolph Sabath, Democrat from Illinois, accused the "Chamber of Commerce, the National Association of Manufacturers, and their lesser but even more virulent satellites" of writing the bill and "ramming it through" the House. Sabath warned the Republicans that the interests who were forcing them to adopt H.R. 3020 would not be able to spend enough money to reelect them because their money could not buy the American people once they found out what happened.[40]

Representative Klein also charged that the bill was written

[36] U.S. House of Representatives, Committee on Education and Labor, *Report No. 245* (80 Cong., 1 Sess., 1947).

[37] *Congressional Record,* 80 Cong., 1 Sess., 1947, XCIII, 3427.

[38] *Ibid.,* 81 Cong., 1 Sess., 1949, XCV, 5144.

[39] *Ibid.,* 80 Cong., 1 Sess., 1947, XCIII, 6391.

[40] *Ibid.,* p. 6388.

with the help of industry representatives and lawyers from the National Association of Manufacturers and the United States Chamber of Commerce. Some of the most valuable assistance, he declared, came from William Ingles, who reported a yearly salary of $24,000 as a lobbyist for Allis-Chalmers, Fruehauf Trailer, J. I. Case, the Falk Corporation, and Inland Steel. Other aid came from Theodore Iserman, who "put aside his rich Chrysler law practice for two weeks" to help the committee. Finally, another "volunteer in the antilabor cause" was Gerald Morgan, who had a law office in Washington with large corporations for clients.[41] Adam Clayton Powell, Jr., Democrat from New York, said the bill "was written on the fifth floor of the Old House Office Building" by "over a score of corporation lawyers . . . paid by big business."[42] To substantiate these indictments, John Blatnik, Democrat from Minnesota, made a point-by-point comparison between H.R. 3020 and the 1946 legislative recommendations of the NAM, which were quite similar. Blatnik stated that he had received, and intimated that all other congressmen had received, a leather-bound booklet from the NAM early in this session. Its title was *Now Let's Build America,* and it contained the NAM's 1946 legislative proposals to Congress; it was the source from which he drew his comparison.[43] The NAM later denied these charges by issuing a statement "Who Wrote the Taft-Hartley Bill?" on January 13, 1948.[44]

In amazingly candid testimony, Gerald Morgan, the lawyer referred to by Klein, later revealed how the Taft-Hartley Act was written in the committees. Morgan had been a legislative counsel for the House from 1935 to 1945 and, according to his statement, had had a "major part" in drafting

41 *Ibid.*, p. 3421.
42 *Ibid.*, p. 3525.
43 *Ibid.*, pp. 3541-42.
44 Millis and Brown, *From the Wagner Act to Taft-Hartley,* pp. 370-71 n.

the Fair Labor Standards Act, the 1940 Smith amendments to the Wagner Act, the War Labor Disputes Act, and the Case bill. Early in 1947 Morgan was requested by Chairman Hartley to serve as a special counsel to the majority members of the Committee on Education and Labor. Previously he had been approached by Charles Halleck, Republican from Indiana, who talked to him "at some length" on this same matter and suggested that he start to work on a proposed draft of labor legislation. Halleck, as mentioned previously, was the Majority Leader in the House but was not even a member of the Labor Committee.

Following this suggestion, Morgan took the defeated Smith amendments of 1940 and the Case bill, combined them, and threw in "a number of additional ideas that Mr. Halleck thought would be appropriate." This working draft was given to Hartley, who called a series of conferences of a few congressmen to discuss the policy issues contained in Morgan's proposal and "substantially revised" his document. Hartley then hired Morgan to continue his good work. Morgan submitted a second draft and the majority members of the committee met with him daily for three weeks. Out of these discussions emerged a "tentative draft of a bill" embodying policy decisions made by these congressmen. The draft was then submitted to the Republican Steering Committee for its consideration and later read to the full Labor Committee. The Labor Committee then added various amendments and it was introduced in the House.

During this time Morgan attended every meeting on the bill, working on it "morning, noon, and night." To aid him in this work, Morgan called upon the technical assistance of two other lawyers. One was Gerard Reilly, a former member of the NLRB who incidentally was greatly disliked by the AFL and CIO. At that time Reilly was serving as special counsel to the Senate Labor Committee, which was working on the Taft bill. The second man was Theodore Iserman, a labor law attorney who had written a book in 1946 entitled *The Wagner Act and Industrial Peace*. According to Morgan's testimony the "technical assistance" these two men rendered concerned NLRB policies, practices, and decisions, and court decisions.

Morgan stated that Hartley originally asked him to go on the professional staff but that he had refused because he would not give up his regular practice. When he was hired, and during the period of his work, Morgan received no compensation. Then "several months" after the passage of the act, "through the good offices of Mr. Halleck," Morgan was paid $7,500 by the Republican National Committee for his services. Morgan had previously declared that he was revealing all this because of the misinformation concerning who wrote the Taft-Hartley Act and that he had received permission from Hartley and Halleck to do so. When asked if he felt he had worked for the Republican National Committee or if the majority committee members had been his clients, he replied that he had been working for the members of the Labor Committee. But he could not explain why he had asked Hartley and Halleck to disregard his lawyer's "ethical seal of secrecy" in giving this testimony instead of the Labor Committee members he had considered as his clients.

Morgan was asked if he had contacted any agents or representatives of the NAM during his work on the Taft-Hartley Act. He replied that he had spoken only to Raymond Smethurst, the NAM counsel, about an antitrust provision but said that particular section was not included in the final act.[45] Three days after these hearings Morgan submitted a letter to the committee chairman. In this letter Morgan remembered that he had talked to employer repre-

[45] U.S. House of Representatives, Subcommittee of the Committee on Education and Labor, *Hearings on H.R. 2032, Labor Relations,* 81 Cong., 1 Sess., 1949, pp. 1160-78.

sentatives while working on the Hartley bill, although not on his own "responsibility." This was done, he said, because he was requested to do so by congressmen in connection with proposals these groups wanted inserted into the law. He had merely consulted these representatives to find out what they proposed in terms of the requests they had made to individual congressmen.[46]

This testimony was apparently designed to clear the NAM of any direct participation in writing the Taft-Hartley Act. However, the fact that there had been a profuse amount of publicity connecting the NAM with the writing of the bill and that the NAM had subsequently sought to exonerate itself from blame, plus the consideration that this revelation came some two years later, suggests a guilty conscience. Also, the business connections of these lawyers leads to the conclusion that they would not be prone to insert anything into the act which the NAM opposed. Ingles' and Iserman's lobbyist connections and Morgan's lucrative corporation law practice were pointed out by Democratic congressmen. Gerard Reilly was serving as the legislative representative for General Motors, General Electric, and the printing industry in 1949.[47] One must arrive at the inescapable conclusion that, in the case of the Taft-Hartley Act, the minds of the Republican congressmen and the NAM were certainly running in the same channels in regard to restrictive labor legislation. However, it should be pointed out that it is a common practice for pressure groups or their representatives to participate in the drafting of legislation that affects their interests.[48] In the case of the Taft-Hartley Act, as is the case in most instances like this, it was politically expedient for the opposition to call attention to these activities.

Chairman Hartley introduced the 67-page measure on

46 *Ibid.*, p. 1185.

47 *Ibid.*, p. 1172.

48 See David B. Truman, *The Governmental Process* (New York: Knopf, 1960), for the role of interest groups on legislation.

April 10. Five days later, when general debate commenced, the House voted to limit debate to a total of six hours with the bill being left open for amendment on the floor. Hartley opened the discussion by declaring that his committee had made "the most exhaustive study" and held the most complete hearings on this complicated matter that had ever been held by any labor committee in the history of Congress.[49] With the imposed limitation, debate on such a long and complicated measure was much too brief. The majority members hinged their defense of the bill on two major factors. They argued that their proposal was a "labor bill of rights" designed to help the individual worker and to "equalize" the Wagner Act and that they had received a "mandate from the people" demanding such legislation. The minority argument was basically that this one-sided bill was written by the NAM and that the 1946 election results stemmed from public dissatisfaction over inflation, housing, and other similar issues. These brief debates create the inescapable impression that from the beginning the majority was quite confident of victory and the minority equally certain of defeat.

The final vote was taken April 17 and the Hartley bill passed by the tremendous majority of 308 to 107—nearly 3 to 1. A majority of 93 Democrats joined the Republicans in voting for the bill with only 84 Democrats against the proposal. Of the Democrats voting for the bill, all but five came from the Southwest or states south of the Mason-Dixon, Ohio River line. Of these five, two came from Missouri and three from California. The Missouri tally was two Democratic votes against and nine Republican and two Democratic votes for it. Only one Representative from Missouri, Republican Dewey Short, voted for the Taft-Hartley Act and was returned to the next Congress. Of the Californians who voted for the bill, only Democratic Clair Engle was

[49] *Congressional Record,* 80 Cong., 1 Sess., 1947, XCIII, 3423.

returned to the next Congress; the other two Californians who voted for it were replaced by Republicans. As will be noted later, Engle changed and voted to recommit the Wood bill in 1949. Only 26 of the 121 Democrats from states south of the Mason-Dixon, Ohio River line and the Southwest voted against the measure. Only 23 Republicans and one American Labor Congressman voted against it while 215 Republicans, or a majority of those voting, favored the measure. Sixteen of these 23 Republicans came from urban, industrial states. Of the remaining seven, one in Kentucky and one in Tennessee represented coal-mining districts, two represented the Seattle, Washington, area and one came from Portland, Oregon. Only the Nevada Republican and one from North Dakota represented rural areas.[50] Twelve of these Republicans were replaced by Democrats in the next Congress. Not one was replaced by another Republican, suggesting that, at least on this one issue, the voters were not dissatisfied over their defection on a major party issue. The New York *Times* reported the House as passing with "exultant shouts . . . a bill embodying the sharpest restriction on labor unions" that had ever been attempted.[51]

On the same day, April 17, Senator Taft introduced his committee's bill, S. 1126, in the Senate. The technical work on the Senate bill had been performed by its counsel Thomas Shroyer, who had formerly served with the NLRB in Taft's home city of Cincinnati. Shroyer was assisted by Gerard Reilly, who also assisted on the Hartley bill. When Reilly was appointed special counsel for the Senate Labor Committee, he temporarily gave up cases and retainers from corporations subject to the Wagner Act but resumed his lobbying activities soon after the passage of the Taft-Hartley Act. Shroyer also received some assistance from Robert N.

50 *Ibid.*, pp. 3670-71.
51 New York *Times*, April 18, 1947.

Denham, an NLRB trial examiner whose anti-Wagner views were well known and of which more will be said later. Denham testified that he had given Senator Forest C. Donnell, Republican from Missouri, a memorandum of desired Wagner Act changes, the "major portion" of which appeared in the Taft-Hartley Act.[52] However, two years later Shroyer denied using the memorandum in preparing the Taft bill, saying that he had received it after the committee bill was substantially in its final form.[53] But since this technical assistance in writing the bill was acknowledged and well known, the bitter criticism leveled at the Hartley bill in the House, that enemies of unions wrote the bill, was not voiced in the Senate.

One of the major problems the Senate committee faced was the decision of whether to use the omnibus approach as the House was doing or to report several separate bills. Taft favored the omnibus plan and on April 12 the GOP Senate Conference Committee approved this arrangement. Senator Morse, who opposed this, revealed what he considered to be the major reason for this decision. Morse said that during this conference there was a great deal of discussion concerning a possible veto and it was decided that an omnibus bill would have a better opportunity of gaining support to override a veto.[54] Taft himself was quoted as saying that he expected a veto which the Senate would sustain. If this occurred, the Republicans could then place the responsibility on the President for failure to enact labor legislation.[55] During the course of Senate debate Morse continued his fight by offering a motion to recommit the bill to committee with instructions to report four

52 U.S. Senate, Committee on Labor and Public Welfare, *Hearings on Confirmation of Nominees for NLRB,* 80 Cong., 1 Sess., 1947, p. 5.

53 U.S. Senate, Committee on Labor and Public Welfare, *Hearings on S. 249, Labor Relations,* 81 Cong., 1 Sess., 1949, pp. 1124-25.

54 *Congressional Record,* 80 Cong., 1 Sess., 1947, XCIII, 4147.

55 New York *Times,* April 6, 1947.

separate bills instead. He argued that the Senate and House could then "pass those bills that can be passed," whereas an omnibus bill might be defeated because of certain objectionable features.[56] Morse was more interested in getting workable labor legislation in this instance than he was in the politics of the matter. However, his motion was defeated by a vote of 35 to 59.[57]

On April 17 Taft introduced his 68-page bill and general debate began April 23. In contrast to the House debates, the Senate had no time limitation and discussion was on a much higher level. There were fewer personal exchanges, compared with those in the House, and the arguments followed more closely the real issues involved. The principal majority argument in the Senate revolved around the fact that the Wagner Act was an experiment and experience had indicated the necessity for certain changes. The minority answered with the claim that an effective labor relations program had been built up over the years and this bill would increase, not decrease, industrial conflict.

In contrast to House action where the liberal minority was completely overwhelmed by the majority, the minority in the Senate introduced a substitute measure. Senator James Murray, Democrat from Montana, introduced a bill on May 9 which would have provided seven major amendments to the Wagner Act. His bill would: (1) give the President seizure powers similar to those in the Smith-Connally Act when a strike endangered public safety; (2) strengthen the federal mediation and conciliation services; (3) make illegal secondary boycotts in furtherance of jurisdictional disputes; (4) permit supervisory employees to organize if no rank-and-file workers were included; (5) provide industrywide bargaining only on a voluntary basis; (6) allow employers to request an election when an unrecognized union or two

[56] *Congressional Record,* 80 Cong., 1 Sess., 1947, XCIII, 4203.
[57] *Ibid.,* p. 4264.

competing unions claimed representation rights; and (7) appoint a temporary joint committee composed of six Senators, six Representatives, and eight people representing labor, management, and the public. This committee would study the whole labor relations problem and make a preliminary report to Congress by January 8, 1948, and a final report by April 15, 1948, in regard to further legislation. However, these provisions were much too mild to suit the temper of the Senate and Murray's proposal was defeated 73 to 19 on May 13. On the same day, a final vote was taken on H.R. 3020 as amended by the Senate. The Senate amendment to H.R. 3020 struck out everything following the enacting clause of Hartley's bill and inserted the provisions of S. 1126.

The Senate vote on Taft's measure was 68 to 24 in favor —more than the two-thirds majority necessary to override a veto. Twenty-one Democrats voted for the bill and only three Republicans, George Malone of Nevada, William Langer of North Dakota, and Wayne Morse of Oregon, voted against it. Twenty of the twenty-one Democrats voting for the bill were from states south of the Mason-Dixon, Ohio River line or the Southwest. The other Democrat, Scott Lucas of Illinois, did not vote to override Truman's veto and became, ironically, Majority Leader of the Senate in the Eighty-first Congress and thus the official leader of the Senate forces that attempted to repeal the Taft-Hartley Act.[58] The New York *Times* reported that this Senate action followed "three weeks of the greatest debate on domestic affairs in the Eightieth Congress."[59]

Following this vote, Taft moved to request a conference with the House to work out a compromise bill. His motion was agreed to and Senators Taft, Ball, Ives, Murray, and Ellender were appointed to represent the Senate.[60] The next

[58] *Ibid.*, p. 5117.
[59] New York *Times*, May 14, 1947.
[60] *Congressional Record*, 80 Cong., 1 Sess., 1947, XCIII, 5118.

day, May 14, the House disagreed with the Senate amendment of H.R. 3020 and agreed to a joint conference. Representatives Hartley, Landis, Hoffman, Lesinski, and Barden were appointed conferees for the House.[61] The legal counsel that assisted this conference committee in drafting the compromise bill consisted of Gerald Morgan, Gerard Reilly, Thomas Shroyer, and Senator Ives' counsel, Dwyer Shugrue.[62]

One of the primary concerns of the conference was the threat of a veto. Although President Truman had made no public statement in this regard while the Hartley and the Taft bills were being debated, it was well understood that, politics permitting, his views concerning labor would not allow him to accept a bill that was too restrictive. Taft was aware of a veto possibility, and Hartley, referring to the conference committee's work, said he knew they "had to write a final bill that would be enacted over a veto."[63] Part of his strategy to accomplish this was to create the general impression that the House bill was "tough" and "harsh" while the Senate measure was "fair" and "mild." This was part of Hartley's "master plan"—to make everyone, especially other congressmen, believe that the harsher provisions of the Hartley bill were discarded in conference "in favor of the so-called milder provisions of Taft's bill." He later complimented the press for the "excellent job" it did in contrasting the two bills. He felt that the mass media contributed a great deal to the generally accepted view that the Senate measure was "weak, confused, and inadequate," which substantially assisted him in this maneuver.[64] Congressman Ray J. Madden, Democrat from Indiana, called

61 *Ibid.*, p. 5275.

62 U.S. House of Representatives, Subcommittee of the Committee on Education and Labor, *Hearings on H.R. 2032, Labor Relations,* 81 Cong., 1 Sess., 1949, p. 1163.

63 Hartley, *Our New National Labor Policy*, p. 70.

64 *Ibid.*, p. 75.

attention to this in the House. Madden noted that "columns of misleading propaganda" were put out by newspapers and commentators to the effect that the conference bill was much milder than Hartley's bill in order "to confuse the Members of Congress and the public" and thus create the impression that the final measure was not as antilabor as Hartley's proposal.[65] Senator Taft denied this, saying that the Senate conferees had "conceded nothing . . . of importance."[66] However, inadvertently Taft had previously given weight to the argument that his bill was not so mild, when he was quoted as saying his bill was "not a milk-toast bill." At this time he conceded that S. 1126 covered about three-fourths of the objectives "pressed on us very strenuously by employers."[67]

Whether Hartley created his master plan before or discovered it after the accomplished fact is immaterial. As Hartley said, he "deliberately put everything" he could into the House bill so he would "have something to concede and still get an adequate bill in the end."[68] His method of getting "everything" possible into his bill was what Congressman Hartley termed "legislative psychology." This maneuver consists of inserting several additional provisions into a measure that a congressman wants enacted that are "obviously undesirable, unworkable, or unconstitutional" and which will then draw the fire of the opposition. These obnoxious features are brought up for a vote, defeated, and the opposition is so relieved over this triumph that the amended version can then be passed. This method was utilized by Hartley on H.R. 3020 simply by putting in several remedies for the same offense. The most offensive ones were stricken out but in the end the bill contained the

65 *Congressional Record,* 80 Cong., 1 Sess., 1947, XCIII, 6385.
66 *Ibid.,* p. 6534.
67 "Back to McKinley," *Nation,* CLXIV (May 3, 1947), 507.
68 New York *Times,* May 30, 1947.

desired provisions and sufficient remedies to carry them out.[69] Hartley's "legislative psychology" also prevailed in the congressional conference that hammered out the compromise.

A comparison of the major features of the two bills when they went to conference reveals a great similarity in goals. The House bill was harsher in listing forbidden union practices with respect to union members since the Senate bill had no such provision. But both bills outlawed secondary boycotts, jurisdictional strikes, the closed shop, and denied employee status under the law to supervisors. Hartley's measure also prohibited mass picketing, featherbedding and brought unions under the antitrust laws. The House measure prohibited industrywide bargaining unless the employers were within a 50-mile radius of each other whereas the Senate bill merely made it an unfair practice for a union to compel choice of employer representative. Both bills removed the United States Conciliation Service from the Department of Labor and created a new agency. The House proposal limited economic strikes with a 75-day cooling-off period and a strike-vote requirement in contrast to the Senate bill, which required a 60-day notice of contract termination and banned strikes during the notice period. Both bills provided for government injunction in "national emergency" strikes and the Hartley version forbade strikes by government employees.

The House measure permitted welfare funds only when the union did not participate in their administration and the Senate bill provided for welfare funds with joint employee-employer administration. Both proposals opened the federal courts for damage suits against unions for unlawful concerted activities and violation of contract. Both the House and Senate provided for denial of bargaining rights

69 Hartley, *Our New National Labor Policy*, pp. 67-68.

to unions whose officers refused to sign a non-communist affidavit. The House bill banned union political expenditures in national elections and required unions to submit annual reports of their finances to the Department of Labor. Hartley's bill increased NLRB membership and provided for two agencies with separate functions, while the Senate merely wanted to increase NLRB membership. The Senate version permitted employees to file petitions for new union elections and employers to file petitions for union decertification elections. Finally, the Taft bill proposed a joint committee to study labor-management relations.

Thus Taft's proposal was mild only when compared to Hartley's bill. The major distinctions between the two bills were the NLRB changes, mass picketing and featherbedding, industrywide bargaining, welfare funds, strike votes, government employee strikes, union political activities and finance reporting, union elections, and the joint committee. With these differences, the House bill was harsher, but the Senate bill, as Taft insisted, was certainly not a "milk-toast" measure.

The conference committee met for two weeks, from May 15 to May 29, and thrashed out their differences. The Taft-Hartley bill they reported to their respective chambers was reputed to be a victory on the part of the Senate managers.

The major changes which the Taft-Hartley Act, an amendment to the Wagner Act, made in the national labor policy were as follows.[70] (1) The NLRB was increased from three to five members and board findings of fact had to be supported by "substantial" evidence; an independent General Counsel would assume the prosecutory functions of the board. (2) The closed shop was outlawed—the union shop being permitted on petition of 30 percent of the workers and a majority of favorable votes cast in an ensuing election.

[70] An outstanding detailed analysis is made of both the Wagner Act and the Taft-Hartley Act by experts with much practical experience in Millis and Brown, *From the Wagner Act to Taft-Hartley*.

(3) Unfair labor practices committed by unions were listed which made it illegal for unions to refuse to bargain, use secondary boycott, try to force an employer to bargain with a union other than the recognized bargaining agent, engage in jurisdictional strikes in violation of board rulings, require exorbitant initiation fees, force employers to pay for services not actually rendered, or curtail the right of free speech of employers. (4) Supervisors were excluded as employees under the act. (5) A new independent Federal Mediation and Conciliation Service was created to replace the United States Conciliation Service. (6) Provision was made to handle "national emergencies"—when a threatened strike endangered a whole industry or a substantial portion thereof, in the President's opinion, he could appoint a board of inquiry to investigate and then direct the Attorney General to seek an injunction forbidding such strike. If a settlement was not reached within sixty days after issuance of this injunction, the board of inquiry would make another report and fifteen days after this report, the NLRB would hold an election on the employer's last offer. If the final offer was rejected the injunction would be dissolved and the right to strike revived. This section thus set up the famous "80-day cooling-off period" for national emergency strikes. (7) Welfare funds were outlawed except when jointly administered by labor and management. (8) Unions were made suable in federal courts for violation of contract and made liable for acts of their agents. (9) Unions were required to make annual financial reports both to the Department of Labor and to their individual members. (10) The checkoff was prohibited except on a voluntary basis. (11) Union officials had to sign a non-communist affidavit annually or their union forfeited its rights under the act. (12) Unions were forbidden to make expenditures or contributions in any national primary or general election. (13) Federal government employees could not strike. (14) A provision which later

became a major issue permitted states to enact "right to work" laws prohibiting compulsory membership in a union shop. (15) Employees could petition for a new union election and employers could petition for a decertification election. (16) A joint congressional committee was established to study labor-management relations and determine how well the new act operated.

In analyzing these major provisions it can be seen that if there were any victory it was largely on the part of the House. The House conferees gave up the ban on industry-wide bargaining, restrictions on nonemergency strikes, bringing unions under the antitrust acts, and welfare funds. They also agreed to the Senate's joint committee. On the other hand, in the final bill the Senate agreed to the House's much harsher provisions in regard to the NLRB, a cooling-off period before striking, specific union activities like featherbedding, certain internal union practices, government employees' striking, union political activities, and union finance reporting. If the deleted House provisions had been included in the final act, the Taft-Hartley Act would have been much harsher, but the inclusion of the House measures made the Taft bill much more antilabor than originally drawn. It is true that the Taft bill was "softer" than the Hartley bill, but the claim that the Taft-Hartley Act was much softer as a result of the Senate victory in the conference must be questioned. Commenting on the supposed mildness of the Taft bill, Senator Harley Kilgore, Democrat from West Virginia, drew the analogy of a 25 percent solution of carbolic acid as being mild compared to a 100 percent solution.[71]

On June 3 the conference report was submitted to the House and the next day, following a one-hour debate, the House passed the Taft-Hartley Act by a vote of 320 to 79.[72] Senate debate on the conference report began on June 5 and

[71] *Congressional Record,* 80 Cong., 1 Sess., 1947, XCIII, 6529.
[72] *Ibid.,* p. 6392.

the next day this body approved the measure 57 to 17.[73] Both houses passed the Taft-Hartley Act by more than the two-thirds majority necessary to override a veto. The bill was sent to President Truman on June 9 for his consideration.[74]

Thus, the first time the Republican party recaptured both houses of Congress following the New Deal it was able to pass, by huge majorities, a bill which would basically alter a New Deal policy. Using the antilabor feeling generated by union abuses of power and the public reaction against the postwar strikes, the drive which began immediately after the Supreme Court validation of the Wagner Act culminated in the passage of legislation, the ostensible purpose of which was to restore the balance of power lost by the Wagner Act. The Republican Eightieth Congress revived restrictive labor measures that had previously failed of enactment, owing either to the defection of one of the houses or a presidential veto, added some new items created by the strife of the war and reconversion period, and amended the Wagner Act, creating a new national labor policy designed to "equalize" bargaining power in the "public interest."

The provisions to create a new five-man National Labor Relations Board and to separate NLRB judicial and prosecutory functions and changes in rules of evidence in NLRB procedures and in employer requests for union elections were taken from the Smith Committee proposals of 1939-1940. The provisions for a new independent agency to handle conciliation, the cooling-off period before striking, suability of unions, exclusion of supervisors, and restricting the use of secondary boycotts came from the vetoed Case bill of 1946. To these were added other NAM and employer proposals to curb union power and activities and to curtail industrial

[73] *Ibid.*, p. 6536.
[74] *Ibid.*, p. 6679.

conflict. With the impending threat of a presidential veto, these provisions were combined into an omnibus bill so that the executive branch would have to accept all of the proposed changes or none. If the bill were accepted by President Truman, it would mean a victory for the antilabor forces, and if he vetoed it, he would receive the onus of having defeated labor legislation demanded by the public. Thus the Truman administration received one of the hottest political domestic issues it was to face. The attention and pressure of the nation was now directed toward the White House for the decision of Harry S. Truman.

4

TRUMAN VETOES THE TAFT-HARTLEY ACT

A TREMENDOUS amount of lobbying and political pressure had been exerted upon Congress during the passage of the Taft-Hartley Act. When Congress sent the approved bill to the President for his consideration on June 9, 1947, this political pressure was then transferred to the White House. The President had ten days, Sundays excluded, to make the decision to sign or veto, during which time individuals and organizations utilized their political power in an effort to influence his decision. Letters, telegrams, and postcards poured into the White House from the nation, almost all viewing the measure as either completely good or completely bad. The Taft-Hartley Act evoked one of the greatest public opinion mail responses that the administrative branch ever endured on a domestic issue. Eben Ayers, a White House assistant press secretary, reported that this "volume of mail was the greatest ever received at the White House on any legislative issue or any other controversy."[1] This response would not again be equalled or exceeded until the controversial dismissal of General Douglas MacArthur by Truman in April 1951.

By June 14 the White House had received over half a million messages—140,000 letters, 460,000 postcards, and 20,000 telegrams—"a vast majority" of which, according to Ayers, urged a veto.[2] The final total of communications numbered over 750,000 and occupied some 300 cubic feet of space in the White House files.[3] Unfortunately, because of the sheer bulk, selections were made from this public opinion mail and the rest was destroyed. Much of this correspondence was "inspired" by labor organizations in an effort to have the bill vetoed, and a majority of the mail retained in the files favored a veto. Whether the items retained were truly representative of the public opinion mail received remains unanswerable. But according to Ayers' estimate, it is an illustrative selection since it shows a preponderance of unfavorable attitude toward the bill.

Many union representatives were already in Washington lobbying against the bill and more arrived after its passage. The labor lobby in the Capitol at this time was compared to "a swarm of locusts" by one newspaper.[4] The White House staff found it impossible to arrange the desired presidential interview for many such delegations because of their numbers.[5]

During the five weeks prior to its final passage, organized labor had staged a huge nationwide campaign in which the AFL alone spent a reported $1,000,000 to sway public opinion

1 New York *Times,* June 19, 1947.

2 New York *Herald Tribune,* June 15, 1947.

3 William D. Hassett to Secretary of Labor Tobin, Memorandum, Sept. 9, 1949, Truman Papers, OF 15, HSTL.

4 Washington *Evening Star,* June 14, 1947.

5 John R. Steelman, Office Memorandum, May 20, 1947, Truman Papers, OF 407, HSTL.

and Congress against the Taft-Hartley bill.[6] This program included five advertisements—one a full-page ad—which were placed in 110 of the nation's leading newspapers. Radio time was purchased on ABC for a series of five-minute talks, a soap opera, and Thursday night variety shows that included such popular stars as Jimmy Durante, Milton Berle, the DeMarco Sisters, Henry Morgan, and Georgia Gibbs.

These pressure activities were now directed toward the White House in an effort to persuade the President to exercise his veto power. Huge labor rallies were held throughout the country to protest against what labor immediately dubbed the "Slave Labor Bill." For example, at a mass meeting of "thousands" at Rochester, New York, workers "unanimously" condemned the bill, urging a veto and demanding that Democratic congressmen uphold the veto.[7] A petition with 115,000 signatures requesting a veto, gathered in forty-five minutes in New York City, was presented to President Truman.[8] On June 11, 60,000 CIO workers paraded down Eighth Avenue to a rally in Madison Square Garden demanding that President Truman veto the measure and that Congress sustain the veto. This followed a similar parade and rally of "35,000 to 50,000" AFL members a week previously on June 4.[9]

The mayor of New York City supported the attitude of these workers. In a radio address of June 3 he condemned the Taft-Hartley bill as being "pushed" by the NAM and the Chamber of Commerce "whose representatives admittedly wrote most of the legislation." He said this was part of the reason why the Republicans now wanted a "thorough-going system of regulation for labor," after fourteen years of

[6] *Newsweek,* XXIX (June 16, 1947), 28-29.

[7] Hugh A. Harley to President Truman, June 10, 1947, Truman Papers, OF 407, HSTL.

[8] Kenneth Sherbell to President Truman, June 9, 1947, Truman Papers, OF 407, HSTL.

[9] New York *Times,* June 11, 1947.

opposition to any and all forms of regulation. Also, he declared, the Republican party feared the working man and wanted to restrict his organizations.[10] The mayor of Detroit proclaimed June 16 as Veto Day. The Taft-Hartley bill, he said, was "inimical" to the interests of organized labor and the public and would generate "more not less" industrial strife.[11] The general reaction of the rank-and-file workers toward the bill, although probably unrecognized by themselves, was summed up best by the Federal Reserve Board which stated that it had "symbolic significance to labor."[12] Although the rank and file complained of abuses at the hands of their leaders, they resented legislation designed to restrict labor and would close ranks against such an outside attack, as they did to a large extent in the election of 1948.

Unions and union officials were most vociferous in denouncing the Taft-Hartley Act. Walter Reuther, president of the UAW-CIO with almost 1,000,000 members, personally requested a presidential veto because its enactment would "set off a whole new era of industrial strife and friction" since its provisions gave "encouragement and new weapons to anti-labor employers."[13] Reuther soon telegraphed another veto request on behalf of the UAW-CIO Executive Board, declaring that the bill, by weakening unions, would subsequently concentrate even more control "of our way of life in the hands of the small number of giant monopolistic corporations." James C. Petrillo, president of the American Federation of Musicians with over 200,000 members, wired Truman that at its annual convention the delegates of this

10 Mayor O'Dwyer, ABC, 8:15 P.M., June 3, 1947, Radio Forums, Office of Government Reports, Division of Press Intelligence, June 5, 1947, Truman Papers, Misc. File, White House Central File, HSTL.

11 George Edward to the President, Telegram, June 16, 1947, Truman Papers, OF 407, HSTL.

12 M.S. Eccles to Harry S. Truman, June 18, 1947, Truman Papers, OF 407, HSTL.

13 The following public opinion mail may be found in the files on the Taft-Hartley Act, Truman Papers, OF 407, HSTL.

union had "unanimously adopted" a resolution urging a veto as the bill was an employers' bill and would make "slaves" of workers. The International Typographical Union, one of the nation's oldest trade unions, was somewhat less emotional in its condemnation. This union felt the bill should be vetoed on the grounds that, in addition to the current arguments, it would lead to "inevitable contempt for law and courts" by the country's 15,000,000 organized workers if and when subjected to the bill's "senseless legal manipulation and litigation." Also, the typographical union said, totalitarian countries could use the enactment of such a "repressive" law as an example of the weakness of democracy in contrast to their own systems which would at least be "consistent with their philosophies" where "the dictators are politically honest" with their people. Philip Murray told the President that the bill not only must be vetoed, but that it must not become law. If it did, it would "engulf not only the labor movement but the entire nation in tragic consequences" since it was the "keystone in a program to legislate a new depression."

Letters and telegrams flooded the White House from hundreds of local unions, state labor councils, and smaller national unions. Most of these messages described the bill as a "Slave Labor Bill" and denounced it as being "class legislation." One union expressed alarm over the current drive of antilabor manufacturers to create "the kind of lynch labor hysteria" which led to the passage of the bill. Another union feared a depression as a consequence of the passage of this legislation. The measure was sponsored by the NAM, they said, and was designed eventually to destroy the American labor movement. The next step, if it became law, it was argued, would be a campaign to cut wages which in turn would lead "headlong into another depression." Another typical example of union response was the expression of fear that the results of the Taft-Hartley bill were "too terrible to contemplate," maintaining that labor relations would be thrust back one hundred years by it. The Foreman's Association of America, however, legitimately complained that if the bill became law, it would deprive some 3,500,000 supervisory employees of employee status under the national labor policy. They were currently engaged in a "bitter struggle against organized employers" to gain union recognition and this bill would deprive them of peaceful methods of gaining that objective.

Individuals and groups, other than organized labor, strongly urged a veto. One citizen, confused as to who vetoes federal legislation, sent his Senator a note on a piece of brown paper torn from a grocery bag which simply said, "Please veto Taft-Hartley measueer [*sic*]." The National Catholic Welfare Conference took an official stand in opposition to the bill. The national conference of the Presbyterian church "unanimously adopted" suggestions for improving labor relations "along Christian principles" and urged a veto on the grounds that the "dangerous phases" of the Taft-Hartley proposal far outweighed its good points. The National Council of Jewish Women asked the President to veto the bill because it would "produce strikes and lockouts that it seeks to eliminate."

The liberal Americans for Democratic Action recommended vetoing both the tax and labor bills since they were elements of "a design for depression." The Union Labor Legionnaires demanded a veto because the Taft-Hartley bill would set collective bargaining back fifty years. "Certainly the 3½ million paid up members of organized labor who fought in World War 2 did not fight and die for this attempted act of American Fascism," they declared. Oddly enough, even some Southerners, where antiunionism was strongest and whose congressional delegations had voted almost unanimously for the measure, found a reason for opposition. The Committee for the Preservation of Southern

Traditions objected to the proposal because it would help abolish "Jim Crow" employment. All members of that organization were requested to wire or write Southern Representatives or Senators who had voted for the bill, expressing their objections to this "Negro Republican trick."

The three leading agricultural organizations took the same stand they had taken on the Case bill of the previous year. The National Farmers Union opposed the Taft-Hartley bill on the grounds that it would create additional labor unrest. This, added to the current inflationary problem, would mean more work stoppages and less production. What was more urgently needed, the Farmers Union felt, was legislation to control prices. But the conservative American Farm Bureau asked Truman to sign the bill because it had "the overwhelming support of the American people." Although the measure was not "exactly" what it preferred, the National Grange recommended approval because it was the best that could be "reasonably" expected from Congress at this time and, in addition, the American people demanded the protection the bill would provide.

Other organizations recommended approval on the basis that it was in the "best interests" of the nation. The American Association of Small Businesses took a poll of its members which represented "a good cross section of the nation's industry" and found that 97 percent favored approval of this or "similar legislation." Samuel Goldwyn, who had suffered union difficulties in his movie studios and had testified accordingly before the two congressional labor committees in their hearings on the Taft and Hartley bills, urged the President to sign the bill in order to stabilize labor relations. Goldwyn felt that the "overwhelming" majorities in Congress in favor of the measure were "an expression of the equally overwhelming will of the American people."

Of more importance, politically speaking, in influencing

the decision of whether or not to veto, were the sentiments expressed by political groups and individuals. John N. Garner, former Vice President, advised Truman to sign the bill. But a more typical message from politicians came from the Democratic members of the Massachusetts legislature who urged a veto on the basis of loyalty to party traditions. The Democratic party represented the common people, they said, whereas the Republican party represented "Big Business, High Finance and Monopoly." Since the Taft-Hartley bill was "admittedly written by the lawyers of Big Business" the Democratic President should veto it. Many county and precinct Democratic clubs also submitted resolutions urging Truman to veto the bill.

Soon after the bill was passed the Democratic National Committee polled the national committeemen to ascertain their views on the advisability of a veto. Of the committeemen polled, 103 favored a veto, 66 wanted Truman to sign the bill, and 4 recommended allowing it to become law without his signature. Of the 66 who urged approval, 40 were from Southern states.[14] In surveying the opinions of the Democratic party workers of the country from the available public opinion mail, the vast majority, excluding the South, recommended a veto of the Taft-Hartley bill for political purposes.

The White House staff was busy evaluating this public opinion, studying the proposal itself, and trying to reach a decision on the best course of action. Even before the final measure was written by the conference committee, *Business Week* claimed that President Truman would soon have to face "the most important political decision" that he had been confronted with since he became President. This magazine reported White House sources at this time as saying that the decision lay between allowing the bill to become law without a signature or writing a veto message

[14] New York *Times*, June 20, 1947.

that would become "one of 1948's hottest campaign documents."[15]

As previously mentioned, the threat of a veto had been one of the considerations weighed by the majority Senators and Representatives when the two bills were in their respective chambers and during the conference. Representative Frank W. Boykin, Democrat from Alabama, had earlier complained to the President that the feeling was common among labor leaders who were lobbying on the Hill that no matter what kind of a labor proposal Congress produced Truman would veto it. Boykin was concerned over this because he had overheard some "staunch party members" saying in the Democratic cloakroom that if Truman did not sign the labor bill the party was "sunk so far as the next election is concerned."[16]

The threat of a veto was brought up several times during congressional debate. Congressman Emanuel Celler, Democrat from New York, speaking on the same day that the Hartley bill passed the House, referred to all the effort put in on the bill going to "naught" because, like the Case bill, this one would also "earn the veto and justifiably so." Celler had just returned from a White House visit and when Charles Halleck asked if he were speaking for the administration, Celler replied that he was not speaking "officially" but that he could put two and two together.[17] Unfortunately, the press took this up and quoted Celler as speaking for Truman. The New Yorker immediately wrote Truman explaining how the misunderstanding had come about and apologized for it.[18] Congressman Henderson Lanham, Democrat from Georgia, in referring to Senate concurrence in

15 "Will the Majority Hold?" *Business Week,* May 17, 1947, p. 70.

16 Frank W. Boykin to the President, May 2, 1947, Truman Papers, OF 407-B, HSTL.

17 *Congressional Record,* 80 Cong., 1 Sess., 1947, XCIII, 3619-20.

18 Emanuel Celler to Harry S. Truman, April 18, 1947, Truman Papers, OF 407, HSTL.

this "evil bill," was thankful that there was a man in the White House with sufficient courage "in the face of the Nation-wide hysteria to veto such an infamous bill as this."[19] Wayne Morse on the Senate side stated that he was not only going to vote against sending the Taft bill to conference, but would also vote to sustain a veto if Truman had "the good judgment to veto it."[20]

It was apparent, then, that a veto was commonly expected. Labor itself was fairly confident of it and the two authors of the legislation, as noted earlier, expected Truman to veto their work. So their strategy was to make the Taft bill appear "mild" in comparison to the Hartley bill and give the impression that the harsher measure was moderated in conference. Thus, they reasoned, the chances were greater that Truman would accept the final version and, if he vetoed it, the general impression in Congress that the compromise bill was mild would win enough support to override the veto. And the press, as Hartley noted, was quite helpful in creating this impression. The *Nation* expressed the earnest hope that President Truman would not allow himself to be taken in by this "brazen campaign now raging in the press to make the bad look good by contrast with the worst."[21]

Truman himself gave no indication of his intentions until the last minute. Thus, although the general impression was current that he would veto, a certain amount of suspense was created because of the uncertainty and because of the importance of his decision. Even before the bill reached the President's desk, the New York *Times* reported a "close associate" of Truman as saying that the President "was leaning toward a veto" but that he would not make up his mind definitely, of course, until he had fully studied the bill. This same news item reported Truman's "inner circle of

[19] *Congressional Record,* 80 Cong., 1 Sess., 1947, XCIII, 3624.
[20] *Ibid.,* p. 5109.
[21] *Nation,* CLXIV (May 31, 1947), 645.

advisers" as "about evenly split" between those favoring a veto and those urging signature.[22]

Even after the bill had been in his possession for eight days, Sunday excepted, Truman told reporters that he did not yet know whether he would veto it.[23] However, a memorandum written by Truman this same day gave an indication of which way he was leaning. George Harrison of the Railroad Brotherhood had sent the President a roster of the Senators and indicated what he believed to be the position of each in regard to overriding a veto. Harrison thought that twenty-nine Senators would uphold a veto, which would not be sufficient if all ninety-six voted, three would possibly support a veto, and eight the President "must see." Truman turned this list over to one of his assistants, Charles Murphy, with instructions to discuss it with Clark Clifford and then make a personal check on the Senators to see how they "really" stood.[24] Also, the next day, June 19, a delegation of Southern Democrats called upon Truman to request his signature on the bill. Truman was reported as telling them that in making his decision he had not listened to any labor leaders or "economic royalists" and he did not want to be pressured by any Democrats either.[25] But by this time the decision undoubtedly had been made even if the veto message had not been drafted.

The Taft-Hartley bill was submitted to the President on June 9, which meant that June 20 would be the final date on which he could make his decision before the bill became law without his signature. In the meantime he had an official visit to Canada scheduled and Congress had sent him the tax reduction bill, which was considered as being almost as important as the labor measure. This measure provided

22 New York *Times*, June 8, 1947.
23 *Ibid.*, June 18, 1947.
24 Harry S. Truman to Charles S. Murphy, Memorandum, June 18, 1947, Truman Papers, OF 407, HSTL.
25 New York *Times*, June 20, 1947.

for a tax reduction of 30 percent on incomes under $1,400, 20 percent up to $136,700, and 15 percent on incomes between $136,700 and $302,000, and 10.5 percent on those above $302,000. Truman decided to veto this bill because he believed it favored the wealthy over the lower income groups and would further stimulate inflation. He submitted the veto message on June 16 to Congress and his veto was barely sustained. Because of these important matters the President could not give his personal attention to the labor bill until the last minute. But in the meantime the spadework of studying the bill was being done for him.

The task of analyzing the Taft-Hartley bill was given to John R. Steelman, who by this time was Truman's top labor adviser. Steelman in turn set the White House staff to work studying the bill and coordinating advisory reports. After this had been completed, a White House official stated that the final report submitted to Truman was "the most detailed analysis he had ever received relating to a bill."[26]

In a letter to Dr. Steelman, Sumner H. Slichter, one of the nation's leading industrial relations experts, expressed the conviction that a veto would be as unfortunate as acceptance. It was easy to find fault with the bill, he said, because it covered too many things. But on the other hand he believed it would deal with certain labor abuses that needed elimination which labor itself had shown no signs of correcting.[27] The Federal Reserve Board was one of the few agencies that favored it. The board decided that it was a choice "between this bill and nothing" and the Taft-Hartley bill would provide increased protection to the public and the workers themselves against "abuses and shortsighted practices" of management and labor.[28]

[26] *Ibid.*

[27] Sumner H. Slichter to John R. Steelman, June 10, 1947, Truman Papers, OF 407, HSTL.

[28] M. S. Eccles to Harry S. Truman, June 18, 1947, Truman Papers, OF 407, HSTL.

Steelman's personal legal adviser, Aaron Lewittes, submitted a 16-page description of the bill's provisions and concluded that although there were some desirable features, it contained too many seriously objectionable features. Lewittes decided that if it became law it would seriously disturb labor relations. Unions would be weakened by "tremendously intensified anti-union activities by employers, material slowing down of Board operations, litigation, cease-and-desist orders, injunctions and damage suits."[29]

NLRB chairman Paul Herzog turned in a report denouncing the bill. Herzog claimed that the Taft-Hartley amendments would transform the Wagner Act from "a shield for the working man" into a "sword" to be used against unions. He felt that although the individual modifications, when considered separately, seemed "innocent," it was the "cumulative impact" of the bill which made it an "anti-labor measure." He maintained that the proposal was "unworkable" because it placed the board in a "rigid procedural strait-jacket" and it was "deliberately calculated" to "encourage litigation" and "stimulate procrastination."[30] Senator Joseph Ball, Taft's right-hand man in the Labor Committee, protested against Herzog's report because it had circulated in the Cabinet and among "various interested persons." Ball argued that this document was a "tissue of distortions" that was "apparently based upon a memorandum written by Lee Pressman."[31] Pressman was at that time CIO general counsel and later resigned from his job because of alleged communist associations.

The Council of Economic Advisers tendered a penetrating analysis of the overall effects of the Taft-Hartley bill. This council, composed of Edwin G. Nourse, Leon H. Keyserling,

29 A. Lewittes to John R. Steelman, June 11, 1947, Truman Papers, OF 407, HSTL.

30 Paul M. Herzog to Harry S. Truman, Memorandum, June 11, 1947, Truman Papers, OF 407, HSTL.

31 Joseph H. Ball to Harry S. Truman, June 16, 1947, Truman Papers, OF 407, HSTL.

and John D. Clark, recommended disapproval of the bill on the basis of two major objections. First of all, they said, the bill provided no real solution to industrial conflicts. Instead of setting up workable procedures or machinery to settle paralyzing strikes, it merely required delay in concerted action. Secondly, it would inject the national government too completely into internal union affairs. The general impression of labor that this was a punitive measure would breed resentment rather than moderation and cooperation in collective bargaining. Also, in this regard, the bill was so complicated and ambiguous that labor-management relations would be unstable for years before returning to normal. The council summed up its objections by saying that the bill would encourage industrial strife and thus would run counter to the objectives of the Employment Act of 1946.[32]

There were conflicting reports of the position of the Cabinet in regard to a veto. The New York *Times* reported unanimity among Cabinet members in favor of a veto.[33] However, another source states that only Postmaster General Robert Hannegan and Secretary Schwellenbach favored a veto.[34] Undoubtedly, many were thinking of a Gallup Poll taken in May 1947. When asked, "If a bill which cuts down labor's power a great deal is passed by Congress, would you like to have President Truman give it his okay or veto it?" 46 percent wanted him to sign it, 38 percent hoped for a veto, and 16 percent had no opinion.[35] In the face of such an apparent public demand for such legislation it seems quite likely that many department heads would favor following the popular demand and recommend approval rather than risk political reprisal in the coming election.

Several quite important political factors indicated that

[32] Council of Economic Advisers to the President, June 16, 1947, John D. Clark Papers, HSTL.

[33] New York *Times*, June 22, 1947.

[34] Robert S. Allen and William V. Shannon, *The Truman Merry-Go-Round* (New York: Vanguard, 1950), p. 27.

[35] *Public Opinion Quarterly*, XI (Fall 1947), 482.

signing the measure would be the wisest course. The manifest desire of the nation for remedial labor legislation, plus the large majorities given the bill by Congress, made it fairly obvious that a veto would be overridden. Thus Truman would be placed in the embarrassing position of having tried to withhold legislation that the people demanded. Then too, there was the President's personal feeling that some labor leaders were acting too arrogantly. Only a year previously he had requested authority to draft strikers, and mail was being received from rank-and-file union members complaining of union abuses. Also, Truman had to consider holding the Democratic party together. The fact that so many Democrats, most of them from the South, had supported the bill in Congress rendered his decision more difficult since the Democratic party would need united support in the national election a year hence. And although union officials were issuing frenzied demands for a veto, there was little that labor could do except remain in the Democratic party, regardless of what happened. Finally, one of the major arguments in favor of signing the bill was the impending coal strike. The government was still operating the coal mines but was scheduled to return them to the operators on June 30. It was generally conceded that John L. Lewis would then call the miners out on strike. If this happened and the Taft-Hartley bill were vetoed, Truman would have no ready weapon to contend with the strike. One presidential adviser expressed the opinion that there was "little doubt" that Truman would have rejected the bill if the coal strike threat had not arisen.[36]

But there were strong factors impelling a veto. Signing the proposal would be inconsistent with the Case bill veto of the previous year and the requests made in the State of the Union message. Also the tax-reduction measure had just been vetoed as favoring the wealthy, so a veto of the

[36] New York *Times*, June 8, 1947.

Taft-Hartley bill would place the President even more on the side of the common man. Then there was the apparently honest conviction that the bill would actually increase industrial strife. Reports of various competent advisers, such as Paul Herzog, indicated that the legislation was fundamentally unworkable and would create not only endless court litigation but resentment on the part of labor itself. Though labor had been traditionally Democratic there were obvious signs that it was moving away from the party. After the strike draft proposal in the 1946 railroad strike, A. F. Whitney pledged his union's entire treasury to the defeat of Truman in 1948. The rift between the President and John L. Lewis was widening as a result of the tense coal situation. So although labor had no immediate political party to turn to, there was the possibility that a liberal third party would arise, drawing some labor votes away from the Democratic party. Robert Hannegan, also serving as Democratic national chairman at this time, warned Truman in a telephone conversation that "signing the bill would give Henry Wallace the domestic issue that he needed to start a third party in 1948."[37]

Finally, there was the danger that labor might prove apathetic in voting in 1948. Labor had stayed home to a large extent in 1946 and the result, as Truman pointed out, was a Republican Congress and the Taft-Hartley bill. A veto might prove extremely stimulating to labor voters in the coming election.

With all these factors in mind and the extremely thorough report prepared by Steelman's staff, President Truman undertook to study the "incomprehensible Taft-Hartley bill" on June 18.[38] Forty-eight hours later he came up with a veto message. This message was composed with the assist-

[37] *Newsweek*, XXIX (June 23, 1947), 15.

[38] Harry S. Truman to Carl A. Hatch, June 23, 1947, Truman Papers, OF 407, HSTL.

ance of John Steelman, Charles Ross, Paul Herzog, and Clark Clifford. Clifford was very perceptive politically and at this time was one of Truman's top advisers, if not the principal one. Clifford was reported to have favored a veto from the beginning[39] and undoubtedly had a great deal of influence in shaping the final decision.

Clark Clifford was a St. Louis attorney who received an appointment as White House naval aide in July 1945 and very rapidly rose to influence in the Truman administration. Although not a flaming crusader, Clifford was a nephew of the liberal editor of the St. Louis *Post-Dispatch* and was thoroughly imbued with the social and economic goals of the New Deal. As special counsel to the President, this "unideological moderate . . . sought . . . to codify the New Deal" by defending it against Republican attack and bringing it up to date after the war interim.[40] As speech writer and political adviser he was to prove extremely instrumental, along with Samuel Rosenman, in shaping the Fair Deal ideology. The 1946 "draft-labor" proposal and Case bill veto were largely his work and he was to play a key part in drafting the 1948 campaign speeches and the 1949 inaugural address.

Truman presented the veto message to Congress June 20, the final day before the bill would become law with or without presidential action. Wayne Morse described the 5,500-word message as "one of the most powerful vetoes in all our history."[41] The New York *Times* reported that Truman castigated the bill with twenty-four different adjectives that had harsh connotations, such as "dangerous," "unworkable," "arbitrary," "discriminatory," "impossible," and "drastic."[42]

President Truman began his veto message by stating

39 New York *Times*, June 8, 1947.
40 Goldman, *The Crucial Decade*, p. 65.
41 New York *Times*, June 21, 1947.
42 *Ibid.*

that, in analyzing the bill, he had subjected it to four major tests and found it wanting in each case. First, it would result in more government intervention, contrary to the national policy of economic freedom, by making the government an "unwarranted participant at every bargaining table." Second, it would not improve labor relations because "cooperation cannot be achieved by law." Instead, it would encourage distrust and suspicion and lead to court settlement of differences. Congress, he said, had paid too much attention to the "inevitable frictions" of the reconversion period when the bill was drafted and "ignored the unmistakable evidence" that labor-management cooperation had improved in recent months. Third, the bill was unworkable because the NLRB would have its tasks greatly expanded and at the same time be restricted in its procedures. This would result in a greatly increased backlog of unsettled cases, a problem which already confronted the board. Also, the national emergency strike provisions would require an immense amount of government work and yet result "almost inevitably in failure." Fourth, the bill was unfair in prescribing unequal penalties for the same offense. Truman pointed out that much had been made of the claim that the bill was intended to equalize bargaining power but that in the case of conflicting charges of unfair labor practices the NLRB would have to give priority to employer claims.

The President then stated his specific objections to the bill. He believed it would increase strikes because unions would be less willing to accept a no-strike clause in contracts since they would be subject to suit in federal courts for breach of contract. Also unions would be forced to strike or boycott to settle jurisdictional disputes as that would be the only way they could force the NLRB to assume jurisdiction. The bill would limit the area of voluntary agreement by restricting union-security provisions and welfare funds, and such items as safety and rest-period rules might be construed as featherbedding. Truman felt that employers would be hampered by increasing the number of union elections which would disturb plant production, inviting employees to sue employers for thousands of minor grievances, and prohibiting the granting of a union shop even if desired by the employer. Truman was convinced that several provisions were unworkable. These included separating the general counsel from the board, setting up procedures contrary to the Administrative Procedures Act of 1946, requiring endless government supervised elections, and necessitating board determination of which employees were entitled to reinstatement and voting privileges after a strike. He also considered the national emergency provisions ineffective and discriminatory since the board of inquiry could only investigate and not even offer its informed judgment after the investigation.

If the proposal became law, Truman said, it would deprive workers of vital protection as the employer would be able to initiate an election at a time advantageous to himself and it would force workers to compete with sweatshop goods by halting all types of secondary boycotts. It would make unions liable for agents' actions whereas, in contrast to employers, unions cannot always control the actions of their agents or members. Also, in regard to its effect on labor, Truman was convinced that the bill was discriminatory. If an existing agreement were violated the employer would only have to restore the previous conditions while the employee could be discharged for violation. It permitted employers to seek restraining orders on the pretext that the workers were using illegal boycotts or jurisdictional strikes and it imposed burdensome reporting requirements on unions only.

Finally, Truman objected to the measure as it raised serious issues of public policy. These issues included the restriction of political contributions and activities of unions, prevention of union certification of an entire national union if one official refused to sign a non-communist affidavit, and giving priority to state laws in regard to union-security provisions. Truman ended by stating that, contrary to his State of the Union recommendations, the bill made drastic changes in the national labor policy and provided for investigation afterward by the joint committee.[43]

That same evening President Truman explained his action to the American people in a nationwide radio address. He had vetoed the Taft-Hartley bill, he said, because it was "bad for labor, bad for management, and bad for the country." He reiterated his State of the Union requests, stating that he believed those proposals had been accepted as "fair and just" by the great majority of the people. Instead of following his recommendations, Congress had produced a "shocking" piece of legislation which he could not have signed under any circumstances. He informed the people that they had been misled in regard to the bill, quoting Hartley's statement, "You are going to find there is more in this bill than may meet the eye." Truman had found no truth in the claim that the Senate had taken the "harsh" House proposal and made it "moderate." He enumerated the various ways in which the bill would weaken labor unions, maintaining that legislation was needed to correct abuses and not to take away the fundamental rights of labor. His address ended with the hope that the bill would not become law "for the sake of the future of this nation."[44]

That same evening Robert Taft answered the President. In a nationwide radio broadcast Taft characterized the veto message as "a complete misrepresentation of both the general character of the bill and of most of its detailed provi-

[43] Veto Message to the House of Representatives, June 20, 1947, *Truman Papers, 1947*, pp. 288-97.

[44] Radio Address, June 20, 1947, Truman Papers, OF 407-B, HSTL.

sions."[45] Hartley maintained that the President did not write the veto message because he was an "honest man." The message, Hartley charged, was "studded with misrepresentations, half truths and distortions" much too similar to those that "Left-Wing lawyers for the CIO and Left-Wing lawyers for the labor board have been circulating for weeks."[46] The reaction of the press to the veto was not too surprising. The New York *Times* declared that the President had never made any move to cooperate with Congress. Labor-management relations under his administration had been "far and away the worst in the nation's history," the *Times* stated, and in two years he had shown no evidence of having a labor policy of his own or of trying to develop one. Yet he "figuratively slapped the Congress in the face" with a veto message that was "a catch-all for every discredited argument advanced against the bill over the past several weeks."[47] The Washington *Times Herald* emphasized that the 1946 elections signified that a majority of the voters wanted such labor legislation. Against this recent expression of the popular will, Truman had to trace his mandate back to Franklin D. Roosevelt's 1944 wartime election. "Yet the President now puts his mouldy second-hand mandate of 1944 against the 1946 Congressional mandate," the *Times Herald* snapped, "and vetoes this labor bill."[48]

The veto message was read to the House of Representatives at 12:05 P.M. Forty-three minutes after the reading commenced, the House of Representatives began a rollcall vote which was completed by 1:17 P.M. The House overrode the veto 331 to 83 with 15 not voting. Of the 331 voting to override, 106 were Democrats and all but 8 of these were from the South or Southwest.[49]

45 New York *Times,* June 21, 1947.
46 *Ibid.,* June 22, 1947.
47 *Ibid.,* June 21, 1947.
48 Washington *Times Herald,* June 21, 1947.
49 *Congressional Record,* 80 Cong., 1 Sess., 1947, XCIII, 7489.

Action in the Senate was less hasty than that of the House because of a filibuster. Three Democratic Senators, Claude Pepper of Florida, Glen Taylor of Idaho, and Harley Kilgore, and one Republican, Wayne Morse, decided to filibuster through the weekend so that the reaction of the nation to the veto could reach the Senate and be assessed. These Senators began at 2:20 P.M. on June 20, after the veto message was read, and held the Senate in continuous session until 4:30 P.M. the next day, which was Saturday. At that time the Senate agreed to vote at 3:00 P.M. the following Monday.

On Friday President Truman invited twelve Senators who had voted for the bill to lunch at the White House in an effort to gain their support.[50] The following Monday the President made a final effort to sway Senate voting. He sent a letter to Senate Leader Alben Barkley reiterating his belief that the bill would seriously harm the country in this "critical period." He commended Barkley and his colleagues who had fought against the bill, wishing them success in their efforts to sustain his veto.[51]

Jack Redding, publicity director of the Democratic National Committee, reported that at this point the administration thought it could hold thirty votes and would probably only need two more to sustain the veto. Senator Robert Wagner, author of the Wagner Act, was extremely ill and Senator Elbert Thomas of Utah was in Switzerland attending a conference of the International Labor Organization. Redding called Thomas, who agreed to fly to Washington, and arrangements were made to bring Wagner from New York to cast the two needed votes. "We had been told that the attempt might kill him," Redding said in regard to the ailing Wagner. "We were also told that the Senator was willing

[50] *Newsweek*, XXIX (June 30, 1947), 15.

[51] Harry S. Truman to Alben Barkley, June 23, 1947, Truman Papers, OF 407-B, HSTL.

to die, if die he must, in casting the deciding vote." However, the administration lost some of the thirty "sure" votes at the last minute and the project was called off.[52]

So on June 23 the Senate overrode the veto by a vote of 68 to 25, with 2 not voting.[53] Twenty Democrats joined the Republicans against sustaining the veto, all of them coming from the South or Southwest. This vote of Congress to override the veto of the Taft-Hartley bill, the *Congressional Digest* recorded, was "about as severe a rebuff as any President has received on major legislation in the present century."[54]

The day after the Senate vote a radio forum was held on the subject, "Will the Taft-Hartley Act Work and How Well Will It Work?" Senator Aiken expressed the opinion that Congress should have made a study of the "basic causes of labor unrest" before taking action but "pressure from the country made this delay impossible." He continued by saying that if and when the act was "properly amended" he thought it would prove just and practical. Paul Herzog, who would have to administer the act, stated his misgivings but said that the NLRB and its staff were pledged to "do their utmost" to make it work as effectively as possible. Lee Pressman of the CIO described it as a "nightmare" that brought government in on the employers' side to repress labor. And Ray Smethurst, NAM general counsel, felt that the act fell short of what the employers wanted in "equalizing" bargaining power, but most of them were "reconciled to the fact that this law is a step in the right direction."[55]

News commentator Eric Sevareid declared that the congressional vote overriding the veto was probably the most

[52] Jack Redding, *Inside the Democratic Party* (New York: Bobbs-Merrill, 1958), pp. 77-79.

[53] *Congressional Record,* 80 Cong., 1 Sess., 1947, XCIII, 7538.

[54] *Congressional Digest,* XXVIII (April 1949), 101.

[55] Radio Forum, Office of Government Reports, Division of Press Intelligence, June 26, 1947, Truman Papers, Misc. File, White House Central Files, HSTL.

important victory of the legislative over the administrative branch since Franklin D. Roosevelt lost the 1937 Supreme Court fight.[56] Edwin C. Hill was certain that the veto defied the 1946 election returns and also the desires of a large segment of the Democratic party. Only a political wizard of Franklin D. Roosevelt's caliber could now fend off a split, Hill stated, that would be disastrous to the party and to Truman's ambitions.[57] The liberal Max Lerner condemned the Taft-Hartley Act and predicted that it would be repealed only by a Congress elected as a part of a liberal victory.[58] The only regret Congressman Hartley had was that the act did not "complete the job the Republican party set out to do in November of 1946."[59]

After the bill was passed over his veto, President Truman issued a statement in which he said that the Taft-Hartley Act was "now the law of the land" which everyone had to respect. He wanted to make it "unmistakably clear" that as President he would see that the law was "well and faithfully administered" and stated that he had received similar reassurances from the NLRB. He then called upon labor and management to exercise "patience and moderation" in living under the law and not seek to take unfair advantage of its provisions. "We must all do our part," he concluded.[60] The National Labor Relations Board, composed of Paul M. Herzog, John M. Houston, and James J. Reynolds, Jr., issued a statement pledging "the fairest and most efficient administration" of the act within its power.[61] All of the provisions of the Labor-Management Relations Act of 1947, by its terms, were to go into effect on August 22, 1947.

56 Radio Comment of June 23, Office of Government Reports, Division of Press Intelligence, June 24, 1947, Truman Papers, Misc. File, White House Central Files, HSTL.

57 *Ibid.*

58 *Ibid.*, June 30, 1947.

59 Hartley, *Our New National Labor Policy*, p. 171.

60 Statement, June 26, 1947, Truman Papers, OF 407, HSTL.

61 Paul M. Herzog, Radio Address, June 24, 1947, Truman Papers, OF 145, HSTL.

The veto of the Taft-Hartley bill was one of the most important domestic decisions made by President Truman during his first administration. As the heir and defender of the New Deal, the President was confronted with the extremely difficult choice of either riding the crest of the popular wave of a postwar reaction against the power of unions or standing firm in the face of it in defense of his sincere convictions. To compound the dilemma of his position, it came at a time when the tense coal situation was again inflaming public emotions against labor. If a coal strike developed, the administration would need a weapon like the Taft-Hartley Act to combat it. If he vetoed the bill and a subsequent coal strike got out of hand, Truman would have no defense for his action.

This decision was further complicated by its political aspects. It came between two election years and in the middle of a postwar conservative reaction. The Republicans were gaining political momentum and could foresee the definite probability of capturing the Presidency in 1948 after sixteen years of drought. If Harry Truman planned to be his party's candidate to succeed himself in 1948 and expected to win, he would need a firmly united party to counteract the growing political conservatism of the nation which was increasing Republican strength. And yet a large segment of his party, Senators and Representatives from the South and Southwest, had joined the Republican majority on this legislation. They not only joined in passing the Taft-Hartley Act, but more important, voted to override the decision of the titular head of their party. In making this decision then, Truman had not only to fly into the face of apparent national public opinion, but also to stand in direct opposition to the desires of an important section of his party.

Furthermore, he had to consider the best course of action in regard to his own constituency, the urban laborers. Southern Senators and Representatives could ignore the outcries of labor, but a Democratic President could not. President Truman was aware of the numerous complaints of union abuses from rank-and-file members but there was the distinct likelihood that if their unions were attacked by an outside force they would unite in opposition to such an onslaught. There was a possibility that they would not only close ranks but that such an assault would provide a stimulus in 1948 to overcome the apathy shown by labor in 1946.[62]

Truman's decision to veto the Taft-Hartley Act marked a major turning point toward domestic liberalism in his Presidency. At this very time the Cold War was unfolding on the international scene; his administration was formulating the policy of containment with the Truman Doctrine and its aid to Greece and Turkey in March 1947; Secretary of State George Marshall first proposed what became known as the Marshall Plan in June 1947. On the domestic scene, the veto of the tax bill and the Taft-Hartley Act, coming within days of each other, established a milestone for Harry S. Truman in his determination to preserve and extend the New Deal in his "domestic cold war" with the Republican Eightieth Congress.

Although he was guided by expert advice, the final determination to veto was his own. And once he made that irrevocable decision he became so emotionally committed to it that he would come to its defense whenever attacked. He had done everything within his power "to prevent an injustice against the laboring men and women of the United States,"[63] and in doing so, Harry S. Truman was to exact retribution from the Republicans in 1948.

[62] Clifton Brock, *Americans for Democratic Action* (Washington, D.C.: Public Affairs Press, 1962), p. 87, notes that the Taft-Hartley veto "soothed the ruffled feelings of labor and his veto of a regressive GOP tax bill had won general acclaim on the left."

[63] Truman, *Memoirs,* II, 30.

5

THE "DO-NOTHING" CONGRESS BECOMES A CAMPAIGN ISSUE

Charles Halleck, House majority leader of the Eightieth Congress, is quoted as saying, "It always galls me to think that Harry Truman won in 1948 by attacking the Congress which gave him his place in history."[1] Truman used the "Do-Nothing Eightieth Congress" as a whipping boy in the campaign of 1948 to arouse the American people into voting for him and the Democratic party; the Taft-Hartley Act was one of the major issues he used in castigating this Congress. Thus when the Republican Eightieth Congress altered the national labor policy over the veto of President Truman, it created a political nemesis that was to play a tremendous role in snatching almost certain victory from the Republican presidential candidate in 1948.

Although the act went into effect on August 22, 1947, it did not actually become much of a political issue until the campaign of 1948. There were a few actions and comments from the executive branch concerning the law during its early operation, but in general the Truman administration remained quiet on the issue until it exploded into criticism in 1948. One month after the law went into effect Philip Hannah, an assistant secretary of labor, resigned his position because he believed it "raised grave issues for the American people." Hannah felt that he could not work under the new policy and his only alternative was to resign from government service and, as a private citizen, carry on "the fight to repeal this anti-labor and undemocratic law."[2] But this incident was scarcely noticed. As noted by Cyrus Ching, director of the new Federal Mediation and Conciliation Service, opponents for the most part were busy adjusting themselves to the new situation and had little time to devote to criticism.[3]

President Truman, while having done everything in his power to prevent the act from becoming law, utilized its national emergency provisions. He invoked these powers six times before the campaign of 1948: three times in maritime strikes, twice with coal mine disputes, and once before an impending strike at the Oak Ridge atomic plant.[4] Although the Taft-Hartley Act prohibited striking against the government, an altercation had developed at the Oak Ridge plant between the company that had leased the government plant and its employees, so the government was only indirectly involved. This Oak Ridge dispute in the spring of 1948 evoked a message from the President to Congress. Truman reported that everyone involved in the controversy had complied with the Labor-Management Relations Act and should be commended for reaching a settlement without

1 Jules Abels, *Out of the Jaws of Victory* (New York: Holt, 1959), p. 139.

2 Philip Hannah to the President, Sept. 26, 1947, Truman Papers, OF 15, HSTL.

3 Cyrus S. Ching to the President, Oct. 29, 1947, Truman Papers, OF 419-F, HSTL.

4 *Congressional Digest*, XXVIII (April 1949), 106.

interruption of work. However, he said, this contention had raised the question of what policy should be followed in settling future labor strife in government-owned, privately-operated, atomic energy plants. He proposed establishing a commission of experts to study the problem and submit recommendations for necessary special legislation "in this new and vital field."[5] A special procedure for handling labor disputes in this area was later set up which subsequently effectively settled a number of controversies.[6]

The 1948 State of the Union message contained Truman's first significant discussion of the Taft-Hartley Act after its enactment. As usual in preparing this message, the various departments and agencies were requested to submit their views on what should be included. Reporting for the NLRB, Paul Herzog concluded that experience under the law had been too brief to permit making a sound judgment on its effectiveness and the board could not present any specific amendments.[7] But Secretary of Labor Schwellenbach submitted several proposals. In addition to recommending that the federal minimum wage be raised to 75 cents per hour and extended to agricultural workers and seamen, he proposed several changes in the Labor-Management Relations Act. These included amendments to liberalize restrictions on union-security agreements, union political contributions, health and welfare funds, return of the conciliation functions to the Department of Labor, and "early amendment or repeal of the provisions of the Act which are found to be unworkable or unfair."[8]

President Truman incorporated the minimum wage raise recommendation into his annual message to Congress. This

5 Statement to Congress, June 18, 1948, *Truman Papers, 1948*, pp. 379-81.

6 John H. Leek, *Government and Labor in the United States* (New York: Rinehart, 1952), p. 266 n.

7 Paul M. Herzog to the President, Nov. 4, 1947, Truman Papers, OF 419-F, HSTL.

8 L. B. Schwellenbach to the President, Oct. 31, 1947, Truman Papers, OF 419-F, HSTL.

increase was justified, he felt, because "the welfare of industry and agriculture depends on high incomes for our workers." In regard to the Labor-Management Relations Act of 1947 he reminded Congress that he had made his attitude quite clear in the veto message and nothing had occurred since then to change his opinion. But he made no specific recommendations for amendments, saying that as long as it remained the law he would carry out his "Constitutional duty to administer it."[9]

While the enactment of the Taft-Hartley Act did not cause many changes or too much apparent consternation in the executive branch during the first few months of its existence, it had an immediate and pronounced effect upon the attitude and policies of labor officials. Immediately after its passage labor turned to politics with a vengeance, the slogan "Repeal the Slave Labor Act" becoming its shibboleth. On the day following the Senate action to override the veto, A. F. Whitney sent a letter to the presidents of the AFL, the CIO, the Locomotive Engineers, and the executive secretary of the Railway Labor Executive Association, pointing out that labor had for many years relied upon the Senate for protection since the House of Representatives was "more or less reactionary." But after the Senate overrode the veto of this cardinal attempt to cripple labor, the "die" was cast and "labor should do something about it." So Whitney suggested that the major groups who were "numerically and financially able" should carry on a fight to correct the damage and develop a program designed for "the mutual advantage of every group of labor."[10] Evidently most union officials felt as he did because labor became more politically active than ever before.

[9] State of the Union message, Jan. 7, 1948, *Truman Papers, 1948*, pp. 1-10.

[10] A. F. Whitney to William Green, Philip Murray, Alvanley Johnston, and E. A. Lyon, June 24, 1947, Secretary Schwellenbach File (Bills, H.R. 3020), R.G. 174, National Archives.

Section 304 of the Taft-Hartley Act forbade unions to make contributions or expenditures in national elections. This provision was inserted in the bill mainly "to help rally timid Congressmen" to support the measure, the idea being that it would give them protection against labor retaliation in subsequent elections.[11] Also the Republican Eightieth Congress realized that labor's political activities in the past had been directed largely toward helping Democrats rather than Republicans. On the basis of this prohibition unions early believed that they would be greatly restricted in national politics, if not completely ejected. For example, the Boilermakers, Iron Shipbuilders and Helpers of America were denied permission to present a program "pointing out the injustices of the Taft-Hartley Act" on this basis by the American Broadcasting Company.[12] However, the law's prohibition defined "labor organization" as one which dealt with employers in regard to wages, hours, and working conditions. Unions soon discovered that this provision could be circumvented by setting up separate political organizations with funds voluntarily contributed and unconnected with their regular treasuries.

The AFL had, with the exception of the election of 1924, always pursued the strategy of "rewarding friends and punishing enemies." It now placed even greater emphasis upon this traditional policy and embarked upon an active political program. When William Green addressed the AFL annual convention in October of 1947 he proposed two great objectives that labor must achieve "at any cost": first, to repeal the Taft-Hartley Act "at the earliest opportunity" and, second, to defeat for reelection every member of Congress who had voted for it. To accomplish these goals, he

11 A. J. Liebling, "The Wayward Press," *New Yorker,* XXIII (Aug. 16, 1947), 67.

12 Clif Langsdale to John R. Steelman, Aug. 11, 1948, Truman Papers, OF 407, HSTL.

asked the convention to declare election day of 1948 a holiday so labor could "march to the polls and vote against their enemies."[13] The convention did this and more. Following a resolution stating that the Taft-Hartley Act confronted labor with a challenge to "immediate political education . . . to differentiate between political friends and enemies," the convention unanimously adopted a resolution to set up such a political education program.[14] The AFL Executive Council then met December 5, 1947, and established Labor's League for Political Education.[15]

Labor's League for Political Education proceeded to set up a branch LLPE in every state prior to the campaign of 1948. The AFL Executive Council suggested that each union try to obtain a voluntary contribution from each member, setting a goal of $1 each, to be used for political purposes.[16] After the Supreme Court removed the restriction on political advocacy by labor newspapers in the spring of 1948, the AFL began issuing the *1948 Campaign News Service,* a newspaper designed to educate its members politically for the coming election. The AFL ultimately spent "over $360,210" in this campaign on the national, state, and local levels.[17]

The CIO enlarged the activities of its Political Action Committee (PAC), which had been functioning since 1944, and conducted a campaign against the "Slave Labor Law" that matched the AFL in aggressiveness. At the 1947 annual CIO convention a resolution was unanimously adopted committing the CIO to work "unceasingly in the political field in complete unity with all other labor organizations and other

13 *Proceedings of the Sixty-Sixth Convention of the American Federation of Labor* (1947), p. 15.

14 *Ibid.,* p. 662.

15 *Proceedings of the Sixty-Seventh Annual Convention of the American Federation of Labor* (1948), p. 65.

16 Philip Taft, *The A.F. of L. from the Death of Gompers to the Merger* (New York: Harper, 1959), p. 312.

17 *Ibid.,* p. 317.

progressive groups to insure the political repudiation of those reactionaries" responsible for the Taft-Hartley Act.[18] The PAC reported spending $446,832 in the 1948 campaign.[19] Also the independent machinists and telephone workers created their own political action organizations and even the railroad workers who were not directly affected by the law organized a political agency.[20]

An indication of labor's position in the coming election was given when several labor leaders early endorsed Truman as a presidential candidate. The general chairman of the International Brotherhood of Firemen and Oilers assured him that labor would make every effort to elect its friends and defeat its enemies and that he would assist Truman in any way possible in the coming election.[21] Following the stand taken by the AFL in its 1947 convention, many federated unions submitted resolutions dedicating themselves to fighting for repeal of the Taft-Hartley Act and defeating congressmen who had voted for it. Even some of the independents, like the Brotherhood of Signalmen of America, sent in similar resolutions "in accordance with the policy of the American Federation of Labor."[22] Long before the 1948 nominating conventions the Maryland and District of Columbia branch of the LLPE approved a resolution lauding Truman for vetoing the bill. And "in appreciation for the known friendship of President Harry S. Truman toward organized labor," it endorsed his reelection, calling upon all members of organized labor to vote for him in November 1948. The Democratic National Committee's director of publicity requested "200 to 250 copies" of this resolution

18 *Proceedings of the Ninth Constitutional Convention of the Congress of Industrial Organizations* (1947), p. 188.

19 New York *Times*, Oct. 31, 1948.

20 Rayback, *A History of American Labor*, p. 400.

21 Lee Anderson to Harry S. Truman, July 7, 1947, Truman Papers, OF 407, HSTL.

22 C. L. Bromley to the President, Aug. 13, 1948, Truman Papers, OF 407, HSTL.

"for distribution to prominent Democratic leaders throughout the country."[23]

Truman decided to seek the presidency in his own right because there was still "unfinished business" needing attention, the most important being the threat of Russian communism and the "coalition of southern Democrats and northern Republicans, who hoped to compel the repeal of a great deal of New Deal legislation."[24] In the coming campaign he decided that the Eightieth Congress was to be his "Exhibit A." This Republican-controlled Congress had ignored his recommendations and "managed to reverse the sound democratic policies of collective bargaining, social security, rent controls, [and] price controls," which proved the Republican party to be the party of "special privilege."[25] Truman was convinced that the American people did not actually realize the significance of what was happening because of the distortion of news by the press. The Republican threat to the New Deal structure coupled with "the influence of a hostile press which promoted the policies of the Republican party" led Truman to conclude that the only way he could win would be to present the "facts to the people."[26]

On June 3 Truman set out on a cross-country jaunt that was to last until June 18. The ostensible purpose of this journey was to receive an honorary degree from the University of California, but this tour proved to be a preview of his presidential campaign. Also on this trip Truman received the news of the death of his Secretary of Labor, Lewis Schwellenbach. At Seattle Truman informed a crowd of the event, paying high tribute to Schwellenbach as the "greatest" Secretary of Labor he had ever known.[27] John R.

[23] John M. Redding to Frank J. Coleman, May 4, 1948, Truman Papers, OF 407, HSTL.

[24] Truman, *Memoirs,* II, 172.

[25] *Ibid.,* pp. 174-75.

[26] *Ibid.,* p. 177.

[27] Remarks at Seattle, Wash., June 10, 1948, Truman Papers, OR, HSTL.

Steelman was asked to fill this vacancy but declined on the grounds that he was more valuable in his current position, and Truman agreed with him.[28] Maurice J. Tobin, governor of Massachusetts, who had a good record as far as labor was concerned, accepted the position. Judging from his activities in the campaign following his acceptance of the post, his ability as a political speaker was one of the major qualifications that determined Tobin's appointment.

During this June tour Truman revealed the two issues on which he later attacked the Republican Eightieth Congress repeatedly—inflation and the Taft-Hartley Act. In a speech delivered at Butte, Montana, he charged that the Eightieth Congress had cut off almost all the appropriations to run the Bureau of Labor Statistics. This was quite important, he insisted, because this bureau studied prices and tried to determine the causes of inflation. So the Eightieth Congress had not only cut off price controls but had also removed the "speedometer" which told how fast prices were rising.[29] The next day he told a gathering of Communications Workers of America that he realized they were unhappy over the Taft-Hartley Act but that as President he had to enforce it. The law came about, he said, because in 1946 only one-third of those eligible had voted and their only remedy now was "November, 1948."[30] From this trip he concluded that the people were interested in issues and in order for them to make the right political decisions, they had to know the "facts."

Soon after the June trip the national conventions were held, with the Republicans leading off.[31] Thomas Dewey,

28 Press Conference, July 1, 1948, Truman Papers, OR 21, HSTL.

29 Remarks at Butte, Mont., June 8, 1948, Truman Papers, OR, HSTL.

30 *Ibid.*, Spokane, Wash., June 9, 1948.

31 Much of the following material on the 1948 campaign is from R. Alton Lee, "The Turnip Session of the Do-Nothing Congress: Presidential Campaign Strategy," *Southwestern Social Science Quarterly*, XLIV (Dec. 1963), 256-67. The author acknowledges with gratitude permission given by this quarterly to use this material.

Robert Taft, and Harold Stassen were the three leading contenders for the nomination in this race. Stassen was eliminated early in the campaign when he lost the Oregon primary. The deciding factor in this primary was a debate between Dewey and Stassen on outlawing the Communist Party, Stassen taking the affirmative. The loss of this race finished Stassen as a potential nominee, leaving Taft as the major competitor for Dewey to defeat at the convention. While Taft was a strong contender, controlling the conservative wing of the party, there was a general feeling among the delegates that "he lacked vote-getting appeal and . . . would jeopardize the sure victory of the G.O.P."[32] As a result, the Republican national convention, meeting in Philadelphia on June 21, nominated as their presidential candidate Thomas Dewey of New York by acclamation on the third ballot. Governor Earl Warren of California, the state with the fourth largest number of electoral votes, was nominated as the vice-presidential candidate to balance the ticket. The Republican platform omitted any mention of the Taft-Hartley Act, stating only that collective bargaining was "an obligation as well as a right" and pledged "continuing study to improve labor-management legislation in the light of experience and changing conditions."[33] The remainder of the platform advocated many of the items that Truman had been requesting of the Republican Eightieth Congress, but discussed them in the nebulous way parties use when extremely confident of victory. With most Republicans firmly united behind Dewey, the party was confident of victory and felt no need to make concessions to labor.

In contrast to this Republican unity, the Democratic party seemed hopelessly splintered. Secretary of Commerce Henry Wallace had split with Truman, disagreeing with the admin-

[32] Abels, *Out of the Jaws of Victory*, pp. 62-63.

[33] *Official Report*, 24th Republican National Convention, Philadelphia, June 21-25, 1948, p. 190.

istration's "get tough" attitude toward Russia. When he spoke out publicly against this policy he was fired in September 1946. Wallace then became editor of the *New Republic,* using this liberal weekly as a sounding board to attract old New Dealers who were disgusted with what they considered Truman's betrayal of the Roosevelt policies. Many of these liberals, dating from the New Deal period, were convinced that Truman was not moving as fast as he could in social and economic policies in the postwar period. With the support of this group, late in 1947 Henry Wallace declared his candidacy on a third party ticket. Reminiscent of the LaFollette movement in 1924, the Progressive party met in Philadelphia in July after the other conventions and nominated Henry Wallace and Senator Glen Taylor as candidates for President and Vice-President. This third party movement persuaded many liberals and "left-wingers" to abandon the Democratic party, but it also helped swing the undecided moderate vote to Truman since the communists noisily supported this Progressive ticket.[34]

In addition, Southern states'-righters withdrew from the Democratic party and formed yet another party, the Dixiecrats. When the Democratic convention, meeting also in Philadelphia on July 12, adopted a strong civil rights plank promoted by the Americans for Democratic Action, many Southern dissidents walked out. At a meeting in Birmingham on July 17, a states'-rights ticket of Governor J. Strom Thurmond of South Carolina and Governor Fielding Wright of Mississippi as presidential and vice-presidential candidates was "recommended" by delegates representing the Southern states plus California and Indiana. Realizing they could not hope to win, the Dixiecrats planned to split the electoral vote so that no candidate would get an electoral

[34] For a rather sympathetic account of Wallace's campaign, see Karl M. Schmidt, *Henry A. Wallace: Quixotic Crusade 1948* (Syracuse, N.Y.: Syracuse, 1960).

majority. The election would then be thrown into the House of Representatives where they would hold the balance of power and support a candidate who would grant them concessions on civil rights legislation. Thus the Democratic party went into the campaign of 1948 with a three-way split. This stacked almost impossible odds against the regular candidate since no Democratic aspirant had won the presidency without the support of the South, not to mention the loss of the extreme liberal element of the party.

Truman's national popularity had plunged rapidly after the initial spurt of sympathy accorded him on his assumption of the terrible burdens of the presidency. In July 1945, public opinion polls indicated that he had the approval of 87 percent of the people, a mark higher than that ever reached by the extremely popular Franklin D. Roosevelt after his first "100 Days." But with the growing frustrations of the postwar world and reconversion problems, the public began directing its bitterness at the White House and Truman's popularity dropped to an all-time low of 32 percent approval in October 1946. His decisive handling of John L. Lewis' injunction violation in November 1946 rallied more national support to his administration, bringing the percentage up to 48 in February 1947,[35] and it continued to fluctuate through 1948. These low ratings in public opinion polls prior to the summer of 1948 led to a brief but powerful movement within the party to block his nomination.

Party regulars who wanted to "dump" Truman centered their support on General Dwight D. Eisenhower, one of the most admired and popular of American figures. In a public opinion poll conducted in June of 1948, it was found that between the three following candidates, the choice was Truman 26 percent, Eisenhower 53 percent, and Wallace 5 percent, with 16 percent expressing no opinion. This same poll showed Truman with only 34 percent against Dewey's

[35] *Newsweek*, XXIX (Feb. 10, 1947), 24.

41 percent and Wallace's 3 percent,[36] indicating Truman's lack of popularity at this time. Although Eisenhower emphatically stated in a letter January 23, 1948, that he would not consider being a candidate, his name continued to arise as a potential Democratic nominee. On July 5, one week before the Democratic convention, Eisenhower reiterated his decision not to run and on this same day the New York *Times* indicated that Truman had the nomination with 809 delegates pledged to him. After Eisenhower's firm declaration, the drop-Truman move switched to Supreme Court Justice William O. Douglas but this also came to naught as Douglas refused the honor. It seemed the Democrats could find no candidate, except Harry S. Truman, who wished to be sacrificed to certain defeat by opposing the Republican nominee.

After Truman decided to run, the possibility of blocking his nomination was almost nil. To have passed over him and nominated another candidate would have meant party repudiation of its leader and program, an almost certain path to defeat. And as Truman himself points out, the incumbent President has much influence with the National Committee, which usually selects a chairman for the convention who meets his approval. This gives the President a great deal of control on the operation of the convention.[37] So Truman went into the Democratic convention in full control of the party machinery, although his popularity was still at low ebb. In fact, even after his nomination, a poll taken of Democratic voters in August indicated that only 46 percent thought he was the best candidate that the party could have selected and that 40 percent felt that someone else should have been nominated.[38] However, owing to the tight reins he held on the party regulars, Truman was able

[36] Elmo Roper, *You and Your Leaders* (New York: Morrow, 1957), pp. 133-34.

[37] Truman, *Memoirs,* II, 186.

[38] Roper, *You and Your Leaders,* p. 134.

to dictate to the convention not only his own nomination but the platform as well, with the exception of the floor fight over the civil rights plank.[39]

In contrast to the Republican platform, the Democratic platform unequivocably declared, "We advocate the repeal of the Taft-Hartley Act." The law had failed, the labor plank said, and labor-management disputes had increased because it encouraged litigation and "undermined the established American policy of collective bargaining." Instead, the Democratic party proposed legislation that would "establish a just body of rules to assure free and effective collective bargaining." This platform also recommended strengthening the Department of Labor and restoring the Federal Mediation and Conciliation Service to the department.[40]

With the incumbent obviously certain of nomination, the Democratic delegates assembled in "an atmosphere of gloom and despondency."[41] Meyer Berger of the New York *Times* gave a vivid description of their convention:

> Democratic delegates wandered deserted streets today without destroying their Sabbath stillness. They seemed like so many mourners.
>
> Caucus rooms were weeping chambers. Lobbies were as soundless as a studio at a broadcasting station. A delegate from Texas sneezed, and the echo thundered and rolled like a cannon shot on a mesa.
>
> Listless cab drivers lolled by empty vehicles at hotel curbs and in the side streets sunning. One said bitterly: "We got the wrong rigs for this convention. They shoulda given us hearses." One of his droopy-eyed fellows retorted: "What convention?"
>
> Delegates meeting on the street or in the lobbies don't say, "Going to the caucus?" or "Coming to the meeting?" They lift

[39] Harold L. Ickes, "Taft Minus Hartley," *New Republic,* CXXI (July 18, 1949), 16.

[40] *Official Report,* Democratic National Convention, Philadelphia, 1948, pp. 530-31.

[41] New York *Times,* July 11, 1948.

their heads off their chests and murmur: "We're going to the wake."[42]

Truman received the nomination with 947 votes on the first ballot with Senator Richard Russell of Georgia, the states'-rights candidate, obtaining only 263 votes. Senator Alben Barkley of Kentucky was nominated for the vice-presidency by acclamation. During this activity, which lasted until two o'clock in the morning, Truman broke precedent by being present in a room below the convention floor.

Immediately after receiving the nomination, Truman appeared before the delegates and delivered a rousing acceptance address. Truman opened his speech with the declaration that he and Barkley were going to *win* in the coming race—a conviction that had not been expressed too hopefully up to that time—which created a new optimism in the party delegates. He told the convention that his June tour revealed that the people wanted to know the facts. He then enumerated these "facts" in a slashing attack on the "Do-Nothing Eightieth Congress." The sins of that Congress, he declared, included killing price controls, failing to pass necessary legislation for housing, minimum wages, social security, national health, and civil rights. In labor relations, where moderate legislation was needed, it passed the Taft-Hartley Act which had disrupted labor-management relations and would "cause bitterness and strife for years to come" if not repealed.

Truman then played his trump card. The Republican platform of 1948 "promised to do . . . a lot of things" he had been requesting of Congress for a long time, he charged. Therefore, he told the convention, he intended to call the "Do-Nothing" Congress into special session "on the twenty-sixth day of July, which out in Missouri they call Turnip

[42] *Ibid.*, July 12, 1948.

Day" and give the Republicans a chance to prove they meant what they said in their platform. He planned to ask that special session to enact adequate legislation for housing, aid to education, improvement of national health, civil rights, curbs on inflation and other items in the Republican platform. If they really wanted to fulfill their promises, he remarked facetiously, they could do the "job in 15 days . . . and still have time to go out and run for office." Of course they would attempt to "dodge their responsibility" by dragging "red herrings across this campaign," but he and Barkley would make certain that they did not "get away with it." The action taken by "that worst 80th Congress" would "be the test" because the American people would "decide on the record," he concluded.[43] Truman's speech, which signaled the opening of the 1948 campaign, had a tonic effect on the delegates. The New York *Times* reported the convention adjourning "with fire in its eye, in place of the glazed look of a week ago."[44] More important, Truman thus set the tone of his campaign which was to be a continuous attack on the Eightieth Congress rather than his actual opponent, Thomas E. Dewey.

Since the concept of calling a special session of Congress proved to be highly valuable in Truman's campaign, claims for authorship of the project are numerous. Margaret L. Coit states that Bernard Baruch was responsible. According to her, Baruch discussed the coming campaign with Samuel Lubell and then informed Truman that he should accept the nomination in person, call a special session of Congress and "dare the Republicans to make their platform good."[45] But Truman insists that the scheme was his own inspiration.[46]

[43] "Acceptance Speech to Democratic Nominating Convention, Philadelphia, July 15, 1948," Truman Papers, OR, HSTL.

[44] New York *Times*, July 18, 1948.

[45] Margaret L. Coit, *Mr. Baruch* (Boston: Houghton Mifflin, 1957), p. 625.

[46] Personal interview of the author with Harry S. Truman, Aug. 3, 1961.

However, it is extremely difficult to attribute the origin of this move to any one person because the idea of a special session was publicly bruited about a great deal in the summer of 1948.

Thus when Congress adjourned on June 20, the New York *Times* had noted that it was "subject to recall by the majority leaders or President Truman" but that otherwise its work was ended.[47] But even prior to June 20, which was before the Republican convention convened, people had called attention to the idea of a special session in letters and telegrams to the White House. The earliest such letter found in the Truman Papers was dated June 16. The writer believed this proposal would be "excellent strategy" since it would probably throw the Republicans into "utter confusion" and also illustrate to the public "their incapacity as well as their stupid insincerity."[48] And on July 5, the New York *Times* reported Truman's telling Frank M. Karsten, Democratic Representative from Missouri, that "he was seriously considering" a special session "to act on housing bills."[49]

On the day after Truman's acceptance speech the *Times* said he had made the decision "at least a week ago."[50] Yet, in a July 13 draft of his acceptance speech there was no mention of a special session. Moreover, since Truman delivered his speech on July 15 from notes gathered by Clark Clifford and Samuel Rosenman, it seems obvious that the final decision to use this strategy was not made until a few hours before the speech and that one of these two men was responsible for influencing the result.

This can be further substantiated by an unsigned memorandum, dated June 29, which sheds much revealing light on the thinking of Truman's political advisers in regard to

[47] New York *Times*, June 21, 1948.

[48] W. Ross Livingston to Harry S. Truman, June 16, 1948, Truman Papers, OF 419-A, HSTL.

[49] New York *Times*, July 7, 1948.

[50] *Ibid.*, July 16, 1948.

the proposed campaign strategy. This document, entitled "Should the President Call Congress Back?" which was found in the Rosenman file, clearly suggests that the special session scheme came from this New Deal adviser of Franklin Roosevelt. The 1948 election, this memorandum shrewdly deduced, could be won only "by bold and daring steps . . . the boldest and most popular" of which would be the calling of a special session of Congress. This reasoning was buttressed by the following points: (1) such action "would focus attention on the rotten record of the 80th Congress," (2) it "would force Dewey and Warren to defend the actions of Congress, and make them accept the Congress as a basic issue," (3) "it would keep a steady glare on the Neanderthal men of the Republican party . . . who will embarrass Dewey and Warren," (4) it would split the Republican party on major issues, and (5) it "would show the President *in action on Capitol Hill,* fighting for the people . . . leading a crusade for the millions of Americans ignored by the 'rich man's Congress.'" The writer agreed that this course would be "hazardous politically," but he pointed out that Truman faced "an uphill fight to win the coming election . . . and the American people love a fighting leader who takes bold action to help the ordinary citizen against the lobbies and the corporations."

The memorandum then went on to answer possible objections to the plan. If a special session were called the Republicans would probably reply with civil rights legislation which would produce a Southern filibuster. But the President could meet this by threatening the southerners with loss of "patronage, their positions of power in the party and their prestige in the event of a Republican victory." The writer continued prophetically, however, the South could not win or lose the election for the Democrats since the outcome would be determined in the Northern, Midwestern, and Western states.

The memorandum also pointed out that some might warn against a special session because it could produce "some genuinely good legislation" for which Dewey and Warren would assume credit. But the writer felt this would not materialize since "reactionaries and lobbyists" controlled Congress, and if a few good bills were passed, the Democratic publicity department should "pound it home to the people that the President" deserved credit.

Finally, the note asserted that while the possibility existed that Congress "might pass phony bills . . . which might fool the people," such action would not materialize because Congress was dominated "by men who cannot pass price-control legislation without losing their financial backers and incurring the wrath of the N.A.M., the U.S. Chamber of Commerce, and other such groups."[51]

Even if Truman did not originate the idea of a special session, it is certain that he added a personal touch by calling it on "Turnip Day." The current adage in Missouri was, "on the twenty-fifth of July, sow turnips wet or dry." Although Truman misnamed the day (the twenty-fifth of July fell on Sunday, hence Congress could not meet until the twenty-sixth), his political reasoning was sound. When he later explained "Turnip Day," he told reporters that "a half pound of seed will sow a couple acres of turnips,"[52] the obvious implication being that from the seeds sowed on July 26, he would reap a substantial harvest the following autumn.

Thus, with this special session of Congress, Truman laid the foundation for his campaign, and his reasons for accepting this approach seem clear. With an extreme low in national popularity and a three-way split in his party, Truman faced almost impossible odds. As Clark Clifford stated,

[51] Memorandum, "Should the President Call Congress Back?" unsigned, June 29, 1948, Rosenman Papers, HSTL.

[52] New York *Times*, July 16, 1948.

"We've got our backs on our own 1-yard line with a minute to play; it has to be razzle-dazzle."[53] To win, Truman had to dwell on domestic issues, and Dewey's record here was not very vulnerable. So he chose to emphasize the conservative character of the Republican Eightieth Congress and to attempt to associate Dewey with it, with special stress on the congressional misdeeds.

The editorial reaction to Truman's acceptance speech is interesting. The New York *Times* declared it to be "unprecedented" for a President to choose the Capitol as "the arena for the opening round of a Presidential campaign."[54] The Baltimore *Sun* pointed out that while Truman had "little or nothing to lose," it still "took considerable nerve to reconvene this Republican Congress."[55] The Chicago *Sun* affirmed that by taking this action Truman immediately shifted "from the defensive to the offensive" in the coming campaign.[56] The *Christian Science Monitor* interpreted the move as having injected "new life and hope" into the Democrats and as "opening the way for an appeal to the independent vote which will decide this election."[57] The New York *Star* believed that Truman thus had given the Democratic party "one chance to save itself," and the Republican party "a chance to fail this year, even now."[58] The Saint Louis *Star Times* was certain that it would be "risky politics" for Congress to ignore his requests because many of them were "close to the hearts of the people."[59] The Chicago *Daily Tribune* lamented that "once more the Republicans have been caught with the wrong candidate" since it now meant that the campaign was between President Truman and

[53] *Newsweek,* XXXII (July 26, 1948), 21.
[54] New York *Times,* July 17, 1948.
[55] Baltimore *Sun,* July 18, 1948.
[56] Chicago *Sun,* July 16, 1948.
[57] *Christian Science Monitor,* July 15, 1948.
[58] New York *Star,* July 28, 1948.
[59] Saint Louis *Star Times,* July 28, 1948.

Senator Taft, "the intellectual and moral leader" of the Republican Congress.[60]

While Democrats were jubilant and regarded calling the special session as "smart politics," the Republicans, needless to say, were less than enthusiastic. Senator Arthur Vandenberg, Republican from Michigan, and other Republican leaders assailed the call as "a last hysterical gasp of an expiring administration."[61] Senator C. Wayland Brooks, Republican from Illinois, averred that never before had an incumbent "stooped so low in his desperation to garner votes."[62] Other congressmen called it "a cheap political trick," and "a cheap and dangerous device." Even Henry A. Wallace, the Progressive candidate for President, declared that Truman called the session in an effort to make Congress the "scapegoat for his own inadequate and often dangerous leadership."[63]

President Truman issued the formal summons, and the Eightieth Congress reluctantly reassembled on "Turnip Day." The reception Congress accorded his message was described as "the most frigid . . . given to a presidential message in modern times."[64] Doris Fleeson compared the situation to a bullfight, with Truman waving his "red flag of recommendations" while Congress "pawed the ground."[65] President Truman greeted the congressmen with the declaration that "the urgent needs of the American people require our presence here today." The people demand legislation, he said, to check inflation and to help meet "the critical housing shortage." He then gave them his recommendations on these two items. These included specifics which he had been requesting of Congress for many months. In addition,

[60] Chicago *Daily Tribune,* July 15, 1948.
[61] New York *Times,* July 16, 1948.
[62] *Ibid.*
[63] *Ibid.,* July 30, 1948.
[64] Baltimore *Sun,* July 28, 1948.
[65] Washington *Star,* July 28, 1948.

he urged legislation dealing with education, minimum wages, social security, displaced persons, a United Nations loan, civil rights, and ratification of the International Wheat Agreement. It would be of tremendous benefit to the nation, he concluded, if Congress had time to enact such legislation. If this was found to be impossible, he added slyly, then "certainly the next Congress should take them up immediately."[66]

Jennings Perry of the New York *Star* was convinced that Truman now had Congress "buffaloed" and guaranteed that the "squirming of its managers" would be "a performance to fascinate the galleries."[67] The Republican leaders received little assistance in the form of advice from Dewey. The day after his nomination Dewey was quoted as saying that it would be "a frightful imposition" to call Congress back for a special session that summer.[68] Now, faced with its actuality, he apparently considered it preferable to keep his campaign separate from the Truman-Congress fight.

Harold Stassen advised Dewey either to lead Congress during the special session or to ignore it, but not to straddle the issue. Most of his advisers recommended that he remain aloof, since he might jeopardize his certain victory, and thus take neither the credit nor the blame for the record of the Eightieth Congress. So the official position of the candidate in regard to the session was announced by his campaign manager, Herbert Brownell, Jr., who declared that "the Republican platform calls for the enactment of a program by a Republican Congress under the leadership of a Republican President. Obviously this cannot be done at a rump session called at a political convention for political purposes in the heat of a political campaign."[69] Although

66 Message to Congress, July 27, 1948, *Truman Papers, 1948,* pp. 416-21.
67 New York *Star,* July 29, 1948.
68 New York *Times,* July 16, 1948.
69 *Newsweek,* XXXII (Aug. 2, 1948), 16.

Dewey repeatedly endorsed the achievements of the Eightieth Congress, he did not bless the Republican congressmen with any positive suggestions for this session. Dewey's forbearance in this matter, the *New Republic* asserted, was caused by a desire "to wait for a Gallup poll" before acting.[70]

The first reaction of many of the Republicans was to adjourn immediately. In fact, on the first day Frederick C. Smith, Republican from Ohio, introduced a resolution calling for adjournment "immediately upon receipt of the President's message."[71] But it was soon decided, with Dewey's approval, that the best strategy would be to consider the proposals and then adjourn as soon as possible. Republican House Speaker Joseph Martin warned of "plenty of action" later, but, he added, "Like the boys at Bunker Hill, we'll wait to see the whites of their eyes."[72]

A memorandum written by William Batt, Jr., of the research division of the Democratic National Committee, indicated that the special session was not a political maneuver *in toto* and that the administration did hope for some accomplishments. In this, Batt emphasized that there was considerable activity to pressure Congress into action. These lobbying activities were being conducted by Lee Johnson of the National Public Housing Conference, the secretary of agriculture through contacts with various farm organizations, the American Association for the United Nations, Americans for Democratic Action, the American Civil Liberties Union, the National Association for the Advancement of Colored People, and various similar pressure groups.[73]

Since both houses of Congress had just been in session and had completed hearings on many of the items Truman had recommended, they could have enacted considerable

[70] *New Republic*, CXIX (July 26, 1948), 3.

[71] *Congressional Record*, 80 Cong., 2 Sess., 1948, XCIV, 9376.

[72] *Time*, LII (July 26, 1948), 15.

[73] Memorandum, William L. Batt, Jr., to Clark Clifford, July 28, 1948, Truman Papers, Murphy File, HSTL.

legislation even in the short time he had proposed. But after eleven days of actual session, Congress adjourned on August 7 despite Truman's plea two days earlier that Congress remain at work since it had "failed to discharge the tasks" for which he had called the special session.[74]

Congress did take some action, however, during this period. It gave the President additional power over inflation by tightening up consumer credit and bank credit controls. Instead of the administration's housing bill, Congress passed an emasculated version sponsored by Senator Joseph R. McCarthy, Republican from Wisconsin. In addition, Congress voted $5 million to purchase automobiles for disabled veterans and provided for a $65 million loan to the United Nations to begin construction of its headquarters in New York City. Committees of both houses also began hearings on communist activities which eventually culminated in the much-publicized Alger Hiss-Whitaker Chambers episode.[75]

But because this session did not enact most of his recommendations, Truman could remain on the offensive in his running battle with the Eightieth Congress. His subsequent campaign was an incessant attack upon the record of the "Do-Nothing" Congress, berating the Republicans for not taking the necessary steps to halt inflation, for passing the Taft-Hartley Act, and for not helping the people by raising minimum wages and by expanding social security coverage, all of these being items that would appeal to the laboring man.

Truman's critics were quick to point out that this "Do-Nothing" appellation was undeserved, particularly in the light of the amount of legislation passed in 1947. And, as Jules Abels points out, in foreign affairs the Eightieth Congress enacted a remarkable program in 1947 and 1948 and

[74] News Release, Aug. 5, 1948, Truman Papers, OE 419-A, HSTL.

[75] News Release, White House, Aug. 12, 1948, Truman Papers, OF 419-A, HSTL.

thus for this reason alone does not completely deserve the label.[76] But in terms of domestic legislation produced or rejected in the second session of this Congress, Truman was rather accurate in his description since very little was accomplished in this "domestic cold war." At any rate, the term proved quite appealing, politically, in the following presidential campaign. Whether accurate or not, this descriptive title enabled Truman to castigate successfully the Republican Congress for its inactivity and to associate Dewey's statements and party platform with this Congress in his campaign.

[76] Abels, *Out of the Jaws of Victory,* pp. 128-30.

6

TRUMAN STUMPS THE NATION

ORGANIZED LABOR played a decisive role in the campaign that followed the 1948 national conventions, particularly in congressional races. Shortly before the Democratic convention it was reported that many union leaders "looked upon Truman's candidacy with skepticism."[1] But after his nomination almost all union officials endorsed him, officially or unofficially. In fact, Jules Abels is persuaded that the PAC and the LLPE each spent over $1,000,000 in the political campaigns of 1948.[2] John L. Lewis was one of the few who refused to support the Democratic candidate. Although Lewis did not formally endorse Dewey, he urged his miners to defeat "Injunction Harry." At the UMW biannual convention in October 1948, Lewis charged Truman with being "cowardly" in his attitude toward labor and a "malignant, scheming sort of individual who is dangerous not only to the United Mine Workers of America but to the United States of America." As the Washington *Star* noted when reporting this speech, this was referring to Harry Truman "as no major figure has referred to a President in modern times."[3] The segment of labor led by Lewis felt that Truman's policies on other issues, such as the use of injunctions in labor disputes, far outweighed his opposition to the Taft-Hartley Act.

But to most leaders of organized labor there was only one basic issue in this presidential campaign and that was the repeal of the Taft-Hartley Act. On this basis labor's choice was easily made. Truman and the Democratic platform were for outright repeal; the Republican candidate and his party advocated "slight changes." But the apparently meager prospect of a Truman victory stimulated a feeling of apathy throughout the nation. When people were asked whom they *thought* would win, in a poll taken in July 1948, Dewey received 64 percent and Truman only 22 percent. Elmo Roper conducted another survey immediately after the election, asking people which candidate they had believed would win just before the election. In this poll the gap was even greater, with Dewey getting 69 percent and Truman only 19 percent.[4] In fact the pollsters had generally given up taking polls some time before the election because it was considered futile since the outcome of the election was already decided.

This general assumption of Dewey's victory made union officials' task of selling Truman to the workers much more difficult. But there was an additional factor which made the union leaders' job even more formidable. As Joseph A. Loftus pointed out at the time, the Taft-Hartley Act had proven to be "an abstract subject" to most workers because

1 "Political Lineup of Union Leaders," *United States News and World Report,* XIV (June 25, 1948), 50.

2 *Out of the Jaws of Victory,* p. 224.

3 Washington *Star,* Oct. 6, 1948.

4 Roper, *You and Your Leaders,* p. 136.

they had not "experienced the Slave Labor penalties" their leaders had predicted.[5] Loftus observed, though, that the campaign had done much to develop cooperation between the AFL and the CIO, with the exception of the "far left" which supported Wallace. This rank-and-file labor indifference to the Taft-Hartley Act was borne out by a public opinion poll taken in September of 1948. Roper asked what should be done with the law. Only 12 percent said repeal it entirely, 11 percent wanted it changed to favor unions more, 25 percent desired only minor improvements, 30 percent would have liked to see it strengthened to check unions further, and 22 percent expressed no opinion.[6]

To help overcome this apathy and make sure the 1946 mistake of labor's staying home was not repeated, there was a strong movement within the ranks of labor to declare election day a labor holiday, as suggested by William Green in the 1947 AFL convention. On Labor Day 1948 Green delivered a speech in which he said labor's keynote should be "Use Your Vote!" He pointed out that if all workers registered and voted they could give the new Congress a "mandate for progress."[7] Union members, therefore, were urged to vote even if it meant being absent from work. However, as Dayton David McKean states, business quickly denounced this holiday tactic and he believes it was not "widely used."[8] But the vigorous campaign by Truman and his forces along with the political efforts of unions brought labor to the polls in greater numbers than expected and achieved much the same results.

Since the polls overwhelmingly predicted a Dewey victory and few people really believed Truman had a chance, labor leaders tended to emphasize the congressional elections.

[5] New York *Times*, Aug. 29, 1948.
[6] Roper, *You and Your Leaders*, pp. 136-37.
[7] William Green, "Labor Day—Use Your Vote," Akron, Ohio, Sept. 6, 1948, *Vital Speeches*, XIV (Sept. 15, 1948), 711.
[8] Dayton David McKean, *Party and Pressure Politics* (Boston: Houghton Mifflin, 1949), p. 476.

The AFL followed its traditional political policy and declined officially to endorse Truman's candidacy but it was obvious and well known that most of the union's officers favored the Democratic candidate rather than Dewey. Most CIO leaders would have preferred that the Democratic party had chosen a stronger candidate than they believed Truman to be, but since he was the chosen standard-bearer and both he and his party had taken such a firm stand against the Taft-Hartley Act, they advocated his election. But Truman's decided and well-publicized handicap in the public opinion polls forced unions to concentrate their money and energy on congressional races out of self-protection.

The widespread belief that Harry Truman was doomed to defeat led to a movement within the CIO, led by Walter Reuther, to lay the groundwork for the future formation of a third party. Since organized labor had placed its confidence in the Democrats as the party to promote its interests, many felt Truman's defeat would leave them unprotected politically. So in March 1948 the CIO's international executive board formulated the long-range objective of developing, following the elections of 1948, "a genuinely progressive political party." Referring to this project in August, Reuther pledged his "complete support, . . . [and] full energy" to effect a "realignment of political forces" in the United States. The first step in implementing this program, Reuther believed, was to concentrate on electing as many prolabor Senators and Representatives as possible in 1948 and use these elections as a nucleus around which to build the new labor party.[9] So the strategy followed by the CIO was to approve Truman but to concentrate its activities on electing favorable congressmen. One magazine reported that the PAC endorsed Harry Truman as the "lesser of two evils but it didn't contribute a nickel to his campaign."[10]

[9] New York *Times,* Aug. 15, 1948. See also *Newsweek,* XXXII (Oct. 25, 1948), 37.

[10] *Newsweek,* XXXII (Nov. 8, 1948 Election Special), 12.

The AFL hierarchy came to much the same conclusion concerning Truman and also concentrated on Congress, following its usual policy of "rewarding friends and punishing enemies." In the subsequent campaigns, the LLPE tried to avoid districts or states that had strongly entrenched anti-labor Senators and Representatives and focused its efforts on those races in which success was considered possible. Particular emphasis was placed upon certain Senate races because of the six-year term of Senators and "because it was believed that the labor vote could frequently have more influence on a state basis rather than in a single district."[11] Both the LLPE and the PAC promoted especially the senatorial candidacies of Hubert Humphrey of Minnesota, James Murray of Montana, Paul Douglas of Illinois, Lester Hunt of Wyoming, and Matthew Neely of West Virginia, in addition to all other candidates who opposed the Taft-Hartley Act.[12]

Even Department of Labor officials campaigned in 1948 against the Taft-Hartley Act. John T. Kmetz, an assistant secretary of labor, informed the Louisiana State Federation of Labor in April 1948 that labor was going to be kept busy on many fronts defending its rights. He pointed out that the Taft-Hartley Act, which was "vindictively passed over one of the strongest Presidential veto messages" in history, had created "excitement and resentment." This, in turn, had distracted public attention from the antiunion drives currently being conducted in the state legislatures.[13] Kmetz made a tour of this area campaigning against the law while ostensibly on official business. After he appeared in Dallas, Texas, an editorial appeared in the Dallas *Times-Herald* charging that as a government official he had attacked the Taft-Hartley Act and the congressmen who had voted for it.

[11] Taft, *The A F of L from the Death of Gompers to the Merger*, pp. 316-17.

[12] *Newsweek*, XXXII (Nov. 8, 1948 Election Special), 12.

[13] Address at Lake Charles, La., April 6, 1948, John T. Kmetz File (Adm.), R.G. 174, National Archives.

Kmetz' defense of his speeches was that he was only expressing the view, gathered at labor conventions, that many congressmen who had voted for the measure were not going to return to Congress. Mrs. Katherine Dillard of the Dallas *News* reported him as saying he was not telling people how to vote but merely advising labor to help defeat representatives "who would destroy labor"[14]—a rather fine distinction. John W. Gibson, acting secretary of labor following Schwellenbach's death, addressed a gathering of workers in July. In this speech he said the "propaganda line" of the framers of the act was that workers wanted and needed "protection" and they were still working "tooth and nail to keep the truth about this vicious anti-labor, undemocratic law from the people."[15]

The new Secretary of Labor, Maurice J. Tobin, threw himself into an all-out campaign against the act. In three months of preelection campaigning he delivered some 150 speeches in more than twenty states and "in every speech he exposed and denounced the iniquitous Taft-Hartley law."[16] The New York *Times* reported that Tobin used his first official news conference as secretary of labor to attack the law. The *Times* recorded him as calling the statute "impractical" and criticizing especially the closed shop and political expenditures bans, advocating changes "along the lines of the Democratic platform."[17] In addressing a rally of the Liberal party in New York City, Tobin charged that the Republican Congress, "urged on by the NAM, took advantage of the emotional and hysterical atmosphere" engendered by the postwar strikes to pass "discriminatory legisla-

14 U.S. House of Representatives, Subcommittee on Expenditures in the Executive Departments, *Hearings*, April 19, 1948, John T. Kmetz File (Adm.), R.G. 174, National Archives.

15 Address at Milwaukee, Wis., July 22, 1948, Assistant Secretary of Labor Gibson File (Speeches), *ibid.*

16 Maurice J. Tobin to Harry Read, Oct. 5, 1949, Secretary Tobin File (1949—CIO), *ibid.*

17 New York *Times*, Aug. 19, 1948.

tion."[18] A few days later he repeated this accusation against the NAM. He said the only "protection" the law gave was to the "rugged individualists of the National Association of Manufacturers," pointing out how these "propaganda experts" had consistently fought against the Wagner Act.[19] Another theme he used was to warn the workers to go to the polls. They must "elect representatives to Congress" who would repeal the Taft-Hartley law.[20]

It was Harry S. Truman, though, who took the issue he had created by vetoing the Taft-Hartley Act and made it "one of the chief political issues" of the 1948 campaign.[21] Accepting the challenge of the tremendous odds against him, Truman undertook the greatest fight of his career. Truman was one of the few that summer who was convinced that he could win. He decided to conduct a "rip-snorting, back-platform campaign" to what Taft derisively termed "whistle-stops" but what to Truman were the "heart of America." "When they count the whistle-stop votes," he declared, "Taft may be in for a big surprise," because they would "make the difference between victory and defeat."[22]

Truman devised his strategy on the basis of his June trip and the impression he received of the people's wanting to know the "facts," plus the inactivity of the "Do-Nothing" Congress. So in his presidential campaign, like a modern-day Paul Revere, Truman criss-crossed the country in an operation resembling "a prolonged midnight ride warning the American people that the Republicans were coming."[23]

The New York *Post* noted, early in the campaign, that

18 Address at New York City, Sept. 1, 1948, Secretary Tobin File (Speeches), R.G. 174, National Archives.

19 Address at Akron, Ohio, Sept. 6, 1948, *ibid.*

20 Address at the Greater Lawrence Area, Sept. 6, 1948, *ibid.*

21 *Congressional Digest,* XXVII (April 1949), 106.

22 Drew Pearson, "The Washington Merry-Go-Round," Washington *Post,* Aug. 15, 1948.

23 Victor L. Albjerg, "Political Realignments," *Current History,* XXIII (Oct. 1952), 244.

there were two factors that gave Democratic leaders "faint new stirrings of hope": Dewey's nomination, which had not stirred any particular enthusiasm among the independent voters, and the President's "fighting tactics" of going on the offensive by attacks on the record of the Republican Eightieth Congress. This held "the promise of a stirring and exciting campaign" that might lead to a large turnout in voting, a traditional advantage for the Democrats. "In the final analysis," the *Post* added, this new hope could be traced to "the fact that Mr. Truman is a fighter who doesn't know when he is licked."[24]

Truman's appeal to labor was keynoted in a letter to be published in the Labor Day issue of the *American Federationist.* In this message he charged that the party which passed the Taft-Hartley Act over his veto was also responsible for the high cost of living. "Having inaugurated in the Republican-controlled 80th Congress a blueprint for tearing down 16 years of progress under the Democratic party," Truman continued, "the Republicans are now asking labor's support for their anti-labor policies." He referred to the Republican platform as being "afraid to mention the Taft-Hartley Act" while the Democratic platform boldly advocated its repeal. This record, the incumbent President summed up, "tells American workers which political party has their best interests at heart year in and year out."[25] In his annual Labor Day statement Truman declared again that the law "which unfairly restricts labor unions and their members . . . should be repealed." He noted that labor was "making great efforts to get out the vote" and expressed the hope that every eligible voter would go to the polls in November. "Then," Truman said, "the outcome will be the decision of all America."[26]

24 "Washington Memo," New York *Post,* July 29, 1948.

25 Truman to William Green, Aug. 19, 1948, Truman Papers, PPF 85, HSTL.

26 Labor Day Statement, 1948, Truman Papers, OF 407, HSTL.

In his actual campaign Truman electioneered thirty-five days, traveling approximately 31,700 miles and delivering 356 speeches.[27] He inaugurated this campaign, significantly, with a Labor Day speech before 100,000 people in Cadillac Square, Detroit. Truman had the assistance of Clark Clifford and John R. Steelman in preparing this speech, asking their advice on "methods for carrying out the Democratic party's pledge to bring about repeal" of the Taft-Hartley Act.[28] Truman told the Detroit workers that a strong and free labor movement was the best bulwark against communism. This necessitated "a friendly Administration and a friendly Congress" to help them remain strong. He declared that, although the Eightieth Congress did not "crack down on prices, it had cracked down on labor" by placing a "dangerous weapon" in the hands of big corporations. This weapon, the Taft-Hartley Act, was only a "foretaste" of what would happen if this Republican "reaction" were allowed to continue. If laborers stayed at home as they did in 1946 and allowed a Republican President to be elected along with a Republican Congress, labor would then be hit by "a steady barrage of body blows," he warned, and it would be deserved. He painted a gloomy picture of labor's position if the administration of the law were in the hands of a Republican, saying that it would bring on another "boom and bust" cycle similar to that of the last Republican administration. Labor must now fight harder than ever before, he cautioned, and "anything short of an all-out vote would be a betrayal by labor of its own interests." "I know we are going to win this crusade for the right!" he concluded.[29] Truman spoke to six Labor Day audiences that day, promising the "most important campaign this country has witnessed since the Lincoln-Douglas debates."[30]

27 Truman, *Memoirs,* II, 219.
28 New York *Times,* Aug. 24, 1948.
29 Address at Detroit, Mich., Sept. 6, 1948, Truman Papers, OR, HSTL.
30 Toledo, Ohio, Sept. 6, 1948, *ibid.*

On September 17 Truman left Washington on an extended tour, but his campaign was curtailed by the Democratic National Committee's lack of sufficient funds. W. H. Lawrence reported that on this September trip the Democrats were unable to "buy a single nationwide 'live' radio broadcast" of any of Truman's speeches.[31] In fact, funds were so limited the campaign train could not pull out of a station in Oklahoma until a collection was taken up by that state's governor, Roy Turner, and W. Elmer Harber of Shawnee, Oklahoma.[32] Nevertheless, what he lacked in the facilities of mass communications and money, Truman made up for in personal appearances and by raising issues which would stimulate voters. At Herrin, Illinois, he said that the first action the Republicans took after winning control of the Eightieth Congress "was to pass the Taft-Hartley Act which was intended to take away some of the rights of labor."[33] In Carbondale, Illinois, he stated that the "puppet Congress" took the Republican way "backward" and "passed the reactionary Taft-Hartley Act."[34] At Evansville, Indiana, he charged that, following the Republican policy of keeping working people in "bounds," this Congress had placed "handcuffs on labor" by taking away its Bill of Rights. "Led by Senator Taft and Representative Hartley—two men who would like to take the United States back to the 1890's," he exclaimed," the Republicans pushed through the Taft-Hartley law which converted the National Labor Relations Board into an agency to hamstring union labor."[35]

Truman delivered several speeches in Kentucky and West Virginia on October 1, stressing the same theme. At Huntington, West Virginia, he said that prices were rising faster than wages. The Republican Eightieth Congress passed the

[31] New York *Times*, Sept. 26, 1948.
[32] Redding, *Inside the Democratic Party*, p. 273.
[33] Remarks at Herrin, Ill., Sept. 30, 1948, Truman Papers, OR, HSTL.
[34] Carbondale, Ill., Sept. 30, 1948, *ibid.*
[35] Evansville, Ind., Sept. 30, 1948, *ibid.*

Taft-Hartley Act to weaken unions, he proclaimed, so that they could not bargain as effectively for better wages.[36] In Philadelphia he reiterated the Democratic plank, advocating repeal of the law. He did not believe that unions should be destroyed, he told this audience, and he did not think the American people thought so either. He did believe though that the American people would "repudiate the enemies of labor at the ballot box."[37]

At Elizabeth, New Jersey, he reminded a gathering that when the "reactionary" Republicans controlled Congress "reactionary laws" were produced. The answer was to vote Democratic and the people would then get "good housing . . . repeal of that vicious Taft-Hartley Act and more social security coverage."[38] At Amsterdam, New York, he repeated his charge that two-thirds of the eligible voters stayed home in 1946 and received a Congress that worked "for special privilege." The first move that Congress made was to amend the Wagner Act so that it would no longer help labor, he said, "but would work in the interests of special privilege."[39] Truman answered Dewey's statement that the Eightieth Congress "delivered" for the future of the country by claiming that it "delivered . . . a body-blow at labor" by passing the Taft-Hartley Act.[40]

By the time Truman reached the Midwest he had added a new note to his theme song. "Our good old mossback friends passed . . . one of the most complicated laws that anybody ever saw," he affirmed, but this Taft-Hartley Act was not the end. Hartley's book, *Our New National Labor Policy,* had been published and Truman gleefully proceeded to quote from it, emphasizing its subtitle, "And the Next Steps." He cited Hartley's statement that the Taft-Hartley

[36] Huntington, W. Va., Oct. 1, 1948, *ibid.*
[37] Philadelphia, Oct. 6, 1948, *ibid.*
[38] Elizabeth, N. J., Oct. 7, 1948, *ibid.*
[39] Amsterdam, N. Y., Oct. 8, 1948, *ibid.*
[40] Dayton, Ohio, Oct. 11, 1948, *ibid.*

Act corrected "in a single piece of legislation the outstanding mistakes of the New Deal." Hartley had insisted in his book that good labor legislation would require "interim treatment" which was the Taft-Hartley law. Truman's warning to labor was that after this interim treatment the Republicans would then "take the gloves off, and give you the bare knuckles."[41] Truman returned from this Midwest tour confident that the crowds he had attracted disproved the polls showing Dewey in the lead.[42]

The President was soon back on the road completing his campaign. In Scranton he compared the "shameful and awful" Taft-Hartley Act to "a termite, undermining and eating away" the "legal protection to organize and bargain collectively."[43] In Chicago he warned that the Taft-Hartley Act was but "the opening gun in the Republican onslaught against the rights of working men in this country."[44] He told New Englanders that if they wanted to know what to expect if the Republicans won they should read Mr. Hartley's book.[45] He reiterated that he wanted the act repealed and the best way to accomplish this was "to elect a Democratic President and a Democratic Congress."[46] He assured a gathering in Yonkers, New York, that the Republicans would "pass even more restrictive labor laws" if they had a chance, while he was working to get the Taft-Hartley Act destroyed.[47] Truman concluded his campaign with a speech in St. Louis and then went home to Independence to await the outcome of the election.

The campaign conducted by the Dewey forces offered a startling contrast to Truman's odyssey. While Truman hit specific issues, Dewey conducted a lofty campaign centering

41 Akron, Ohio, Oct. 17, 1948, *ibid.*
42 New York *Herald Tribune,* Oct. 17, 1948.
43 Remarks at Scranton, Pa., Oct. 23, 1948, Truman Papers, OR, HSTL.
44 Chicago, Oct. 25, 1948, *ibid.*
45 Worcester, Mass., Oct. 27, 1948, *ibid.*
46 Taunton, Mass., Oct. 28, 1948, *ibid.*
47 Yonkers, N. Y., Oct. 29, 1948, *ibid.*

on the theme of "unity" and speaking in generalities. Taft did not like this "Me, too" campaign and after the election told William S. White that he had known three weeks before the election that Dewey would lose.[48] But even the day before the election a Gallup Poll showed Dewey with 49.5 percent of the votes, Truman 44.5 percent, Wallace 4 percent, and Thurmond 2 percent.[49] Elmo Roper had announced his "final" poll in August, with Truman receiving 37.1 percent of the popular vote, Dewey 52.2 percent, Thurmond 5.2 percent, Wallace 4.3 percent, and others 1.2 percent.[50] The results of these polls helped to determine Dewey's "Me, too" strategy.

Roper insists that all the polls failed, exploding the persistent myth that the famous political pollster Louis Bean correctly predicted Truman's victory. Roper attributes this tremendous polling error to four factors: (1) figures were gathered too early, (2) Truman's hard-hitting campaign changed votes late, (3) contrary to the assumption that the "don't know" vote would divide evenly, most of it went to Truman, and (4) more labor voted than expected.[51] Truman later said that the polls had been wrong because he had been willing to go out and tell the people what was "good" for them. "You have to sell yourself, and what you stand for," he declared.[52] Truman sold himself to the American people with speeches delivered in language the common man could understand, punctuated with color, humor, and facts.

Richard Rovere, a reporter who covered both campaign trains, recorded Truman's campaign having an air of "general dowdiness and good-natured slovenliness" while Dewey's

48 White, *The Taft Story*, p. 83.

49 Stefan Lorant, *The Presidency*, (New York: Macmillan, 1957), p. 712.

50 Roper, *You and Your Leaders*, p. 111. For a complete survey of these polls see Frederick Mosteller and others of Social Science Research Council, *The Pre-Election Polls of 1948* (New York: Social Science Research Council, 1949).

51 Roper, *You and Your Leaders*, pp. 117-19.

52 Address, Washington, D.C., May 17, 1952, Truman Papers, OR HSTL.

was "slick and snappy." To illustrate, he reported the Kentucky bourbon highball as "the favorite beverage" and poker the major diversion on the Truman train, but on the Dewey train martinis and manhattans were "more in vogue" and "several spirited bridge games [were] going on all the time."[53] Dewey's strategy in this campaign was devised from his bitter experience while running against "The Champ" in 1944. In that campaign Franklin Roosevelt's taunting "Fala" speech stimulated Dewey to come back swinging and, it was believed, by thus losing his temper, helped contribute to his own defeat. So his campaign in 1948, it was determined from the outset, would avoid personalities and issues that might arouse heated dispute or create enemies. Naturally, if Truman were to overcome the Republican lead in the course of the campaign, Dewey could then start slugging. But since the newspapers, pollsters, indeed, almost everyone except Truman, insisted to the end that there was no doubt concerning Dewey's victory, "such a switch in tactics did not become necessary."[54]

In fact, Dewey was so confident that he " 'leaked' his Cabinet choices" to reporters traveling on his train several days before the election.[55] While Truman hopped around the countryside in his "Give Them Hell" campaign, it almost seemed as if he were ignoring his actual opponent, Dewey, and was campaigning against the Eightieth Congress. Dewey also appeared to ignore his opponent, only occasionally referring to the administration in Washington, the major concern seeming to be how much further damage the Democrats could impose upon the country before the next January.

The issue of *Life* magazine published just before the election carried a series of campaign pictures, one of which

[53] Richard Rovere, *The American Establishment* (New York: Harcourt Brace, 1962), pp. 76-81.

[54] *United States News and World Report,* XXV (Nov. 5, 1948), 37-38.

[55] Jack Bell, *The Splendid Misery* (Garden City, N. Y.: Doubleday, 1960), p. 166.

showed Dewey on a ferry boat in San Francisco Bay with the caption, "The Next President."[56] The Chicago *Daily Tribune* courageously released its issue the night of the election with the headline "Dewey Defeats Truman."[57] Even after the election returns began showing Truman with a substantial lead, news commentators could not accept the possibility of his winning. "Wait for the rural vote to come in," they said with knowing assurance. But the returns kept mounting an even greater lead for Truman. The incumbent had slipped away from reporters on election night, going to Excelsior Springs, Missouri. He went to bed confident that when he awoke he would have been elected. He had listened to the broadcast of H. V. Kaltenborn at midnight when he was ahead by 1,200,000 but according to that august commentator Truman undoubtedly would still be beaten. At 4:30 A.M. he awoke finding himself with 2,000,000 votes in the lead and decided he had won. At 10:00 A.M. November 3 he received a telegram of congratulations from Thomas Dewey.[58] The Eightieth Congress, so certain of a Republican victory, had conveniently voted an appropriation of $108,000 for an impressive inauguration which the Democratic party proceeded to make plans to utilize.

As the memorandum in the Rosenman file predicted, the South did not win or lose the election for the Democratic party. And, as it also observed, the American people favor the underdog and love a fighter. The final popular vote made Truman a minority President with 24,104,836 votes or 49.4 percent. Dewey received 21,969,500 votes or 45 percent, Thurmond 1,169,021 votes, and Wallace 1,157,172. Truman won in twenty-eight states with 303 electoral votes, Dewey sixteen states with 189 votes, and Thurmond received the electoral votes of four Southern states and one elector

56 *Life*, XXV (Nov. 1, 1948), 37.
57 Chicago *Daily Tribune*, Nov. 3, 1948.
58 Truman, *Memoirs*, II, 220-21.

from Tennessee for a total of 39. Truman had carried several large agricultural states and Jules Abels states that this unexpected switch in the farm vote was "the prime cause of the upset."[59] Samuel Lubell, in *The Future of American Politics,* claims that, owing to the closeness of the vote, Truman's victory could "definitely be credited" to the German-American vote that switched to Truman.[60] This writer observes that the German-American vote, which had swung away from Roosevelt in 1940 and 1944 because of the war, began returning to the Democratic party in 1948. It seems there are almost as many interpretations of the results of this election as there are analysts studying it.

Unions did not hesitate to take credit for Truman's victory, agreeing with the *New Republic* declaration that "the main credit goes to organized labor."[61] Truman himself told intimates that "labor did it."[62] To substantiate this view, *Newsweek* later stated that three out of every four union members voted for Harry S. Truman.[63] Truman points out that he carried the thirteen largest cities, which had a heavy labor vote, and if he had received the American Labor party votes in New York that went to Wallace he would have defeated Dewey in his home state. Truman insists that the two key states in this election were Ohio and California because without them he would have fallen short of a majority by 12 votes less than the required 266.[64] The vote in these two states was close–Truman beat Dewey by only 17,865 in California and 7,107 in Ohio–and certainly the labor vote in these states played a decisive role.

Although Abels declares that the farm vote was the prin-

59 Abels, *Out of the Jaws of Victory,* p. 290.

60 P. 134. For a good survey of the Democratic party's appeal to ethnic voters in this campaign see, Louis L. Gerson, *The Hyphenate in Recent American Politics and Diplomacy* (Lawrence, Kan.: Kansas, 1964), chap. 9.

61 *New Republic,* CXIX (Nov. 15, 1948), 6.

62 *Ibid.* (Nov. 22, 1948), p. 16.

63 *Newsweek,* XL (Sept. 15, 1952), 21.

64 Truman, *Memoirs,* II, 221.

cipal factor in the upset, he agrees that, with the vote being so close in Ohio and California, "the union vote undoubtedly made the difference" in these two states.[65] Abels quotes an analysis made by William Lawrence in the New York *Times* of the returns of the nine largest industrial counties in Ohio. This study indicated that the Democratic percentage shrank from 55.2 in 1944 to 52.7 in 1948 in these areas. Abels concluded then that the farm vote gave Ohio to Truman,[66] which would not necessarily contradict his previous declaration that labor "made the difference." At the same time Lubell decided that the German-American vote was the decisive factor in Ohio with Truman gaining over Roosevelt's showing in 1944 in those areas predominantly German-American.[67]

Dewey's popular vote in Ohio dropped from 50.1 percent in 1944 to 49 percent in 1948 whereas Truman's percentage was 49.5 compared to Roosevelt's 49.9 in 1944. The deciding factor in Ohio could have been the 0.5 percent vote that went to Wallace. If Dewey had received Wallace's 37,596 votes he would have carried Ohio, yet Truman would have undoubtedly received these votes if Wallace had not been on the ticket. Truman's percentage in California dropped from Roosevelt's 56 in 1944 to 47.84; Dewey's rose from 43 percent in 1944 to 47.39 percent. However, this 17,865 vote difference still gave California's 25 electoral votes to Truman.

The election returns of the six largest industrial counties of Ohio and the five largest industrial counties of California gave Truman a substantial lead in those areas. But Dewey polled fewer votes than he did in 1944 and Truman fewer than Roosevelt in 1944. The important conclusion to be drawn from the role of labor in this presidential race is that labor returned its support to the Democratic party after

[65] Abels, *Out of the Jaws of Victory*, p. 293.
[66] *Ibid.*, p. 294.
[67] Lubell, *The Future of American Politics*, p. 134.

having strayed briefly from the fold. Truman had alienated unions to a great extent by his strike draft proposal in 1946 and as a result labor did not go to the polls to support the Democrats in such large numbers in the elections of that year. With his veto of the Taft-Hartley Act and his vigorous campaign pledging repeal of the law in 1948, Truman recaptured the support of most of organized labor. But too often, in attempting to determine decisive factors in elections, the importance of every state and every vote is overlooked. Labor's votes throughout the nation were extremely important in this election, as was the farm vote.

The part played by organized labor in this campaign can best be seen in the results of congressional elections, where its efforts had been concentrated. Seventy-five Democrats replaced Republican Representatives and eight Democrats replaced Republican Senators, so that the Eighty-first Congress was composed of 262 Democrats and 171 Republicans in the House and 42 Republicans and 54 Democrats in the Senate. More important, to labor, a total of 115 Senators and Representatives who voted for the Taft-Hartley Act either retired, died, or were defeated in primaries or the general election.[68] The PAC endorsed 215 candidates for the House in this election and 144 of them were victorious. Of these, 64 were incumbents, 57 of whom had voted against the Taft-Hartley Act. Of the remaining 80, 79 replaced incumbents who voted for the law.[69] Twelve of the 84 Democrats who voted against the act were defeated for reelection but not one of these lost to a Republican, all being replaced by other Democrats.

Organized labor claimed credit for the election of sixteen

[68] *Time*, LII (Nov. 15, 1948), 25, lists the number as 121. Perhaps the Illinois situation explains some of this difference; in addition to the fact that returns were incomplete Illinois was redistricted in 1948 and some pro-Taft-Hartley congressmen were reelected but from different numbered districts.

[69] Mosteller and others, *The Pre-Election Polls of 1948*, pp. 231-34.

prolabor Senators and the defeat of nine Taft-Hartley Senators.[70] The result of some of these senatorial elections obviously was due to union activity. Robert Kerr of Oklahoma had the support of labor as well as farmers in his state and Lester Hunt of Wyoming, Paul Douglas of Illinois, James Murray of Montana, and Matthew Neely of West Virginia campaigned on a platform to repeal the act.[71] Only Virgil Chapman of Kentucky, who voted for the act as a member of the House of Representatives, won his Senate race and by this time he was promising to support any "necessary changes" in the law.[72] In one election in particular labor could claim credit since the Taft-Hartley Act was the basic issue in the campaign. Senator Joseph Ball of Minnesota, who had done so much to assist Taft in producing the statute, ran against the liberal Hubert Humphrey. By 1948 Humphrey had managed to weld together a coalition of the remnants of the old Farmer-Labor movement and the Democratic party in Minnesota. With this support, Humphrey defeated Ball, using the Taft-Hartley law as the "sole issue" on which to campaign.[73]

In the House of Representatives, two of the three Democrats replacing Republicans in Connecticut came from predominantly industrial districts and the same was true for New Jersey. Eight of the eleven Republicans in Pennsylvania who lost to Democrats came from industrial areas and eight of the nine Democrats who replaced New York Republicans came from industrial areas. In addition, twenty-two Democrats replaced Republicans in Illinois, Indiana, Ohio, and West Virginia in industrial districts. A combination of farm and labor support added another thirteen to the list

70 Rayback, *A History of American Labor*, pp. 402-403.

71 *Time*, LII (Oct. 11, 1948), 23.

72 *United States News and World Report*, XXV (Nov. 12, 1948), 43.

73 U.S. House of Representatives, Subcommittee of the Committee on Education and Labor, *Hearings on H.R. 2032, Labor Relations*, 81 Cong., 1 Sess., 1949, p. 843.

of Democrats replacing Republicans in mixed agricultural-industrial districts in Minnesota, Missouri, and Wisconsin.

Truman lost the 146 electoral votes of the states of Oregon, Michigan, Maryland, Delaware, New Hampshire, Connecticut, New York, New Jersey, and Pennsylvania that Roosevelt carried in 1944, in addition to the 39 Dixiecrat votes. But he picked up the states of Wyoming, Colorado, Iowa, Wisconsin, and Ohio, with 56 electoral votes, that Dewey had won in 1944. In spite of a plurality of 489,000 in New York City, Truman lost the state to the upstate Republican vote and to Wallace. Although Truman got a plurality of 6,000 in Philadelphia and the Democrats captured four House seats there, and Pittsburgh gave him a 72,000 plurality, this was not enough to carry Pennsylvania. Democrats replaced two Republican Representatives in Michigan, both of them in Detroit where Walter Reuther was quite active, but this was not enough for Truman to win the state. Truman carried Chicago but still ran 60,000 votes behind Paul Douglas in Illinois and won the state electoral votes by only a 33,600 plurality. In addition to Wallace's giving New York to Dewey, the 9,900 votes given the Progressive candidate in Maryland left Dewey with a plurality of 8,300 votes in that state and the 40,000 votes Wallace received in Michigan gave Dewey that state's electoral vote with a 34,400 plurality over Truman. In every state that labor and farmers did not work together for the Democrats, Dewey won.

The labor vote was decisive in Truman's carrying the industrial states of Illinois, Massachusetts, Ohio, Rhode Island, and West Virginia with their 81 electoral votes. The rural population of Massachusetts and Rhode Island was 8 and 11 percent respectively, which makes the urban vote decisive in these states. As noted previously, the labor vote was vital in swinging Ohio to Truman, and his 200,000 plurality in Chicago and Cook County more than offset his rural losses in downstate Illinois to give him a

33,600 plurality in that state. If Dewey had carried these states, the electoral count would have been Dewey 270, Truman 222, and Thurmond 39.

Union efforts on behalf of congressional candidates were highly effective in this campaign, but with their lack of emphasis on Truman, he lost some states in spite of this activity. Labor was unable to carry Truman to victory in the industrial states of Michigan, Indiana, Pennsylvania, New York, New Jersey, and Connecticut, despite their congressional victories in these states. Part of this can be attributed to Wallace's candidacy and the inability of labor to decide which of the two to support. In all these states, except New York, Truman ran behind his congressional ticket. He even polled fewer votes than Democratic congressional candidates in Rhode Island, Illinois, Ohio, and West Virginia—states that labor had managed to carry for him anyway and that gave him the margin of victory. On a nationwide basis, Truman ran 0.04 percent behind his congressional ticket.[74] So in one of those rare instances of a "reverse coattail" phenomenon, a presidential candidate won by virtue of his congressional ticket's running better than he did. Although "backhanded" in intent, organized labor thus supplied the margin needed for Truman's victory through its exertions in congressional races.

A closer examination of the votes in the congressional districts of the industrial states adds emphasis to this coattail conclusion.[75] The Democrats gained two House seats in urban districts of Connecticut and Truman ran 3.2 percent ahead of his congressional ticket in the Second District and 1 percent behind in the First District. The Democrats picked up five seats in Indiana and Truman ran behind in all, as

74 Malcolm Moos, *Politics, Presidents and Coattails* (Baltimore: Johns Hopkins, 1952), p. 14.

75 The following statistics are from *ibid.*, Appendix 1, pp. 179-215, which lists the Republican percentages of the two-party vote. I have subtracted these figures from 100 percent to arrive at the Truman percentage of the two-party vote.

much as 7.4 percent in the Fourth District and as little as 1 percent in the Eighth District. Truman ran ahead of his congressional candidates in the Tenth and Eleventh districts and in New Jersey by 2.3 and 4.1 percent respectively. The two Detroit districts that Reuther helped Democrats win gave Truman 11.5 and 5.9 percent fewer votes than for their congressmen. In five of the eight New York districts that Democrats won, Truman ran behind by as much as 12.5 percent; in the other three he ran ahead of his ticket by as much as 6.5 percent. Truman ran behind his ticket in the four Philadelphia districts by 0.5 percent, in four other Pennsylvania districts by as much as 7 percent, and ahead in three Pennsylvania districts by as much as 2.7 percent. So in the industrial states that the Democrats won with the help of labor, but Truman lost, he ran ahead of his Democratic congressmen in eight districts and behind in twenty-two others.

In the four industrial states labor carried for Truman and also gained House seats for the Democrats (the two Rhode Island seats remained Democratic), he ran behind his ticket in twelve districts and ahead in six. He ran behind the Illinois Democratic congressmen and also behind other Democrats in five Ohio districts; in the Second District in Ohio by 5.6 percent and by 1.9 percent in the Chicago area. He ran ahead of his ticket in Massachusetts by 5.8 percent and in two Ohio districts. In West Virginia he ran behind in the Fourth District and ahead in the First, Second, and Third districts.

Regardless of the focus of union political efforts, they gave Truman his margin of victory in certain areas, either directly or indirectly, and undoubtedly had as much effect on the outcome as did the candidate's own vigorous campaigning. By 1948 Truman was at an all-time low in popularity and after sixteen years of Democratic Presidents the people seemed ready for a change in administration. By fighting against almost overwhelming odds, and almost alone in the belief that he could win, Harry S. Truman brought about one of the most smashing upsets in the history of presidential elections. The total popular vote in this election was 48,402,070, or over 1,000,000 less than the 1944 vote and much smaller than expected. That a Democratic candidate could win with such a small turnout of voters made this election result even more surprising to many political analysts.

Truman was able to overcome these handicaps because of his fighting spirit, because he did not know when he was licked. In this campaign he convinced the American people that Harry S. Truman was just "plain folks" who would fight for them against the special interests. This appeal to the common man was significant in winning the laboring man's support. As Samuel Lubell maintains, it is highly questionable that labor leaders have too much influence on the rank-and-file workers in an election. His thesis is that the factors tying laborers to the Democratic party "are ethnic and religious as well as economic."[76] Therefore, regardless of the official position of a union, a successful candidate must still sell himself and his program to the rank and file.

Truman's sincere commitment to repeal of the Taft-Hartley Act, which was a very personal thing to him, won the almost unanimous support of labor throughout the nation and turned the tide in his favor in several key states. It is impossible to point to any one factor as the deciding one in an election of this magnitude and scope. Truman states that labor was responsible for his election and is convinced that he won by using the Taft-Hartley Act as an issue.[77] Abels declares that the farm vote turned the tide and Lubell maintains that the German-American vote was the deciding element. All of these votes were necessary. But it is obvious that Harry S. Truman could not have won in 1948 without

[76] Lubell, *The Future of American Politics*, p. 185.
[77] Personal interview of the author with Harry S. Truman, Aug. 3, 1961.

union activity in congressional elections or without the tremendous endorsement he received from laborers and farmers. The statistics of this election demonstrate, as well as any recent election, that the urban industrial areas control the election of the Presidency and at the same time offer a simple explanation to Truman's smashing victory in 1948.

Of utmost importance in winning this election was the whistlestop campaign against the Eightieth Congress.[78] The political tactic of calling the "Turnip Session" enabled Truman to set the tone for the election of 1948, to dramatize the issue he wanted to campaign on, and to create a sounding board for his speeches. And by bringing his "facts" to the people in this manner he was able to capture the imagination and support of enough voters to bring about his astounding victory.

Using these "facts," which to Truman consisted of the danger which lay in allowing the national government to be controlled by a party bent on reversing the New Deal, he was able to stem the conservative political trend of the postwar period. Immediately after the election, as an indication of the sincerity of his intention to carry out the major promise he made in 1948, one of his first actions upon returning to Washington after the election was to call "a Cabinet meeting and a series of conferences to plan immediate repeal of the Taft-Hartley Act."[79] There seemed to be a good possibility that he would be successful in this endeavor since Dewey had inadvertently brought "unity" to the national government. Truman now had a Democratic Congress to work with when his party recaptured control of both houses of Congress in 1948.

[78] Richard O. Davies, "Whistle-Stopping Through Ohio," *Ohio History* LXXI (July 1962), 113-23, declares that Truman's whistlestop campaign in this crucial state was "an important factor in determining the final outcome."

[79] Truman, *Memoirs,* II, 222.

7

THE ADMINISTRATION FAILS TO REDEEM A PLEDGE

LABOR LEADERS immediately hailed the election of Harry S. Truman to the presidency as a signal for the eradication of the "Slave Labor Law." Labor assumed credit for his election and, as repeal of the Taft-Hartley Act had been one of Truman's major campaign issues, organized labor was certain that his triumph meant the American people endorsed repeal of the detested statute. The AFL and CIO annual conventions in the fall of 1948, following the election, were joyous celebrations. Jack Kroll, director of the PAC, told the CIO meeting that the people had "given their mandate for the repeal of the Taft-Hartley Act" by voting the platform of the Democratic party. The people, he said, "confidently expect fulfillment of that platform."[1] William Green reminded the AFL convention that Democratic leaders had continuously repeated in the campaign that they would repeal the act, if elected. The Democrats had won, Green declared, so there should be no qualification of that promise.[2]

Secretary of Labor Tobin agreed with these expressions, saying that when labor took its "case to the people," the response had been "a clear mandate to wipe out the Taft-Hartley law."[3] President Truman vowed that he would carry out his party's platform to the best of his ability. However, he said that repeal of the Taft-Hartley Act might require rewriting of the Wagner Act as they were "so tangled up" he could not "tell one from the other."[4] *Life* magazine prophetically cautioned that these optimistic declarations might be "premature" since the Southern Democrats would still have "a swing vote in Congress."[5] But labor was too pleased over the election results to heed.

Even before the election of 1948 the joint congressional committee, provided for by the Taft-Hartley Act, had been conducting hearings for the purpose of proposing necessary amendments to the law. This "watchdog" committee, with Senator Joseph Ball as chairman and Representative Fred Hartley as vice chairman, was concerned basically in its early investigations with the problem of the overload of work facing the NLRB. There was a need for accelerating NLRB action on representation and unfair-practice cases and the board was flooded with petitions for elections authorizing the union shop. Paul Herzog informed this committee in June of 1948 that the number of representation and unfair labor-practice cases filed with the NLRB in the previous six months equalled those of the year 1947.[6]

1 *Proceedings of the Tenth Constitutional Convention of the Congress of Industrial Organizations*, Nov. 22-26, 1948, p. 275.

2 *Proceedings of the Sixty-Seventh Convention of the American Federation of Labor*, Nov. 15-22, 1948, p. 9.

3 Maurice J. Tobin, Address to the AF of L Convention, Nov. 15, 1948, Secretary Tobin File (Speeches), R.G. 174, National Archives.

4 Press Conference, Key West, Fla., Nov. 15, 1948, Truman Papers, OR 21, HSTL.

5 *Life*, XXV (Nov. 29, 1948), 36.

6 Statement of NLRB to Joint Congressional Committee on Labor-Management Relations, June 11, 1948, Truman Papers, OF 407, HSTL.

The petitions for union shop elections presented an even more pressing problem. In these same hearings Robert N. Denham, the NLRB general counsel, testified that in the first nine months of operation under the act, 18,407 petitions were filed for union shop elections. The NLRB held 9,105 such elections covering 1,195,843 employees eligible to vote. The results of these elections must have been disappointing to the proponents of the Taft-Hartley Act who had hoped to curtail union-security provisions, for 98.2 percent of the employees involved voted to retain the union shop.[7] Denham concluded from the results of these elections that workers did not want to accept the "so-called emancipation" from their union bosses as provided by the act.[8] However, Raymond Smethurst, NAM general counsel, replied that the suggestion for discontinuing such elections was "too specious to receive serious attention." He maintained that there had been no real test on the issue in "large industrial plants" where the provision held greater significance.[9]

William Green, testifying before the committee, recommended complete repeal of the act. He described a national survey taken by his union among AFL members on the Taft-Hartley issue. The response to this poll was a vote of "15 to 1 against the Taft-Hartley bill."[10] However, the committee voted unanimously against recommending any changes in the policy at this time.[11] And when the committee made a final report on December 31, 1948, it found the law "to be working well, without undue hardship upon labor organizations, employers, or employees."[12]

After the new policy had been in operation for a year

[7] U.S. Congress, Joint Committee on Labor-Management Relations, *Hearings on Operation of Labor-Management Relations Act of 1947*, 80 Cong., 2 Sess., 1948, p. 50.

[8] *Ibid.*, p. 61.

[9] *Ibid.*, p. 132.

[10] *Ibid.*, p. 1050.

[11] New York *Times*, June 2, 1948.

[12] *Congressional Digest*, XXVIII (April 1949), 112.

there were, of course, conflicting opinions in regard to its efficacy. After ten months, the New York *Times* editorialized, it was "beyond question" that the law contained anything "to justify even faintly the dire prophecies of its extreme critics," including those in President Truman's veto message.[13] *United States News and World Report* believed that after a year's experience unions were stronger than ever. This magazine pointed out that union treasuries and membership were larger, there had been fewer strikes, wages were higher, and communist infiltration into unions had been checked. These were quite positive results even though the act was supposed to hurt labor.[14] Professor Sumner Slichter compared union membership figures of 14,841,000 in the fall of 1947 with those of 15,070,000 in the fall of 1948, figures which revealed only a slight rise. But, he added, this slower expansion was to be expected since union membership had more than doubled from 1937 to 1945. Slichter declared that a decline in the rate of growth was inevitable.[15] He felt that one of the most important effects of the law had been to make union officials realize they could not "lean too heavily on the government, and that they must avoid too flagrant a disregard for the welfare and convenience of the community."[16] These were two extremely important factors that had helped bring about the Taft-Hartley Act, and labor's cognizance of public concern about industrial strife was a healthy improvement.

As for management reaction, employers indicated relative satisfaction with the law during the first year. *Business Week* conducted a poll of management in August of 1948, using the sampling method to obtain "a fair measure" of

[13] New York *Times,* June 4, 1948.

[14] "Union Gains Under Taft-Hartley Act," *United States News and World Report,* XXV (Aug. 20, 1948), 20.

[15] Sumner Slichter, "The Taft-Hartley Act," *The Quarterly Journal of Economics,* LXIII (Feb. 1949), 12.

[16] *Ibid.,* p. 16.

attitude toward the new labor policy. In this poll 73 percent indicated that the act had not changed labor relations, 24 percent felt it had eased labor relations, and 3 percent said labor problems had been made "tougher." In contrast to the 8 percent who felt the board was unfair, 74 percent affirmed that the NLRB was administering the statute "in a fair and proper way"; 18 percent expressed no opinion. Of those polled, 50 percent believed the act should be amended, 42 percent wanted it retained with no change, and only 1 percent favored repeal, with 7 percent expressing no opinion. Of those who advocated amendments, 75 percent wanted compulsory arbitration, 75 percent wished to ban industry-wide strikes, and 53 percent indicated a desire to ban industrywide bargaining.[17] While many employers were convinced the law did not go far enough in restricting labor, management in general was satisfied with the new "balance" and was reluctant to utilize the provisions which might hurt the unions with whom they had to negotiate.

One of the purported goals of the policy had been to free members from control of labor bosses by making unions more democratic. But as Philip Taft has illustrated, the Eightieth Congress erred in assuming a conflict between rank-and-file members and their officials. That this was a misconception was borne out by the large favorable votes in union shop elections, the negligible use of decertification procedures, and the large majorities by which members had voted against employers' last offers.[18] Another problem noted by unions came from the Taft-Hartley provision which prohibited an employer's firing an employee for non-payment of union fines. Under the Wagner Act unions had fined members for not attending meetings but were now restricted in this practice. As union leaders pointed out, this

17 "What 528 Management Men Think of Taft-Hartley Law," *Business Week*, Aug. 21, 1948, p. 19.

18 Philip Taft, "Internal Affairs of Unions and the Taft-Hartley Act," *Industrial and Labor Relations Review*, XI (April 1958), 358-59.

provision curtailed enforced democratic participation and yet was included in the law to "protect" members. However, as one writer put it, the shoe was now "on the other foot."[19] Management had disliked the Wagner Act and endeavored to change it just as labor now bewailed the Taft-Hartley Act and fought for its repeal.

The basic motivation behind labor's desire to repeal the Taft-Hartley Act stemmed not so much from the current abridgement of union activities but from fear of what the future might produce under operation of the law. As *Life* magazine stated, labor did not "mind," and had no reason to resent, the statute during a period of relatively full employment. But if unemployment were to rise as a result of an economic slump in the future, management might be able to take advantage of certain phases of the law's "gimmicks to bust the unions."[20] If the economy were to go into a sharp decline and mass unemployment were to follow, labor leaders feared that antiunion employers could utilize the act's restrictive provisions to destroy union effectiveness. But this argument could be answered by the fact that the elements determining union bargaining power, such as the level of economic activity, industrial costs, product market structures, nonunion competition, and quality of union leadership, were only slightly affected by the law. One labor relations expert asserted that, although union gains would slow down in a future depression, this would result from "the relevant factors in the economic environment impinging on union bargaining power," and not from the Taft-Hartley Act as such.[21]

Even *Business Week*, the eminent periodical of businessmen, lent credence to this fear of labor. Soon after the

[19] Edwin E. Witte, "An Appraisal of the Taft-Hartley Act," *American Economic Review*, XXXVIII (May 1948), 381.

[20] *Life*, XXV (Nov. 29, 1948), 36.

[21] Joseph Shister, "The Impact of the Taft-Hartley Act on Union Strength and Collective Bargaining," *Industrial and Labor Relations Review*, XI (April 1958), 346.

results of the election of 1948 were known, and it was clear that the Democrats would attempt to repeal the statute, this periodical lamented its coming extinction by stating that the act had been a failure because of lack of consent. "Only a police state can enforce a law which is believed to be unjust by the people it affects," *Business Week* observed. The mistake committed by the Taft-Hartley Act was that it went too far in crossing "the narrow line separating a law which aims only to regulate from one which could destroy." To prove its argument, this article then drew up a blueprint by which unions could be wiped out in a period of unemployment. Whenever a pool of surplus labor existed from which to hire strike replacements, employers could use four provisions of the law to break unions. When a strike occurred, management could hire replacements and then follow these steps: (1) restrain picketing by injunction, (2) petition for a collective bargaining election, (3) hold strikers ineligible to vote—while the replacements cast the only ballots, and (4) if the election outcome was "no union," the government would have to certify and enforce it.[22] This article did nothing to quiet union suspicions and was widely quoted by those attempting to illustrate how the law could wreck organized labor.

After the election of 1948, even management accepted the fact that the national labor policy would be changed by the new Congress. *Business Week* unequivocally declared that the Taft-Hartley law would "give way before a new Thomas-Lesinski act early in 1949" and stated that employers were signing new contracts contingent on a change in the statute. The fact that contracts with union-shop agreements were being signed following the election of 1948 without the formality of a union-shop election required by the Taft-Hartley Act was given as an example.[23]

22 "Why the Taft-Hartley Act Failed," *Business Week,* Dec. 18, 1948, p. 124.

23 *Ibid.,* Nov. 20, 1948, p. 119.

Labor leaders were even more certain that they would soon be free of the hated law. The New York *Times* reported that an AFL delegation called at the White House before Christmas, 1948, and five officials of the CIO were Truman's first White House visitors after his return from a holiday in Missouri. Both of these delegations "received his assurance that labor legislation headed the agenda he would ask Congress to approve."[24] Unions throughout the country were quick to remind the administration of the campaign promise to repeal the Taft-Hartley Act. Even the new Senate Majority Leader, Scott Lucas of Illinois, had his attention called to this vow by the president of the Communications Workers of America, who stressed the point that the law was "one of the most talked of issues" in that campaign and that the Democrats had pledged repeal.[25] The peak of this mail, requesting repeal of the statute, was reached in April and May of 1949 when the White House mailroom reported about 3,000 letters and postcards received in these two months.[26]

The New York *Times* announced in December of 1948 that organized labor was agreed on the "main outlines of legislative policy" it expected the Eighty-first Congress to enact. Labor was now ready to accept bans on jurisdictional strikes and secondary boycotts involving unjustifiable objectives if it could get the Taft-Hartley Act repealed and the Wagner Act reenacted.[27] These were the two major changes President Truman had requested of the Eightieth Congress in his 1947 State of the Union message.

Secretary of Labor Tobin, who had toiled so diligently to make the Taft-Hartley Act an issue in the campaign of

24 New York *Times,* Dec. 30, 1948.

25 J. A. Beirne to Scott W. Lucas, March 10, 1949, Truman Papers, OF 407, HSTL.

26 Mailroom to William Hopkins, Memorandum, n.d., Truman Papers, OF 550, HSTL.

27 New York *Times,* Dec. 14, 1948.

1948, was completely convinced that the results of the election indicated a mandate for repeal. Tobin believed that the Taft-Hartley Act had created "a situation more dangerous than the open-shop drive and the so-called rights of the individual worker campaigns" of the twenties and must be stricken from the statutes.[28] In a speech delivered to the annual Jefferson-Jackson Day Dinner in 1949, Secretary Tobin emphasized that the administration intended to carry out "the solemn pledges made to the people" in the election and pointedly added that even Senator Taft had "abandoned much of his own law." "The Taft-Hartley law will be repealed," he proclaimed.[29]

President Truman addressed this same gathering with the announcement that the Democratic party was working, and would continue to work, until the law was replaced with one that was "fair and decent." The Taft-Hartley Act was "an insult to the working men and women of the country," he declared, and they would not rest until it was "repealed and destroyed." Truman said he assumed that after the outcome of the preceding election the Republicans would want "to throw the Taft-Hartley Act overboard faster than the sailors got rid of Jonah." Instead, he had found that the "special interests" were waging a campaign to convince everyone that it was a good law and thus obstruct its repeal.[30] Administration efforts to carry out the Fair Deal were bogging down by this time, with most of the measures bottled up in committees. In this speech Truman "lambasted" Congress for its inactivity with terms "as vigorous as any he ever used in denouncing" the Eightieth Congress.[31]

28 Maurice J. Tobin, "Town Meeting of the Air," March 15, 1949, Secretary Tobin File (Speeches), R.G. 174, National Archives.

29 Remarks at Jefferson-Jackson Day Dinner, Mayflower Hotel, Washington, D. C., Feb. 24, 1949, *ibid.*

30 Address at Jefferson-Jackson Day Dinner, Mayflower Hotel, Washington, D. C., Feb. 24, 1949, Truman Papers, OR, HSTL.

31 *Newsweek*, XXXIII (March 7, 1949), 23.

Truman's response to a letter maintaining that labor was not the only group that helped to elect him President was to send the writer a copy of the Democratic platform with the section on repeal of the act underlined.[32] Even Scott Lucas agreed that as a result of the election revocation of this law was "one of the most crucial problems facing the Eighty-First Congress."[33]

When the Eighty-first Congress met in January of 1949 President Truman submitted a program to carry out his campaign promises. Cyrus S. Ching had suggested some items he wanted included in the annual message to Congress. Ching believed that the national labor policy would be strengthened if the boards of inquiry, provided for by the Taft-Hartley Act, were permitted to make recommendations for settlement of labor disputes rather than merely reporting the facts. In addition, Ching wanted amendments to eliminate the secret vote on the employer's last offer, to shorten the injunction to less than eighty days, and to provide that Federal Mediation and Conciliation Service employees should not testify before courts, boards, or agencies with regard to service records.[34] Secretary of Labor Tobin proposed a sweeping two-point program to carry out the administration's campaign promises to labor in his recommendations for this message. Tobin wanted to transfer the Federal Mediation and Conciliation Service and the National Labor Relations Board directly to the Department of Labor, and he proposed repeal of the Taft-Hartley Act and reenactment of the Wagner Act.[35]

In his State of the Union message to Congress Truman

32 Truman to Clarence F. Lea, Dec. 2, 1948, Truman Papers, OF 407, HSTL.

33 Scott W. Lucas to John R. Steelman, Nov. 20, 1948, Truman Papers, OF 407, HSTL.

34 Ching to the President, Dec. 14, 1948, Truman Papers, OF 419-F, HSTL.

35 Maurice J. Tobin to James E. Webb, Dec. 30, 1948, Truman Papers, OF 419-F, HSTL.

observed that workers were "unfairly discriminated against" by the Labor-Management Relations Act of 1947 and he recommended its repeal. He requested that Congress then reenact the Wagner Act with amendments prohibiting jurisdictional strikes, unjustified secondary boycotts, and the use of economic force in interpreting existing contracts. These were items he had been requesting of Congress since he vetoed the Case bill in 1946. Truman also asked that the Department of Labor be "rebuilt and strengthened" with "those units properly belonging" to it placed under its jurisdiction, but he did not specify any agencies.[36] The New York *Times* presented an interesting graph illustrating congressional reaction to this annual message. On a ten-point scale, Truman's reference to repeal of the Taft-Hartley Act brought a response of eight points of applause, equalled only when he expressed a hope of "cooperation with Congress," and exceeded only at the conclusion of his message.[37]

The Chicago *Daily Tribune*, in a fantastic analysis, interpreted Truman's labor proposals to "boil down almost to a design" to remove the names of Senator Taft and Representative Hartley from the law and "re-enact some of its more important provisions." The *Tribune* did note important omissions in the message such as the non-communist affidavit and union financial reports. The writer sarcastically deduced that President Truman therefore believed it "all right for Communists to run unions . . . and union bosses to loot union treasuries without being embarrassed."[38] The New York *Star* believed that the proposal to reenact the Wagner Act with improvements made "sense." The Eightieth Congress had produced a statute that challenged "the wit of the best Philadelphia lawyer" and "new patches on such a bad patchwork" would be a "waste of effort," this tabloid ob-

[36] State of the Union message to Congress, Jan. 5, 1949, *Truman Papers, 1949*, pp. 1-7.
[37] New York *Times*, Jan. 9, 1949.
[38] Chicago *Daily Tribune*, Jan. 6, 1949.

served.[39] The *Wall Street Journal* agreed that Truman could expect repeal of the Taft-Hartley Act but that Congress might modify the Wagner Act more than "Mr. Truman and labor leaders want." This newspaper anticipated a "big fight" in Congress over the issues of the closed shop, the antistrike injunction, an independent NLRB, and separation of NLRB judicial and prosecutory functions.[40]

Newspaper columnist Peter Edson was the first to note President Truman's declaration that "every segment of our population and every individual has a right to expect from the government a fair deal" and felt this would be a good name to describe his program. It was not a "new" New Deal, Edson insisted, because everything in Truman's program had been mentioned in the 1948 campaign, and it was not the "old" New Deal because it went "far beyond anything Franklin D. Roosevelt ever thought of."[41] The same issue of this newspaper that carried the Edson article observed that Truman's message indicated the administration was "intent on moving first and fastest on new labor legislation to replace the Taft-Hartley law."[42]

While the administration and labor leaders were unanimous on the objectives of the desired labor policy, a disagreement developed as to means of achievement. It was agreed that the Taft-Hartley Act should be repealed and the Wagner Act reenacted with improvements. But labor leaders wanted the Wagner Act to be reinstated and amended later, whereas the administration preferred the strategy of completing the entire program in one bill. The New York *Times* noted that President Truman failed to tell Congress in his message whether the "one package" or "two package" method should be followed in enacting new legislation. The *Times* stated that the AFL and CIO presidents

39 New York *Star*, Jan. 6, 1949.
40 *Wall Street Journal*, Jan. 6, 1949.
41 Washington *News*, Jan. 6, 1949.
42 *Ibid.*

interpreted the State of the Union message as favoring the two-step procedure.[43] However, labor was soon disillusioned as the administration pursued the "one package" approach. As the *New Republic* pointed out, the administration believed that something was needed immediately to replace the national-emergency section of the Taft-Hartley law, which had proved so useful. The motivation behind this conviction was a "political fear that Truman would be badly hurt" if he lacked the power "to deal with a hypothetical John L. Lewis coal strike,"[44] a possibility that proved quite real.

The 1948 elections had returned control of Congress to the Democrats. The Eighty-first Congress was composed of 262 Democrats in the House and 54 in the Senate against 42 Republican Senators and 171 Representatives, with one American Labor party Representative and one vacancy in the House. In tabulating the members of this new Congress in terms of their stand on the Taft-Hartley Act, the *Congressional Digest* found that 222 of the 331 Representatives who voted to override the veto had returned and 54 of the 68 Senators who voted to override were still members.[45] A congressional majority of those who favored the act in 1947 reappeared in Congress in 1949, a rather pessimistic picture to anyone who analyzed the congressional situation closely. But the administration had pledged repeal of the act, so it remained to be seen whether enough congressmen had changed their minds in two years, or if the administration could exert enough pressure to obtain sufficient votes for repeal.

When the Eighty-first Congress was organized, the administration Democrats were quick to fill the vacancies on the Senate Labor Committee with prolabor men like Humphrey

[43] New York *Times*, Jan. 6, 1949.
[44] "One Package or Two?" *New Republic*, CXX (Jan. 24, 1949), 7.
[45] *Congressional Digest*, XXVIII (April 1949), 101.

and Paul Douglas of Illinois. Senator Elbert Thomas, the new committee chairman, made immediate plans to secure repeal of the Taft-Hartley Act. On January 6 Thomas introduced S. 249 and it was referred to his committee. Hearings were held from January 31 to February 26 and the Thomas bill was reported favorably out of committee on March 4, 1949. Thomas' counterpart in the House, Representative John Lesinski, introduced an identical bill, H.R. 2032, on January 31. The House Labor Committee conducted hearings from March 8 to March 21, 1949, and favorably reported the Lesinski bill with no amendments. The Thomas-Lesinski bill was the administration's attempt to fulfill its promise to labor.

The administration measure was drawn up under the supervision of Secretary of Labor Tobin. Senator Thomas, who directed the administration's legislative forces in this project, held a meeting with Ching, Herzog, Tobin, and Clark Clifford the second week of January to discuss the proposed legislation. After these discussions Tobin was asked by Thomas to draft the bill and the result was the proposed National Labor Relations Act of 1949, "designed to return to the policy first declared in the National Labor Relations Act of 1935."[46] The New York *Times* charged that labor union lawyers were consulted in the drafting and as a result the bill bore "virtually no substantial resemblance to the Taft-Hartley law."[47]

The Thomas-Lesinski bill provided for the repeal of the Taft-Hartley Act and reenactment of the Wagner Act with certain amendments. The national labor policy would revert to that from 1935 to 1947, but in addition secondary boycotts with unjustifiable objectives and jurisdictional strikes would be prohibited. Parties to a collective bargaining agreement

[46] U.S. Senate, Committee on Labor and Public Welfare, *Hearings on S. 249, Labor Relations,* 81 Cong., 1 Sess., 1949, pp. 19-20.
[47] New York *Times,* Jan. 30, 1949.

would have to give the Conciliation Service thirty days' notice prior to modification or termination of a contract to allow the setting up of a board of inquiry to investigate the proposed changes. The scope of free collective bargaining would be expanded by again allowing the checkoff and union-security provisions. The measure also provided procedures to avert national emergencies arising out of work stoppages during the thirty-day period when a board of inquiry would be investigating the dispute. The Thomas-Lesinski bill would have returned federal conciliation services to the Department of Labor but retained the independent five-man NLRB set up by the Taft-Hartley Act. Finally, the bill provided for a Labor-Management Advisory Committee composed of representatives from labor, management, and the public to advise the secretary of labor in regard to policy and administration of the Conciliation Service.

Secretary of Labor Tobin was the first to testify before the Senate committee. Tobin listed several "important" reasons why he felt the Taft-Hartley Act should be repealed. The ban on the closed shop had outlawed collective bargaining agreements that had been "mutually beneficial to both labor and management" and had helped to keep industrial peace for over one hundred years. The law was pernicious in emphasizing the use of injunctions to settle labor disputes, he said. The act abandoned the principles of the Administrative Procedures Act of 1946, singling out the NLRB as the only regulatory agency to have its functions separated. By providing for so many elections, employer-employee relations were kept in an unstable condition, and Tobin pointed out that it was unjust to allow strikebreakers to vote while denying this privilege to strikers who had not been reinstated. The law was unreasonable in restricting peaceful picketing and certain aspects of collective bargaining agreements like the checkoff and welfare funds.

The Taft-Hartley Act was unfair, Tobin charged, in banning union political expenditures and all secondary boycotts and in allowing unions to be used in federal courts. And an error had been made in removing the Conciliation Service from the Department of Labor where it had functioned successfully for thirty-four years. Tobin summed up his criticisms of the Taft-Hartley Act by blaming its bad features on the atmosphere of the times that gave it birth. Had Congress been faced with "different economic and psychological conditions" in 1947, Tobin explained "the result would undoubtedly have been very different from that Act."[48]

Cyrus S. Ching, director of the Federal Mediation and Conciliation Service, testified that it would be a mistake to restore his service to the Department of Labor. Experience as an independent agency, he explained, had indicated that the new system was more effective. Management regarded the Department of Labor as "the spokesman for labor" and this had tainted the service when it was under the department's jurisdiction. As an independent agency, Ching stated, his employees now found many employers' "doors ajar" that had previously been closed to them. Management was now more willing to use his agency's services than they had been under the Wagner Act.[49]

The CIO filed a 112-page statement with the committee describing its adverse views on the Taft-Hartley Act. Arthur J. Goldberg explained that CIO had "not had access to the avenues of public opinion" and resorted to this lengthy testimony as a means of expressing his organization's views. He stated that the *Saturday Evening Post* had published two pro-Taft-Hartley articles—one on the eve of the 1948 election—but when the CIO asked to submit a report describ-

[48] U.S. Senate, Committee on Labor and Public Welfare, *Hearings on S. 249, Labor Relations*, 81 Cong., 1 Sess., 1949, pp. 19-29.

[49] *Ibid.*, pp. 55-56.

ing the faults of the statute, the *Post* replied that it would solicit only those articles it desired. Goldberg also pointed out that the New York *Times* had published several editorials favorable to the act but, when he sent the *Times* a letter presenting his viewpoint, it was not printed.[50]

The strategy of those who opposed the Thomas-Lesinski bill in the House took the form of introducing a counter-proposal. The coalition of Republicans and Southern Democrats desiring to keep the Taft-Hartley law intact sponsored a bill introduced by John S. Wood of Georgia in March which contained all the major provisions of the Labor-Management Relations Act of 1947. Their plan, which was carried out, was to offer a motion to substitute the Wood bill for Lesinski's; the administration congressmen would then have to amend the Wood bill piece by piece to restore the Lesinski bill.[51] The administration's reaction to the Wood bill was typified by Secretary Tobin's description of it as being "as objectionable as the Taft-Hartley Act."[52]

Despite the dilatoriness of Congress, Tobin still believed in April that the administration's bill would be enacted. He based this opinion on the fact that he had been keeping "a close check on practically every member on the hill." He said this check revealed that "a great many" Democrats and Republicans who had voted for the Taft-Hartley Act were now ready to vote for the Thomas-Lesinski bill as they now realized the "unfairness of the Taft-Hartley law."[53] This conviction was either bluster or wishful thinking. A White House memorandum drawn up in May indicated that the administration could count on only 38 Senators and 200 Representatives for support of the Thomas-Lesinski bill and this House count was probably "overoptimistic."

50 *Ibid.*, pp. 535-36.
51 New York *Times*, April 2, 1949.
52 Maurice J. Tobin, Press Conference, April 13, 1949, Secretary Tobin File (Press Conferences), R.G. 174, National Archives.
53 *Ibid.*

This memorandum emphasized that the entire state Democratic delegations from Alabama, South Carolina, Virginia, Georgia, Mississippi, North Carolina, Texas, and Arkansas would vote against Taft-Hartley repeal.[54]

This conservative coalition was again given assistance by John L. Lewis. While Congress was delaying action, the UMW president called out 400,000 miners east of the Mississippi on a two-week "memorial" stoppage to illustrate UMW opposition to the appointment of James Boyd as director of the Federal Bureau of Mines. Probably the actual motive in calling this walkout was the current coal stockpile of 70,000,000 tons and a two-week layout would reduce this to the normal stockpile of 45,000,000 tons. But whatever his motive, the result was to hurt chances of repeal of the Taft-Hartley Act. After Lewis' action it was reported that "prospects" were "the law would suffer nothing more drastic than modification . . . acceptable to its partisans."[55]

The "modification" proposed in the Wood bill would: remove NLRB supervision of union shop elections, permit hiring halls, allow striking workers to vote in representation elections, allow the issuance of injunctions on secondary boycotts, and allow unfair labor practices to be determined on the basis of discretion rather than making it mandatory, and extend the non-communist affidavit to employers. These changes would have removed most of the really objectionable features of the law. The original Wood bill was described as "a Taft-Hartley with long sharp teeth" but it was modified to include the above changes by its sponsors. Republican Floor Leader Joseph Martin and Charles Halleck met in April and hammered out these changes and persuaded their Southern allies, Wood, Howard Smith of

[54] Memorandum, unsigned (file date May 6, 1949), Truman Papers, OF 407, HSTL.

[55] *Newsweek*, XXXIII (March 21, 1949), 21.

Virginia, and Graham Barden to accept them. This change in strategy was necessitated by the pressure of Republicans from industrial areas who were "feeling organized labor's hot breath on their necks" and threatening withdrawal of support if the Wood bill was not "weakened."[56]

House debate on the proposed new labor law began on April 26. Lesinski defended the committee bill on the grounds that the 1948 election was a mandate for repeal. "After months of debate, after more than a year's experience, after a public scrutiny of the law that was detailed and painstaking, the voters of the Nation expressed their opinion" by electing the presidential candidate who advocated repeal, Lesinski maintained.[57] The argument for the Wood bill as a substitution, led by Samuel McConnell of Pennsylvania, centered on the point that the 1946 elections were a mandate for the Taft-Hartley Act whereas the 1948 elections gave no mandate for repeal. It was also claimed that, irrespective of a popular mandate, the Taft-Hartley Act protected individual workers and was good for the country.

House Speaker Sam Rayburn used his persuasive powers and, taking advantage of the many friendships he had built up over the years, particularly among Southern Representatives, tried to win support for the administration measure. He persuaded those who disliked both the Wood and Lesinski bills to vote against both if they must; he persuaded some who felt they could not vote against the Wood bill to be absent when the vote was taken. And for those who wanted changes in the Lesinski bill, he promised amendments. As a result of this strategy, Southern votes for the Wood measure melted from 75 to 58. Just at this crucial point Truman torpedoed everything Rayburn had done. At a press conference the President was asked if he would determine patronage on the basis of voting for repeal of the

[56] *Ibid.* (April 25, 1949), p. 24.
[57] *Congressional Record,* 81 Cong., 1 Sess., 1949, XCV, 5064.

Taft-Hartley Act. He replied that he certainly would,[58] and this indelicate observation and obvious pressure from the White House mended the coalition that Rayburn had successfully broken. Southerners, irritated by this threat from the White House, swung back to support the Wood bill which was then substituted for the Lesinski measure.

On May 3 the House voted 217 to 203 for the Wood bill. Then, just before the third and final vote, Vito Marcantonio, American Labor Party Representative from New York, demanded an engrossed bill and this delayed voting for another day. On May 4 the House voted 212 to 209 to recommit the Wood bill to committee.[59] The administration forces had used this time to entice a sufficient number of Southerners to vote to recommit. Four Representatives from Arkansas who voted for the Wood bill May 3 now voted to send it back to committee. Brooks Hays, Oren Harris, W. F. Morrell, and Boyd Tackett were lured to the administration side by the promise of pork-barrel legislation, which included large appropriations for the Arkansas River Basin project and Federal Works Administration plans to build several post offices in that state.[60]

Following this administration "victory," Donald L. Jackson, California Republican, triumphantly mailed the following poem to his constituents:

> The tumult and the shouting die,
> The lobbyists in haste depart,
> Still stands that ancient labor law,
> T-H intact in every part.[61]

The administration had successfully stopped the Wood bill, which would have changed some of the restrictive features of the Taft-Hartley Act, still insisting upon complete repeal.

58 Press Conference, April 28, 1949, Truman Papers, OR, HSTL.
59 *Congressional Record,* 81 Cong., 1 Sess., 1949, XCV, 5597-98.
60 *Newsweek,* XXXIII (May 23, 1949), 16-17.
61 *Ibid.* (May 16, 1949), p. 20.

The New York *Times* reported that this "hairline" decision gave the Democratic leaders and "labor chieftains little more than a chance to fight another day."[62] The *New Republic* stated that only this last-minute moves to recommit had prevented the adoption of the Wood bill. One writer blamed the failure on "Secretary of Labor Tobin for premature and maladroit efforts to compromise, and to Speaker Sam Rayburn for lack of support of the President's programs,"[63] which was an inaccurate assessment of Rayburn's activities. For this and similar actions, many were referring to this Congress by this time as the "Eighty-Worst."

The changes in Congressional personnel wrought by the elections of 1948 showed up in this vote on this measure. Of the twenty-three Republicans who voted against the Taft-Hartley Act eleven were replaced by Democrats and ten of these voted for committing the Wood bill. The other, Robert Coffey of Pennsylvania, did not vote. Of the eighty-four Democrats who voted against the Taft-Hartley law, not one was replaced by a Republican. Twelve were replaced by other Democrats, all of whom voted to recommit the Wood proposal except Thurmond Chathan of North Carolina. Two of the three California Democrats who voted for the 1947 act were replaced by Republicans. Clair Engle, the third one, voted in 1949 to recommit the Wood measure.

The Senate did not begin debate on the Thomas bill until June 2. In the meantime, the opposition coalition under the leadership of Taft followed the strategy of offering a series of amendments to the Thomas bill on May 4. However, Taft's changes were a more sincere attempt to correct some of the imperfections which by this time he realized existed in the Taft-Hartley Act. Taft's amendments to the Thomas bill would have changed the Taft-Hartley law in some thirty ways. The major alterations he presented included changing

62 New York *Times*, May 5, 1949.
63 "The Lesson of Defeat," *New Republic*, CXX (May 16, 1949), 5.

definitions so that only actual foremen would be considered supervisors and unions would be responsible only for actions of their actual agents and not their entire membership. His bill proposed enlarging the NLRB to seven members and making it bipartisan, putting the board back under the Administrative Procedures Act, and abolishing the independent general counsel. Taft also wanted to eliminate the voting requirement to authorize the union shop, featherbedding restrictions, the prohibition against striking employees' not being eligible to vote if ineligible for reinstatement, and he now would permit a limited use of the secondary boycott. His amendments would have simplified union financial reports, extended the non-communist oath to employers, allowed the checkoff on a yearly basis, and kept the prohibition on union political contributions in elections but permit union political expenditures. Finally, Taft wanted to change the national emergency provisions to give the President, during such a strike, the alternative of referring to Congress for special legislation, applying for a court injunction for sixty days, or seizure.[64] These provisions, if enacted, would have eliminated the most objectionable features of the Taft-Hartley Act.

Thomas opened Senate debate by stating that with S. 249 the Democratic party was thus fulfilling its campaign promise. Although he admitted that the election results could not be attributed to any single issue or factor, still "perhaps no single question . . . in that election more clearly demonstrated the character of choice the people had" than the Taft-Hartley law.[65] Taft replied that, however bound the President might be by his promise to repeal the statute, there was no such mandate on Congress. He defended this by pointing out that the present Congress contained 222 Representatives and 54 Senators, or more than a majority,

[64] *Congressional Record,* 81 Cong., 1 Sess., 1949, XCV, 5590.
[65] *Ibid.,* p. 7237.

who had voted to override President Truman's veto. Taft agreed that his proposed amendments would help labor relations but argued that "except for the rather violent labor propaganda," the Taft-Hartley Act had, without these changes, "entirely satisfied the people of the United States."[66]

Again the Taft forces were given an assist by John L. Lewis. In the midst of debate on the Thomas bill, the UMW leader announced that, beginning June 13, the miners would leave the pits for one week. The coal stockpile was again up to 65,000,000 tons and many miners were on a part-time basis, so Lewis called this walkout "a stabilizing period of inaction." Following this announcement, Taft was reported to be "grinning broadly" and the administration Senators "sputtering in rage."[67]

A final vote was taken on the labor bill on June 30, 1949. Taft's amendments to the Thomas bill were approved 49 to 44 and the Thomas bill then passed the Senate 51 to 42.[68] Many of the administration Democrats, wanting complete repeal, voted against the amended bill and thus almost defeated it. The Thomas bill was then sent to the House where it was referred to the Committee on Education and Labor on July 1. However, it was never reported to the House floor.[69]

Three Democrats, Lucas, John Sparkman of Alabama, and Kenneth McKellar of Tennessee, who voted for the Taft-Hartley Act now voted against Taft's bill. The seven Democrats who defeated Republicans in 1948 who had voted for the Taft-Hartley Act and voted against this measure were Bert Miller of Idaho, Paul Douglas of Illinois, Guy Gillette of Iowa, Hubert Humphrey of Minnesota, Robert Kerr of Oklahoma, Matthew Neely of West Virginia, and Lester Hunt of Wyoming. Four Republicans who had voted

66 *Ibid.*, pp. 7400-401.
67 *Newsweek*, XXXIII (June 20, 1949), 22.
68 *Congressional Record*, 81 Cong., 1 Sess., 1949, XCV, 8717.
69 *Ibid.*, p. 8808.

for the 1947 law now reversed and voted against Taft. They were Henry Lodge of Massachusetts, Zales Ecton of Montana, Irving Ives of New York, and George Aiken of Vermont.

The New York *Times* described the Senate action as having wrecked "the Administration's six months effort to repeal the Taft-Hartley Act."[70] Truman's immediate reply was that he would continue to fight as "hard" as he could to carry out the Democratic platform.[71] James C. Petrillo assured the President that labor did not feel it had been betrayed by the administration but by John L. Lewis because of his previous heedless actions.[72] Harold L. Ickes agreed with this opinion that Lewis' disregard for public opinion had assisted Taft in defeating the Thomas bill.[73] Benjamin Aaron summed up the failure on the grounds that there was no "popular mandate" for repeal because much of the voting public was indifferent to the issue.[74] Also, Southern Democrats, who were generally beyond the political reach of unions, could indulge their desires and did so even in the face of Truman's threat that he would use voting on the Thomas-Lesinski bill as a test of party loyalty for patronage. But the basic cause for failure can be attributed to the fact that the strongest administration supporters refused to accept any compromise. It proved impossible to obtain the necessary votes to repeal the Taft-Hartley Act, but if the administration had been willing to compromise on half a loaf some of the worst features of the law would have been removed by Taft's proposed amendments or the Wood bill. The *Saturday Evening Post* declared

70 New York *Times*, July 1, 1949.

71 Press Conference, June 30, 1949, Truman Papers, OR, HSTL.

72 James C. Petrillo to the President, Telegram, June 30, 1949, Truman Papers, OF 407, HSTL.

73 Harold L. Ickes, "Taft Minus Hartley," *New Republic*, CXXI (July 18, 1949), 16.

74 Benjamin Aaron, "Amending the Taft-Hartley Act: A Decade of Frustration," *Industrial and Labor Relations Review*, XI (April 1958), 330.

that the administration had not attempted to write a workable labor law but was trying "to pay off its debt to labor's leaders" and that the result was inevitable.[75]

William Green insisted that the defeat of repeal of the "treacherous" law was due to "obstructionists" who "were able to deny a fair deal to the American people." Green declared that the "leaders of Toryism welded the surviving remnants of the Republican forces into a tight coalition with the Southern Democrats" in the Eighty-first Congress and thus checked the 1948 mandate for "progress and social justice."[76] President Truman refused to concede that the battle was lost. Although the "special interests" managed to prevent repeal of the Taft-Hartley Act, the issue was "far from settled." "We are going to continue the fight for the repeal of that repressive law," he promised, "until it is wiped off the statute books."[77] Almost a year after the Thomas-Lesinski failure Truman reiterated his dedication to continue the fight, saying that the people had elected him on the Democratic platform which called for repeal.[78] A few days after this speech he reminded the Democratic party of its promise, vowing to repeal the statute and "replace it with a law that is fair to both management and labor."[79]

It was not until 1951 that the Taft-Hartley Act was amended for the first and only time during the Truman administration. This change came in the provision requiring union shop authorization elections, a result of a Supreme Court decision. Between the passage of the act and the time it was amended, 46,146 such authorization elections were conducted and the union shop was rejected in only 2.9 percent of these elections. Of the 5,069,261 workers who

75 "Truman's Labor Advisors Weave a Tangled Web," *Saturday Evening Post*, CCXXI (March 5, 1949), 10.

76 William Green, "American Labor Must be Strong and Free," Speech at San Diego, Cal., Sept. 5, 1949, *Vital Speeches*, XV (Sept. 14, 1949), 715.

77 Address at Pittsburgh, Pa., Sept. 5, 1949, Truman Papers, OR, HSTL.

78 Butte, Mont., May 12, 1950, *ibid.*

79 National Democratic Conference, May 15, 1950, *ibid.*

voted, 85.7 percent approved the union shop, substantiating the conviction that this provision was useless.[80] A number of these elections had been held in 1948 under NLRB auspices before CIO officials had signed the non-communist oath. The Taft-Hartley Act required union officials to sign such an affidavit or their union would be ineligible for benefits under the law, such as NLRB-sponsored elections. In May 1951, in what was known as the Highland Park Case, the Supreme Court ruled these elections invalid because the union officials had not signed the affidavit prior to the voting, thus nullifying some 4,700 such elections.[81] It was estimated that the cost of holding new elections would run "in excess of $3,000,000 of public funds,"[82] so Congress decided to validate them with special legislation.

In August 1951, bipartisan S. 1959, sponsored by Robert Taft and Hubert Humphrey, was unanimously approved by the Senate Labor Committee. The bill would validate the outlawed elections and remove the Taft-Hartley requirement for union shop elections. As Representative Richard Nixon stated, the bill had "the additional merit of having the support of both industry representatives" as well as unions.[83] The bill passed the Senate on August 21 by unanimous consent and was sent to the House of Representatives.[84] The House approved the measure, without amendments, on October 9 by a vote of 307 to 18, with 103 not voting.[85]

President Truman signed the bill on October 22, 1951. He used the occasion to strike again at the Taft-Hartley Act, saying that while S. 1959 was "desirable," it eliminated

[80] Philip Taft, "Internal Affairs of Unions and the Taft-Hartley Act," *Industrial and Labor Relations Review*, XI (April 1958), 354.

[81] *National Labor Relations Board v. Highland Park Manufacturing Company*, 341 U.S. 322 (1951).

[82] Harry S. Truman, Statement, Oct. 22, 1951, Truman Papers, OF 145, HSTL.

[83] *Congressional Record*, 82 Cong., 1 Sess., 1951, XCVII, 10462.

[84] *Ibid.*, p. 10464.

[85] *Ibid.*, p. 12864.

"only one of the Act's defects." He expressed the hope that this change would be "the forerunner of the future development of sound legislation behind which labor, management, government and the people may unite to achieve industrial peace and economic progress in the national interest."[86]

The election of 1948 and the action of Congress in 1949 on labor legislation proved a striking example of the "double constituency" in American politics. When the Republicans won control of Congress in 1946 they claimed it was a mandate for the Taft-Hartley Act. When Harry S. Truman was elected President in 1948, mainly because of his opposition to the law, he claimed a mandate for repeal. On both occasions the defeated insisted that the election results stemmed from factors other than those which the victors maintained. In both instances there was a manifest edict from the people. However, the different results in 1947 and 1949 can be attributed to the fact that Congress was elected by and represented the interests of the business, middle-class, and agrarian groups of the nation who favored retention of the new policy.

A review of the administration's attempt to repeal the Taft-Hartley Act in 1949 makes it obvious that Truman sincerely tried to fulfill his 1948 campaign promise. But it is equally obvious that he would not be too disappointed in this failure for political reasons. This law did much to win the election for him in 1948 and as long as it remained on the statute books it could serve as a perennial issue for Democrats to be used in future campaigns. Believing that Northern urban areas really desired its repeal, Truman could help liberal Democrats campaign on this issue in the North in 1950 if it were still the law. Conceivably, the administration's "success" in defeating the Wood bill and Taft amendments in 1949 was not a Pyrrhic victory after all. Perhaps, in terms of the political future, success here would

[86] Statement, Oct. 22, 1951, Truman Papers, OF 145, HSTL.

have been discouraging. In any case, failing in this frontal attack on the Taft-Hartley Act, the administration next turned to an indirect means to achieve its objective—the operation of a national labor policy which would not be prejudicial to labor unions.

8

TRUMAN ALTERS NLRB ADMINISTRATION

When the Truman administration failed in its assault on the Taft-Hartley Act in 1949 it turned to the use of flanking maneuvers to achieve its objective. Organized labor was convinced that the law was designed to hurt it and wanted to return to the policy of a paternalistic government under the Wagner Act. The Democrats, desirous of assisting unions, were unable to obtain the necessary congressional support to repeal the act outright, so they attempted to circumvent the intentions of the statute's framers. Congress had enacted the labor policy but the executive branch could, with discretion, administer that law in such a way as to lessen the harshness of its restrictive provisions against its constituency, the laborers.

The philosophy of the New Deal Wagner Act, created by Democrats, was to foster and promote union organization in order to elevate union power to the level of that of industry. The philosophy behind the Taft-Hartley Act, devised by Republicans, contained the premise that by coddling and protecting organized labor under the Wagner Act, union power had grown out of proportion and a new balance needed to be struck. Under the Wagner Act the government restricted management activities to assist unions; under the Taft-Hartley Act the government was expected to restrict union activities to equalize the contest between labor and management. But where a Democratic administration had vigorously applied the New Deal policy, obviously it would not execute with equal vigor a Republican policy that was antipathetic to its philosophy.

The early NLRB, established by the Wagner Act to administer the national labor policy, had been criticized as being too prolabor by those who endorsed Taft-Hartley principles. New Dealers who staffed this agency were largely crusaders for organized labor and, using administrative discretion in applying and interpreting the Wagner Act provisions, tended to determine unfair labor practices, for example, in favor of unions if any doubt existed as to guilt. After the passage of the Taft-Hartley Act this same agency was expected to play a neutral role in umpiring labor-management conflicts. But it could be expected that the Democratic executive branch, in administering this new policy, would continue to favor organized labor whenever possible. Although President Truman emphasized that it would be executed fairly, the administrative discretion inherent in interpreting and applying a policy of such magnitude would allow sufficient latitude to administer the law "fairly" and still be partial to unions. The NLRB was a unified agency under the Wagner Act and could coordinate the administration of the labor policy. The Taft-Hartley Act made it a bifurcated commission with divided powers and authority, thus creating a situation fraught with possibilities of internal dissension.

As long as the two divisions of the agency agreed on principles and objectives there would be little conflict. But when the two disagreed over philosophy and interpretation of the statute, collision would be inevitable. Such disagreement did develop and the administration took advantage of this strife, attempting to subvert the designers' objectives contained in the new policy.

One of the chief criticisms of the original NLRB had been that it was a combination of judge, jury, and prosecutor. Conforming with the pattern of other governmental regulatory agencies, board decisions had been final and could be appealed only in the federal courts. When the Administrative Procedures Act was passed in 1946, the NLRB had altered its organization to accommodate the new principles. Thus, after 1946 NLRB practices and procedures complied "fully . . . with the letter and spirit . . . of the Administrative Procedures Act."[1] Under the revised system, when a charge of unfair practice was brought, it was heard by a representative of the Trial Examining Division. This division was a separate, autonomous unit of the board, operating under the supervision of a chief trial examiner. Decisions by this division were based on NLRB interpretations but either party could file exceptions and appeal to the board with, of course, final appeal lying in the federal courts. But critics of the board, disregarding this conformable procedure, disliked what they considered the board's dictatorial powers and voiced their resentment to the writers of the Taft-Hartley Act. This law answered their criticism by dividing board functions. This concept of dividing NLRB powers and functions was not new in 1947, having been advocated by the NAM as early as 1935.[2] An independent NLRB counsel was created and the prosecutory functions assigned to him. The

[1] U.S. Senate, Committee on Labor and Public Welfare, *Hearings on S. 55 and S.J. Res. 22, Labor Relations*, 80 Cong., 1 Sess., 1947, p. 1926.

[2] *Congressional Record*, 81 Cong., 1 Sess., 1949, XCV, 7379.

board, after 1947, was merely judge and jury. This unique division created administrative problems which were left to the agency to solve.

When the Taft-Hartley Act went into effect on August 22, 1947, the board members met with the new general counsel and drew up a Statement of Delegation agreement. Under this agreement, necessitated by the new law, the board delegated to the general counsel authority over the trial examiners, or field personnel, representation cases, and applications for discretionary injunctions.[3] The board recognized that if the function of the general counsel was to prosecute, this would necessitate his having control over personnel of the agency's prosecutory arm. During the early operation of the law this arrangement seemed satisfactory. Seven months after the agreement was made, Paul Herzog reported that this "common-sense allocation of responsibility had worked well so far."[4] As long as the board and the general counsel were harmonious in interpretation of the statute the arrangement worked smoothly. It soon became apparent, though, that General Counsel Denham's philosophy of the function of government in labor relations was antagonistic to that held by the board.

President Truman appointed Robert N. Denham as the first general counsel in July of 1947. Denham, a Republican, was a lawyer with some forty years experience, having served the last nine of these as an NLRB trial examiner. Denham declared that in June of 1947 he was approached by James J. Reynolds and asked if he were interested in the new position. Reynolds informed Denham that he was the unanimous choice of the NLRB to fill this office. Denham maintained that he "was not interested" but John R. Steel-

[3] NLRB Release, Address of Paul Herzog to Industrial Relations Conference of United States Chamber of Commerce, Chicago, March 18, 1948, Truman Papers, OF 145, HSTL.

[4] *Ibid.*

man persuaded him to take the job until he could "get things running."[5]

Reynolds has a different recollection of what transpired. According to Reynolds, Denham actively sought the position and asked for his assistance in securing it, which he gave. Reynolds supported his nomination mainly because he believed Denham to be "competent" and was "impressed by his sincerity and his devotion to the principles of the new legislation." But it also occurred to Reynolds that the appointment of a Republican "would conceivably be good strategy to shelter the Administration from criticism that might be directed at the NLRB" by Senator Ball's "watchdog" committee, which was studying the operation of the act during its first year.[6] It was the impression of Stephen Spingarn, a White House aide, that this was one of the major reasons for Denham's selection. President Truman did not want to be subject to criticism that he had placed administration of the law "in the hands of an unfriendly official," because of his well-known opposition to the Taft-Hartley Act, so the appointment of a Republican was desirable.[7] Denham's subsequent actions would indicate that he was the pursuer of the position much more than he was the pursued.

The fact that Denham's concept of the role of government in labor disputes was radically different from that of the administration was not immediately apparent. But when Denham assumed his new position he brought with him preconceived notions concerning the fallacy of the old NLRB New Deal philosophy. He believed that these early boards had been too sympathetic to unions and had had inclinations

[5] Robert N. Denham, as told to Stacy V. Jones, "And So I Was Purged," *Saturday Evening Post,* CCXXIII (Dec. 30, 1950), 23.

[6] James J. Reynolds to the author, Sept. 19, 1961.

[7] Stephen J. Spingarn to Clark Clifford, Memorandum, Nov. 17, 1948, Truman Papers, Charles S. Murphy File, HSTL.

"to protect labor even in its excesses, and the privileges thus given by the Wagner Act grew into license."[8] Denham readily admitted that during the time he was a trial examiner he "was in almost continuous conflict" with the NLRB over labor relations philosophy.[9] He declared that when he took over the office of general counsel, the staff which he inherited was convinced that "labor was a sacred cow . . . and an employer was regarded as guilty merely because he was an employer."[10] On another occasion he remarked that labor had "been pampered and spoiled by political influences and governmental favor" under the Wagner Act.[11]

With this philosophy, it is not surprising that Denham wholeheartedly endorsed the principles of the Taft-Hartley Act. In fact, as noted previously, he had assisted Senator Donnell, whom he had met while a law student at the University of Missouri, with a memorandum on changes to be incorporated when the Labor-Management Relations Act of 1947 was being written. Unlike most NLRB personnel, he did not believe the new law was "partisan legislation" but agreed with the authors of the act that it equalized or tended "to equalize the balance" between labor and management. Although it had a few "bugs," it was a "magnificent piece of legislative machinery" to Denham.[12]

While the administration was fighting to repeal the law, Robert Denham as NLRB general counsel was campaigning in support of the act. When he was appointed, Truman told him that, although he did not like the act, it was the law and he expected Denham to administer it "in accordance with its terms, and in the way Congress intended it to be

[8] NLRB Release, Remarks of Robert N. Denham to Metal Trades Association, Chicago, Nov. 6, 1947, Truman Papers, OF 145, HSTL.

[9] Denham and Jones, "And So I Was Purged," p. 23.

[10] *Ibid.*, p. 73.

[11] Stephen J. Spingarn to Clark Clifford, Memorandum, Nov. 17, 1949, Truman Papers, Charles S. Murphy File, HSTL.

[12] NLRB Release, Remarks of Robert N. Denham to Metal Trades Association, Chicago, Nov. 6, 1947, Truman Papers, OF 145, HSTL.

administered."[13] Denham took these instructions literally. As general counsel, with the extensive powers given that office by the new act, he was ready to apply this law covering "that part of our economic structure which probably has more far-reaching ramifications than any other" and which covered "them thoroughly and well," according to the intent of the authors.[14] One of his first actions upon assumption of his new position was to "invite" the personnel working under him "who were unwilling to subscribe to Taft-Hartley to get out."[15] When the Senate Labor Committee conducted hearings on the Thomas-Lesinski bill, Denham was the star witness from the administrative branch who supported the Taft-Hartley Act. He was asked by the committee why he had assembled three or four hundred pages of data as evidence to oppose any changes when he did not know whether he would be summoned by the committee. Denham responded that he had relied upon what he "conceived to be the good judgment of the committee" and was therefore certain he would be called to testify.[16]

As the rift between Robert Denham and the board widened, he delivered an increasing number of speeches to management in which he expressed his support of the Taft-Hartley Act. In one of these addresses Denham stated his conviction that the Wagner Act was definitely social legislation "designed and administered for the benefit of one branch of our labor-management economy, at the expense of another." In contrast, the Taft-Hartley Act was "balanced, regulating legislation." In this address he reminded his

13 Robert N. Denham to the President, Sept. 15, 1950, Truman Papers, OF 145, HSTL.

14 NLRB Release, Remarks of Robert N. Denham to New York Personnel Management Association, New York City, Nov. 24, 1947, Truman Papers, OF 145, HSTL.

15 Denham and Jones, "And So I Was Purged," p. 73.

16 U.S. Senate, Committee on Labor and Public Welfare, *Hearings on S. 249, Labor Relations*, 81 Cong., 1 Sess., 1949, pp. 1724-26.

audience that the personnel of the entire NLRB structure was made up of "persons who were raised in the climate of the philosophy and . . . religion of the Wagner Act" and it was difficult to get "a divorcement of thinking . . . from their old Wagner Act formulae." These people had "found a further deterrent to changing their ways," he said, "in the still unfulfilled expectation that the Taft-Hartley Act would be repealed . . . and the salubrious clime of the Wagner Act restored to them—sans the incubus of a General Counsel." The General Counsel felt that the trend of NLRB decisions served "markedly to restrict application of the law concerning unfair labor practices" committed by unions, a trend to which he could not acquiesce. But he generously conceded that perhaps the board "*honestly held*" these opinions.[17]

The Washington *Post* comment on this speech was that conflict between Denham and the board was inevitable because of the nature of the General Counsel's separate status set up by the Taft-Hartley law. But the *Post* added that it was doubtful whether Congress contemplated the General Counsel's attacking the board "in public in this fashion." Even more serious, according to this newspaper, was the fact that when board decisions were appealed to the federal courts, the General Counsel represented the board in these cases. The General Counsel was thus inviting "employers dissatisfied with the Board's rulings to appeal . . . knowing that he himself will represent" the NLRB in the resulting cases.[18]

In another speech in his campaign to discredit the NLRB, Denham claimed that under the Wagner Act the board had no difficulty in finding "almost any conduct charged to an employer . . . as a violation . . . of the unfair labor practices."

17 NLRB Release, Remarks of Robert N. Denham to Building Trades Employers' Association, New York City, Jan. 12, 1950, Truman Papers, Charles S. Murphy File, HSTL.

18 Washington *Post*, Jan. 18, 1950.

"Now, however, it has become more difficult to classify the unfair labor practices" of unions, he charged, because the board narrowly construed the unfair practices provisions in regard to labor organizations.[19] He later repeated the indictment that the Wagner Act was "class" and "pure social" legislation which made "12 years of rough-going for the employers." But "the demand from an irate public that the scales be reset and that some degree of balance be established" brought about the Taft-Hartley Act which was "regulatory legislation in the full sense." This law set down "the rules of the game for employer and employee," he declared. As for policy disagreements between himself and the board, Denham quoted Justice Louis Brandeis' reasoning on the dominant attribute of the doctrine of separation of powers —"to preclude the exercise of arbitrary power . . . to save the people from autocracy."[20] Denham believed that his position was established to save management from NLRB autocracy and that he was correctly interpreting congressional intent in the Taft-Hartley Act.

Denham's differing interpretation of the function of the NLRB in labor relations both embarrassed and assisted the administration in its struggle against the Taft-Hartley Act. For instance, although both the Wagner and Taft-Hartley acts used identical language in regard to the term "affecting commerce," Denham decided, in opposition to the hands-off policy of the old NLRB, that this should apply to the hotel industry. Therefore, as general counsel he assumed jurisdiction over representation cases in this industry that had hitherto been regarded as intrastate commerce and not subject to the national labor law. Thus he inadvertently

[19] NLRB Release, Remarks of Robert N. Denham to American Trucking Association, Washington, D. C., Jan. 30, 1950, Truman Papers, Charles S. Murphy File, HSTL.

[20] NLRB Release, Remarks of Robert N. Denham to Bronx Board of Trade, March 30, 1950, Truman Papers, Charles S. Murphy File, HSTL.

assisted the campaign for repeal of the law. An interdepartmental memorandum noted that on November 23, 1948, Denham directed the NLRB field offices "to take jurisdiction of any cases 'affecting commerce' even though only one employee was involved." At the bottom of this memorandum John R. Steelman noted that this policy and Denham's position was helping the administration "by setting various people *outside labor,* to help kill the Taft-Hartley law."[21]

But Denham's support of the law led him to adopt extreme positions in its defense. In a speech in San Francisco, he had characterized the law as being "legislation which, if fairly administered," could "do more to bring about industrial peace than any other legislation we have ever had, or which has been proposed up to this time." Referring to this speech, Stephen J. Spingarn maintained that it was one thing for Denham to favor the law but quite another "for him to go out on the stump and propagandize for the continuation of the Act in direct opposition to the President's and the Administration's oft-enunciated position." Spingarn felt that this attitude and conduct could serve as a basis for requesting Denham's resignation or removal.[22]

Denham's attitude and policies naturally brought outcries from organized labor. As he increased his activity in what labor considered to be promanagement policies, the number of union requests and demands increased for the President to remove him as general counsel. One congresswoman from California decided that, on the basis of complaints from her constituents, Denham was abusing his powers by using "deliberate procrastination and delay" when it would help management and by applying for injunctions "to assist employers in breaking strikes even when such injunctions were not justified." She asked Truman to investigate these

21 Russell P. Andrews to John R. Steelman, Memorandum, March 30, 1949, Truman Papers, OF 407, HSTL.

22 Stephen J. Spingarn to Clark Clifford, Memorandum, Nov. 17, 1949, Truman Papers, Charles S. Murphy File, HSTL.

charges and if proven true, "retire him to private life."[23] In November of 1949, Philip Murray publicly requested Truman to remove Denham from office on the grounds that he had used "his vast powers to aid employers bent on destroying free unions." Spingarn noted that this request would make it more difficult for the President to remove him because of public reaction to such a request from a union official, but Spingarn was satisfied that the proposal still deserved "serious consideration." Another alternative, this official observed, would be to reorganize the NLRB by abolishing the office of general counsel.[24] But when questioned by the press in February 1950 on whether he was considering a CIO Executive Board demand that Denham be dismissed, the President replied in the negative.[25]

With General Counsel Denham following an apparently promanagement course in administering the national labor policy and the NLRB continuing its interpretations, insofar as possible, along its traditional prolabor lines, conflict was inevitable. This discord was especially noticeable when the board had to depend upon the General Counsel and staff to prosecute cases. The gulf between these two divisions widened until in the fall of 1949 the board and the General Counsel held several meetings and exchanged memoranda concerning changes to be made in the Statement of Delegation. In a memorandum of September 20, 1949, the board informed Denham that it wanted to assume control over "the selection, retention, transfer, promotion, demotion, discipline and discharge" of all NLRB regional directors and officers. When Denham refused to be swayed by hints and threats in this series of meetings, the board informed him on February 23, 1950, that it was putting a revised State-

[23] Helen Gahagan Douglas to Harry S. Truman, Dec. 2, 1949, Truman Papers, OF 145, HSTL.

[24] Stephen J. Spingarn to Clark Clifford, Memorandum, Nov. 17, 1949, Truman Papers, Charles S. Murphy File, HSTL.

[25] Press Conference, Feb. 16, 1950, Truman Papers, OR, HSTL.

ment of Delegation into effect which contained the proposed changes of the previous September.[26] Denham's reply was a public statement in which he vowed he would not "submit to such action." He would not agree to this revision, he declared, because if the board possessed the authority it was seeking the general counsel, through the regional directors, would lose his "independence of action" as prosecutor for the NLRB.[27] Although Denham protested this unilateral change in the Statement of Delegation, it went into effect anyway, and the administration then turned to more direct means to bring NLBR administration in line with its labor policies.

In July of 1947 Congress established the Commission on Organization of the Executive Branch of the Government, headed by former President Herbert Hoover and popularly known as the Hoover Commission. This commission made a comprehensive study and in January 1949 made its recommendations for reorganizing the departments and agencies of the executive branch to obtain more efficiency with less expense. On June 20, 1949, Congress passed the Reorganization Act which authorized the President to reorganize a department or agency and submit such plan to Congress for approval. If neither house rejected the plan by a majority vote, it would go into operation. After the failure to replace the Taft-Hartley Act with the Thomas-Lesinski bill, and with the deepening antagonism between General Counsel Denham and the NLRB, the administration decided to utilize the Reorganization Act and revamp the National Labor Relations Board by abolishing its bifurcated nature and returning it approximately to its original form under the Wagner Act.

The administration, desirous of canceling the powers of

[26] NLRB to Robert N. Denham, Feb. 23, 1950, Truman Papers, Charles S. Murphy File, HSTL.

[27] NLRB Release, Statement by Robert N. Denham, March 2, 1950, Truman Papers, OF 145, HSTL.

the general counsel, could find justification for this action in the Hoover report. After studying the NLRB organization and administration, the Hoover Commission noted that the general counsel's office, independent of both the board and the secretary of labor, marked a "departure from previous administrative practice." "If permitted to set a pattern for future Governmental organization," the report continued, "it may lead to a diffusion of responsibility." The report observed that the nature and power of the general counsel's office gave rise to "several internal administrative problems," using as an illustration the handling of unfair labor practice cases. Regional directors issued some types of unfair labor practice complaints only with the approval of the general counsel. If a refusal to issue the complaint were forthcoming, appeal had to be made to the same unit from which the rejection originated. The report concluded that "the present position of the General Counsel is an unstable one" and recommended creating a Council of Labor under the chairmanship of the secretary of labor which would include all federal officials concerned with labor problems.[28]

President Truman submitted Reorganization Plan XII to Congress for approval on March 13, 1950. This plan proposed abolishing the office of general counsel and transferring his powers to the chairman of the National Labor Relations Board. The proposal was assigned to the Senate and House Committees on Expenditures in Executive Departments for hearings. Paul M. Herzog gave a lengthy testimony in defense of the plan, on behalf of the NLRB, saying that board support was "unanimous" and "unequivocal." Herzog stated that the President's plan was propounded so that the NLRB would once again function as the Hoover Commission recommended regulatory commissions should operate. Herzog pointed out that, although the board

[28] Commission on Organization of the Executive Branch of the Government, *Task Force Report on Regulatory Commissions* (Appendix N), (Washington, D. C., Jan., 1949), pp. 139-40.

had disagreed with the wisdom of separating their functions at the time the Taft-Hartley Act was passed, it had gone even further than the statute required to make the plan work by delegating additional duties and functions to the general counsel. But when the board tried to correct one of their mistakes by issuing a revised Statement of Delegation, General Counsel Denham refused to accede to the change and it had to be made without his consent.

Herzog stressed that the general counsel had "unlimited authority" to frustrate enforcement of the public labor policy by his refusal to act, and even though this action were arbitrary, it was "subject to no review whatever." The nature of the general counsel's office embarrassed the board at times by the fact that when it disagreed with a complaint issued by the general counsel and the plaintiff appealed, the board had to rely upon the general counsel for its courtroom defense. In some of these appealed cases General Counsel Denham had also stated his contrary views to the court, Herzog said, and thus created the strange anomaly of the federal government's being on both sides of the same case. Herzog summed up the NLRB testimony by stating that "the experiment of the past 30 months has . . . shown that separation of functions creates a nearly insoluble dilemma in internal administration."[29]

In testifying against Reorganization Plan XII, Denham declared that the only "completely satisfactory answer" to the problem was for Congress to "define the area as precisely as possible within which the Board must and must not assert federal jurisdiction." The abolition of his independent office would not solve the difficulty, Denham insisted, but would "merely give the Board the unfettered power to perpetuate the confusion, inconsistencies, and contradictions implicit in its decisions." Denham was certain that destroying the

[29] Paul M. Herzog, Statement to House of Representatives Committee on Expenditures in Executive Departments, March 23, 1950, Truman Papers, OF 145, HSTL.

separation of judicial and prosecutory functions under the authority of the Reorganization Act would be deprivation of due process. He questioned whether the President had the authority to do this with a reorganization plan when this particular due process was "deliberately created" by Congress. If the board received this additional function, Denham said, there was not "the slightest doubt" in his mind that the issue would be taken to the courts. It would then take "a considerable period of time" to get a Supreme Court decision, he warned, and all board decisions rendered in the meantime "would be illegal and void."[30] Paul Herzog's reaction to this testimony was that "once more the General Counsel seems to be inciting litigation."[31]

Although Reorganization Plan XII of 1950 proposed doing almost exactly what Taft wanted to do in 1949 when he amended the Thomas bill so as to abolish the office of general counsel, Senator Taft opposed the idea in 1950. He submitted Senate Resolution 248, on April 3, opposing the plan.[32] Taft said he disapproved of the plan for four reasons: (1) it was not in accord with the Hoover Commission recommendations; (2) it attempted to reverse a basic matter of congressional policy by executive action; (3) it proposed an unsound mixing of judicial and prosecutory functions "similar to that responsible for the greatest miscarriage of justice this country has even seen under the Wagner Act"; and (4) it attempted to use the Hoover report for political purposes.[33]

The administration defense of Reorganization Plan XII was undertaken by Senator John Sparkman, Democrat from Alabama, who was furnished a speech by the White House

[30] Robert N. Denham, Statement to Senate Committee on Expenditures in Executive Departments, April 6, 1950, Truman Papers, Charles S. Murphy File, HSTL.

[31] Paul Herzog to Charles Murphy, April 17, 1950, Truman Papers, Charles S. Murphy File, HSTL.

[32] *Congressional Record,* 81 Con., 2 Sess., 1950, XCVI, 4575.

[33] *Ibid.,* p. 3703.

for this purpose.[34] Sparkman argued that the plan sought to provide "exactly what the senior Senator from Ohio was arguing for less than a year ago."[35] But Taft had pointed out the major deviation from his proposal which to him was the weakness of Reorganization Plan XII, namely, that all of the general counsel's powers were going to be transferred to the chairman of the NLRB. If these functions were going to be entrusted to the entire board, Taft might have agreed, but he felt that this was concentrating too much power in the hands of one man.[36]

As it had done with the Thomas-Lesinski bill in 1949, the administration now placed its full support behind Reorganization Plan XII of 1950. Stephen J. Spingarn reported that unions were "working feverishly" and the secretary of labor was "cooperating" 100 percent in the attempt to get the plan approved. Spingarn had given Tobin a list of Senators "to talk to." He was very concerned about this issue as "it would be the only important labor victory" the administration could take into the elections of 1950.[37] The day before the Senate took a final vote on the plan, Spingarn decided that "five to eight votes" still needed to be won. He pointed out this deficiency to W. Stuart Symington, Democrat from Missouri, noting that it was immaterial whether Senators voted for the plan. As long as there were not 49 votes against it, under the terms of the Reorganization Act it would go into effect. Spingarn asked Symington to try persuading Senators not to vote at all rather than to vote against the plan. This plan was "by far the most important of the Reorganization Plans from the standpoint of the President and the Administration," he reminded Symington, and "its

34 John Sparkman to Stephen Spingarn, May 15, 1950, Spingarn Papers (General Government–Plan 12), HSTL.

35 *Congressional Record,* 81 Cong., 2 Sess., 1950, XCVI, 6877.

36 *Ibid.*, p. 6680.

37 Stephen J. Spingarn to Charles Murphy, Memorandum, May 8, 1950, Spingarn Papers (General Government–Plan 12), HSTL.

victory or defeat will mean a lot in November" since it was the "only significant labor victory which the Administration has a chance of getting this year."[38]

Taft's resolution against Reorganization Plan XII came up for a final vote in the Senate on May 11, 1950. On this same day President Truman sent a telegram to Alben Barkley urging the Senate's approval. Truman declared in this communication that the plan would "correct an administratively unworkable organizational set-up" and bring the NLRB procedures into conformity with the other independent regulatory agencies. He insisted that the issues involved were "not matters of personalities, neither do they go to the substance of the controversy over the Taft-Hartley Act," quoting Taft's 1949 statement when the Senator argued for his amendment abolishing the general counsel's office.[39] But the final Senate vote approved Taft's resolution 53 to 30, thus blocking Reorganization Plan XII.[40] Of these 53 votes of approval 19 came from Southern Senators. The plan was reported to the House from committee but no further action was taken. However, after the Senate killed the plan, what occurred in the House of Representatives was irrelevant since either house could stop a reorganization plan.

The day after the Senate rejected the plan Denham sent the NLRB a note saying that since the plan was now "behind" them, the time was appropriate for making serious efforts "to find a basis for more effective cooperation."[41] Spingarn observed that Denham was apparently going to be "magnanimous about his victory" and the note would deny rumors that Denham planned to "resign now in a blaze of glory."[42]

38 Stephen Spingarn to W. Stuart Symington, May 10, 1950, Spingarn Papers (General Government—Plan 12), HSTL.

39 Press Release, Telegram from the President to the Vice-President, May 11, 1950, Truman Papers, OF 145, HSTL.

40 *Congressional Record,* 81 Cong., 2 Sess., 1950, XCVI, 6886.

41 Stephen Spingarn to Charles Murphy, Memorandum, May 16, 1950, Truman Papers, Charles S. Murphy File, HSTL.

42 *Ibid.*

The board's response to the general counsel's note was that the time had "always been appropriate." The board had, since August 22, 1947, "consistently sought to find a basis for effective cooperation of the Agency" and it would "continue to be glad to do so."[43] Denham got in the last word in this exchange, replying to the board's rather "sassy" note that he did not recall the board's ever trying to compose differences within the commission "except by its mandate that its own terms must govern."[44]

The administration considered the idea of resubmitting a revised plan to Congress. This revision would have made the reorganization conform to Taft's amendment of 1949 by giving the general counsel's powers to the board rather than to the chairman. It was believed that by doing this, it could make Taft "do a lot of wriggling . . . and . . . might be able to pick up the five votes or so necessary to put it through."[45] After discussing this with Senators, Tobin found three who had voted against Reorganization Plan XII and might "go along" but who wanted to see the new proposal before committing themselves.[46] A revised plan was drawn up, ready to transmit to Congress, abolishing the office of general counsel and transferring his functions to the board. But both Stephen Spingarn and Charles Murphy decided "it seemed to be too late" to submit the plan and both Secretary Tobin and Paul Herzog were "reconciled to dropping the idea," so the project was abandoned.[47]

Following the failure of Reorganization Plan XII, strife between the two branches of the NLRB continued until it reached a climax in August 1950. On August 8 the board

[43] *Ibid.*

[44] Robert N. Denham to the NLRB, Memorandum, May 19, 1950, Spingarn Papers (General Government—Plan 12), HSTL.

[45] Stephen J. Spingarn to William Hopkins, May 12, 1950, Spingarn Papers (General Government—Plan 12), HSTL.

[46] Stephen J. Spingarn, Memorandum for the Files, June 7, 1950, Spingarn Papers (General Government—Plan 12), HSTL.

[47] June 22, 1950, *ibid.*

was notified that General Counsel Denham had demoted Ida Klaus and William Consedine, NLRB solicitor and associate solicitor respectively, to assistant solicitors. The board decided that he had acted "without authority" and "accordingly directed Miss Klaus and Mr. Consedine to ignore the General Counsel's invalid and unauthorized instructions."[48]

When this arbitrary attempt to demote personnel under direct board control failed, Denham proposed a plan to help resolve the conflict. He suggested to a third party, John R. Steelman, that he trade supervision over the NLRB Enforcement Division for return of his powers over appointment of field personnel lost by the revised Statement of Delegation.[49] Steelman had one of his aides, Russell P. Andrews, analyze the proposal. This assistant decided that Denham was setting a snare by asking the White House to direct and be a party to a transaction that was favorable to Denham and would discomfit the board. It was Andrews' opinion that "good faith" in the NLRB had deteriorated to the point where the only workable measure would be removal of one of the contending sides and his "personal nominee would be on the non-plural side." He went on to remind Steelman that Truman had instructed the board the previous May not to recede from the amendments made in the revised Statement of Delegation and if the board accepted this "compromise" it would be "ignoring the desires of the President." Also, it was not a problem of reconciling conflict of interest but of dealing with an offender, Denham, who had been "guilty of malfeasance in office in several instances."[50]

Charles Murphy suggested that the administration proceed with a "project of sicking the Senate Committee" on Denham to investigate his administration. Paul Herzog,

[48] NLRB, Minutes of Board Action, Aug. 8, 1950, Truman Papers, Charles S. Murphy File, HSTL.

[49] Robert N. Denham to John R. Steelman, Aug. 8, 1950, Truman Papers, Charles S. Murphy File, HSTL.

[50] Russell P. Andrews to John R. Steelman, Confidential Memorandum, Aug. 17, 1950, Truman Papers, Charles S. Murphy File, HSTL.

however, did not favor the idea because it would give Denham "a soapbox of official character, from which to vent his spleen." Also, Herzog felt, such an investigation would assume the aspects of a new controversy over the Taft-Hartley Act and Denham's "later removal would appear to flow from evidence of his pro-Act and pro-employer bias, rather than be on the basis of his impossible administration, as now." In this same memorandum Herzog enclosed a copy of a recent issue of "The Joe Ball Washington Letter" as an "example of the stuff D. is feeding Joe Ball right now for his weekly 'labor letter.'" Ball had written that the campaign to get Denham fired had been revived but whereas the unions had sparked the demand before, the "present intrigue" was the work of Paul Herzog and Ida Klaus. "Reports are that the President is about ready to move," Ball had proclaimed.[51]

President Truman was ready to move and in September he asked Denham to resign. In his ensuing letter of resignation Denham described his adversities to Truman. He admitted that in his three years' tenure, no one from the White House "offered any suggestion" on how he should treat any matter that came before him. He had "tried to obtain the cooperation of the Board" but failed, he complained, and this lack of concerted action had deprived the public of good administration. It had produced "a situation that should not be allowed to exist in a governmental agency." A few weeks previously he had "made a final offer to bring about a readjustment," he informed Truman, but had "heard nothing from it." Since the President had asked for his resignation "forthwith," he had no choice but to comply, his resignation to become effective at Truman's "convenience."[52] Truman accepted his resignation effective

[51] Paul Herzog to Charles Murphy, Aug. 17, 1950, Truman Papers, Charles S. Murphy File, HSTL.

[52] Robert N. Denham to the President, Sept. 15, 1950, Truman Papers, OF 145, HSTL.

September 18, 1950, being "grateful for the frankness and spirit of fair play with which it was offered." Truman told Denham in his acceptance note it was his view that the situation was caused by the Taft-Hartley Act creating "an administratively unworkable arrangement." Nevertheless, it was his duty as President to try to make it work.[53] George J. Bott, one of Denham's assistants, became the new general counsel.

Senator Taft called Truman's request for Denham's resignation "another surrender" to the CIO-PAC and an attempt "to nullify the Taft-Hartley Act." Taft concluded that this was "only another evidence that the CIO-PAC is making steady progress toward taking over control of the Democratic party." The Senator based his conclusions on the fact that a week before Denham's resignation Truman attended a private dinner of leaders of the AFL and the CIO in Washington, D. C.[54] Denham was convinced that this dinner sealed a bargain exchanging his "political head for the promise of votes—which did not materialize."[55] He described his successor, George Bott, as "a Fair Deal Democrat" who indicated that he would "do nothing to prevent the board from turning Taft-Hartley back to Wagner." "Bott had already surrendered much of his independence," Denham charged.[56] The *New Republic* later characterized Denham's administration by accusing him of having "harangued employers to prosecute under the new law, ignored the five-man Board in initiating his own prosecutions of unions, and all but destroyed the NLRB's function as an agent for industrial peace."[57]

The elections of 1950 were held soon after the fight over

[53] Truman to Robert N. Denham, Sept. 16, 1950, Truman Papers, OF 145, HSTL.
[54] New York *Times*, Sept. 17, 1950.
[55] Denham and Jones, "And So I Was Purged," p. 22.
[56] *Ibid.*, p. 74.
[57] *New Republic*, CXXIII (Nov. 13, 1950), 8.

Denham's resignation. The most important race in these elections, as far as organized labor was concerned, was the campaign of Robert Taft for reelection to the Senate. Being coauthor of the Taft-Hartley Act, leader of the forces that blocked repeal of the law in 1949, and also the one who stopped Reorganization Plan XII in 1950, Taft was labor's "Number One Enemy." Labor therefore was determined to employ all its forces to defeat him. Labor men and labor money poured into Ohio in an all-out attempt to retire Taft from the Senate. Taft answered labor's challenge in the most direct manner possible. According to one of his biographers, Taft ignored all advice to soft-pedal the Taft-Hartley Act and campaigned in every county in Ohio, carrying the fight into the enemy camp by making his labor law the principal issue.[58] But Ernest K. Lindley, describing this race as "the closest thing to a national contest" in this election year, reported that Taft emphasized "the Communist 'origin' and 'inspiration' of the CIO-PAC" in his campaign. And Lindley pointed out that the anti-Taft forces subordinated the Taft-Hartley issue and attacked his record as a whole instead since rank-and-file union members did not "sharply resent" the law and "other issues have more appeal to nonlabor voters."[59] Taft won the election however, with a majority of over 430,000, the widest margin Ohio ever gave a senatorial candidate, dealing organized labor "one of its worst defeats since the Roosevelt era began in 1932."[60]

Samuel Lubell attributed part of this large majority to the weakness of Taft's opponent. The Democratic candidate, Joseph Ferguson, proved to be an impotent campaigner and in addition received no support from Governor Frank

58 White, *The Taft Story,* 95. A good coverage of the election can be found in Fay Caulkens, *The CIO and the Democratic Party* (Chicago: Chicago, 1952), chap. 2.

59 *Newsweek,* XXXVI (Oct. 30, 1950), 20.

60 New York *Times,* Nov. 8, 1950.

Lausche, the titular head of the Democratic party in Ohio.[61] William S. White believed that labor defeated its own objective in this election by overzealousness. It was "widely publicized that the powerful unions were sending in non-Ohio money and non-Ohio workers" which resulted in helping Taft by making him appear a "victim of foreign forces."[62] This election, which labor hoped would be a demonstration of its power, instead indicated labor's political weaknesses. Lubell summed up these weaknesses: (1) "an overly militant labor campaign" evokes in turn an antilabor coalition; (2) labor and the Democrats are "uneasy, mutually suspicious allies"; (3) rank-and-file labor votes its natural inclinations regardless of the official stand; and (4) there is a fear even among rank-and-file workers of labor's becoming too powerful.[63]

The results of the elections of 1950 were a slight victory for the Republican party. The Eighty-second Congress, meeting in January 1951, was composed of 49 Democrats and 47 Republicans in the Senate and 235 Democrats and 199 Republicans in the House. In these elections the Democrats lost five Senate seats and twenty-seven in the House, thus reducing the majority they had won in 1948. Yet the Republican victory was not so great as could have been expected. The party in power traditionally loses congressional seats in midterm elections, but Democratic losses in Congress in 1950 were "less than any previous midterm election since 1938" and "only half the average loss in the last three mid-term tests."[64] In elections of the preceding decade, the Democratic party had made gains in the presidential election years and suffered losses in the midterm

[61] Lubell, *The Future of American Politics*, presents a good analysis of this important election, pp. 189-97.

[62] White, *The Taft Story*, p. 99.

[63] Lubell, *The Future of American Politics*, p. 190.

[64] Gus Tyler, "The Midterm Paradox," *New Republic*, CXXIII (Nov. 27, 1950), 14.

elections. This was attributed to, and helped give rise to, the political theory that fewer people voted in midterm elections and therefore a small vote favored the Republicans. Gus Tyler, a political writer for *New Republic,* decided that Democratic losses in 1950 were smaller than could have been expected because of an above-normal vote.[65] Forty million voted in the 1950 congressional elections, compared to 34,000,000 in 1946 and 28,000,000 in 1942. These numbers, when contrasted with the 46,000,000 votes in 1948 congressional elections, 45,000,000 in 1944 congressional elections, and 46,000,000 in 1940 congressional elections, illustrate that there is much less voter interest in midterm elections than in presidential races.

It was estimated that the AFL and CIO spent about $1 million on political activities in 1950 and with some success. Seventeen out of thirty-one "labor-backed Senate candidates" won and the CIO-PAC "fought in 150 Congressional districts and its candidates won more than 50 seats."[66] But the loss in Ohio with Taft's victory undoubtedly offset these gains in the eyes of union leaders. So by the end of 1950 organized labor had little to show for its political efforts. After extravagant promises in 1948, the Truman administration had been unable to reward labor's loyalty by giving unions what they most desired. Reorganization Plan XII would have helped, but as a result of labor's demands for removal of the General Counsel and the fact that this reorganization resembled another attack on the Taft-Hartley Act, the Senate refused to approve the plan. Failing in this, the only alternative left to the administration was to remove the General Counsel and replace him with one whose labor relations philosophy would be in line with that of the board. The labor policy could then be administered in a way favorable to labor and the administration could mark time until future elections

65 *Ibid.,* p. 15.
66 *Newsweek,* XXXVI (Nov. 20, 1950), 25.

sent more liberals to Congress. But the tide continued against unions and the Democratic party in the 1950 elections. The only thing then left for the Democrats and labor to anticipate was the hope that they could stage a political resurgence in the election of 1952.

9

THE TAFT-HARTLEY ACT WANES AS A POLITICAL ISSUE

By 1952 the attitude of Taft-Hartley opponents had undergone a limited change. After four years of vain endeavor to secure repeal of the hated statute, critics gradually realized that complete destruction of the act was probably impossible. Their collective attitude progressively transformed into the more realistic approach of amending the law so as to remove the more drastic antiunion provisions. In the presidential campaign of 1952 both major candidates advocated change; the Republican by amending the existing law and the Democrat by rewriting the statute. But neither candidate recommended a return to the Wagner Act "with improvements" as had been demanded by Harry S. Truman in 1948.

Even President Truman gave no outward indication that he was still insisting upon outright repeal of the Taft-Hartley Act until the campaign of 1952 had begun. His statements in reference to the law no longer contained the word "repeal." In his 1951 State of the Union message, in the midst of the Korean crisis, he asked Congress for "improvement" in the policy "to help provide stable labor-management relations and to make sure that we have steady production in this emergency."[1] When he signed the Taft-Humphrey amendment in October 1951, he stated that he hoped this would be "the forerunner of . . . future . . . sound legislation." In this same month Truman dedicated Gompers Square in Washington, D. C., with a speech that omitted mention of repeal. Instead, he said the objective should be "a law that will insure free unions and free collective bargaining, and be fair to both employers and employees."[2]

Truman was asked at a press conference in November 1951 if he anticipated the Taft-Hartley Act's becoming an issue in the election campaign of the coming year. He replied that he could not answer until he had analyzed any amendments that might be made by Congress before the election.[3] And he declared in the 1952 State of the Union message that the law had "many serious and far-reaching defects." Truman pledged continuation of his effort to get "a fair law—fair to both management and labor."[4] When challenged by reporters that he had asked for improvements and not repeal in this message, Truman countered by saying, "if that requires repeal of the Taft-Hartley Act, why that's it."[5] However, while campaigning for the Democratic candidate in 1952, he again repeatedly demanded repeal.

The New York *Times* reported in December 1951 that there were "signs" that even organized labor was abandon-

[1] Jan. 8, 1951, Truman Papers, OF 419-B, HSTL; *Congressional Record,* 82 Cong., 1 Sess., 1951, XCVII, 98-101.

[2] Oct. 27, 1951, Truman Papers, OR, HSTL.

[3] Key West, Fla., Nov. 15, 1951, Truman Papers, OR, HSTL.

[4] Jan. 9, 1952, Truman Papers, OF 419-B, HSTL; *Congressional Record,* 82 Cong., 2 Sess., 1952, XCVIII, 31-35.

[5] Press Conference, Old State Department Building, Jan. 11, 1952, Truman Papers, OR 22, HSTL.

ing its drive for repeal and was "ready to cooperate in working out acceptable amendments on a piecemeal basis."[6] This labor acceptance of the inevitable was clearly demonstrated when, after the Republican success in 1952, the leaders of the two largest international federations of unions asked Congress to make specific amendments in the law. AFL president George Meany requested changes to: (1) remove antiunion security clauses, (2) ease restrictions on secondary boycotts, (3) provide better distinction between representation and jurisdiction cases, (4) remove the national emergency injunction, (5) eliminate the provision for union damage suits, (6) renovate the NLRB, and (7) remove exemption of supervisors and agricultural workers.[7] CIO president Walter P. Reuther urged Congress "to redeem President Eisenhower's promise" by proposing modifications similar to those Meany requested for the closed shop, injunction, secondary boycott, and union suability provisions. In addition, Reuther wanted to remove the non-communist affidavit requirement and the employer "free speech" clause.[8]

Although the Taft-Hartley Act was discussed in the election of 1952, it did not play the major role it had in 1948. Five years after the enactment of the law, during which there were repeated failures to achieve repeal, the opposition was beginning to concede that it would be more practical to work for improvement by amendment. However, the act could still stimulate fiery denunciation from Harry Truman and was again used by the Democrats to solicit the support of labor in the 1952 election. But before the campaign got underway, the Taft-Hartley Act became an issue in one

[6] New York *Times*, Dec. 18, 1951.

[7] AF of L News Release, Statement of George Meany, March 3, 1953, Lloyd A. Mashburn File, R.G. 174, National Archives.

[8] CIO News Release, Statement of Walter P. Reuther, March 30, 1953, Lloyd A. Mashburn File, R.G. 174, National Archives.

of the most famous strikes in American history. This was the steel strike of 1952 and the role of the Taft-Hartley Act in this strike had an important influence on the presidential race that followed.

This labor dispute originated in the demand of the steelworkers for a wage increase. The steel industry refused to grant the requested raise since the government would not allow what the industry considered a sufficient compensatory price increase in steel. On November 1, 1951, the United Steel Workers of America, CIO, notified the steel industry that it was ready to begin negotiations for a new contract to replace the existing one that would expire on December 31. The union asked for an 18½-cent wage increase. In addition, requests were submitted for a union shop, six paid holidays annually, double time on Sundays, and a guaranteed annual wage. It was estimated that these supplementary benefits would amount to 5.4 cents per hour in increased wages in the first year and 3.5 cents per hour the second year.[9]

In resisting these demands, Benjamin F. Fairless, president of U. S. Steel, appealed to the principle accepted by the general public that a raise in wages would mean a rise in the cost of living. In a public statement Fairless said that labor had received "a general round of wage increases" on five different occasions since V-J Day, "and five times the cost of living has shot upward in the wake of the pay boost." These new economic demands, Fairless insisted, would raise the industry's employment costs over 50 cents per man-hour. Steel profits for the first nine months of 1951 were 25 percent lower than for the same period in 1950, he stated, because of higher federal income taxes, higher employment costs, and higher prices for purchased goods. Negotiations with the

[9] Mary K. Hammond, "The Steel Strike of 1952," *Current History,* XXIII (Nov., 1952), 285.

union had made "little progress . . . to date," Fairless complained, "because the Union flatly refuses to trim down its financial demands to what will fit into the Government's wage stabilization rules."[10]

Collective bargaining negotiations produced no results and the union announced a strike for December 31, 1951. The union blamed the steel industry for the failure of these negotiations. Philip Murray, the CIO president, accused the steel companies of "acting in concert" and engaging "in an industry-wide strike against collective bargaining." The companies, Murray charged, would not even discuss the proposals or submit counterproposals. He emphasized that "they simply said NO." In this same statement Murray pointed out that the meetings held by Cyrus S. Ching on December 20 with representatives of the two sides were terminated by Ching after two days "when it became apparent that the companies would not even make serious counter-proposals."[11] Because of this serious threat to national defense, President Truman referred the dispute to the Wage Stabilization Board. This action opened an extended controversy over his refusal to invoke the Taft-Hartley law.

With the outbreak of the Korean war steady production and stable labor relations in vital industries assumed paramount importance. To meet this crisis President Truman reconstituted the Wage Stabilization Board on April 22, 1951, by executive order, basing his authority to do so on his constitutional powers as Chief Executive and Commander-in-Chief, and on the Defense Production Act of 1950. This new board was composed of eighteen members with labor, management, and the public being equally

[10] Benjamin F. Fairless, Statement, Dec. 22, 1952, Truman Papers, OF 419-B, HSTL.

[11] Philip Murray, Statement to Wage Stabilization Board in Steel Strike (filing date Feb. 5, 1952), Truman Papers, OF 407-B, HSTL.

represented. The board was empowered to investigate both economic and noneconomic issues in disputes threatening national defense and to make recommendations to the disputants. It was given "virtual assurance from the Economic Stabilization Administrator" that if it "recommended certain changes in wage policy" he would approve them.[12] Truman thus had an "administrative alternative" to use in the place of the Taft-Hartley Act in case of a threatened strike in vital industries.[13]

When Murray announced the strike for December 31 Truman immediately referred the dispute to the Wage Stabilization Board, requesting "promptly . . . its recommendations . . . as to fair and equitable terms of settlement."[14] The President publicly announced his action the same day, saying that negotiations were "at an impasse," with apparently "no hope of settlement through mediation." Therefore he had to find some means of avoiding a shutdown of the steel industry.[15] Truman requested that the workers continue on the job because he had "confidence in the Wage Stabilization Board and . . . the parties . . . to arrive at a fair settlement," to which the union promptly complied.[16] Truman later said he had considered using the Taft-Hartley Act in this dispute, but since the WSB "had been established especially for defense labor disputes and had been reaffirmed by Congress in this function within the year," he decided this "situation" would be better handled by the board than by a Taft-Hartley injunction.[17] A factor equally important

12 New York *Times*, April 22, 1951.

13 Frederick H. Harbison and Robert C. Spencer, "The Politics of Collective Bargaining: The Postwar Record in Steel," *American Political Science Review*, XLVIII (Sept., 1954), 713.

14 Harry S. Truman to Nathan P. Feinsinger, Dec. 22, 1951, Truman Papers, OF 407-B, HSTL.

15 Statement, Dec. 22, 1951, Truman Papers, OF 407-B, HSTL.

16 Harry S. Truman to Philip Murray, Dec. 31, 1951, Truman Papers, OF 407-B, HSTL.

17 Truman, *Memoirs*, II, 467.

in making this decision, undoubtedly, was the probability that if the Taft-Hartley Act were invoked, the union would strike at the end of the eighty-day period if no settlement were reached. By using the Wage Stabilization Board, Truman could request both sides to continue production during the emergency while negotiations continued and thus avert a strike for a longer period, possibly, than by using the eighty-day injunction approach.

In November 1951, prior to the steel controversy, the Council of Economic Advisers had established a national wage-price policy based on: (1) wage adjustments subject to general restraint, (2) maintenance of real wages based on cost of living adjustments, (3) correction of unmistakable inequities, (4) some productivity increases, and (5) restraint of fringe benefits. This council had concluded that the government's position in the steel dispute should be based upon "a tight application" of this policy and no general price increase. Then, in contrast to Fairless' declaration of falling profits, the council pointed out that U. S. Steel's profits before taxes in the first half of 1951 were at the annual rate of $574 million or 26.6 percent on net worth compared to their 1950 earnings of $450 million before taxes, or 22.9 percent on net worth.[18]

After more than two months of investigation the Wage Stabilization Board presented its recommendations on the steel dispute. The board recommended, although not unanimously, that the workers be given a 12½-cent-per-hour raise immediately with another 2½-cent raise July 1, followed by 2½ cents more on January 1, 1953. The board approved the union shop request and advised further discussions on the demand that employers pay 7 cents per hour into a trust fund for the guaranteed annual wage. The chairman,

18 Council of Economic Advisers, Memorandum, Nov. 14, 1951, Truman Papers, David D. Lloyd File, HSTL.

Nathan P. Feinsinger, defended these proposals on the grounds that the increases would merely permit steel workers to catch up with other major segments of industry and not start another "round" of wage increases.[19]

Steel industry officials estimated that a 15-cent wage increase would necessitate raising the price of steel, already at $110 per ton, another $6.60. But the Office of Price Administration would allow only a $2.86-per-ton increase.[20] The industry accordingly refused to accede to the WSB proposals, offering instead the 13½-cent package raise advocated by the industrial members of the Wage Stabilization Board who had not agreed to the recommendations of the majority. Benjamin Fairless denounced the board's wage recommendation, complaining that this would constitute a greater increase than steelworkers ever received "in normal times when no governmental wage and price controls were in effect." He further pleaded that this raise would "gravely impair and perhaps destroy" the steel industry's ability to maintain and expand its plants at a time "when free men are still fighting in Korea and a Free World needs our strength."[21] Further negotiations produced no results and the union prepared to strike on April 8, presenting a crisis to the administration since continued steel production was vital to the war effort in Korea.

A White House memorandum had suggested several bases for emergency seizure of an industry by the President. These included: (1) Section 18 of the Selective Service Act of 1950, (2) Title II of the Defense Production Act of 1950, (3) inherent executive powers found in Article II of the Constitution, and (4) a possible additional statutory basis

19 "Report and Recommendations," Wage Stabilization Board, Steel Strike, March 22, 1952, Truman Papers, OF 407-B, HSTL.

20 Mary K. Hammond, "The Steel Strike of 1952," p. 286.

21 Benjamin F. Fairless, Radio Address, April 6, 1952, Truman Papers, Charles S. Murphy File, HSTL.

in the emergency injunction provisions of the Taft-Hartley Act.[22] In an unprecedented action on April 8, 1952, President Truman ordered Secretary of Commerce Charles Sawyer to seize and operate the nation's steel mills involved in the dispute.[23] The next day Truman informed Congress that he had made this decision "with the utmost reluctance." He said the only alternative to seizure was to grant the industry's demand "for a large price increase," but he and the stabilization officials believed that such a concession "would have wrecked our stabilization program." He hoped congressional action would be taken to settle the dispute, but if not, or until such necessary legislation was enacted, he would "keep the steel industry operating and . . . bring about a settlement . . . as soon as possible."[24]

From this point on the issue became a legal and political battle. Truman "sided squarely with the Steelworkers and verbally blasted the steel industry" while the steel industry countered with the charge that the seizure was a "political deal between the CIO and the administration."[25] Clarence B. Randall, President of Inland Steel, was certain that this "evil deed" of presidential seizure discharged "a political debt to the CIO" and warned the American housewife that this wage increase would start "the whole giddy spiral of inflation . . . again." "To freedom loving people it means the closed shop and compulsory unionism," Randall lamented, and "to the businessman it is the threat of nationalism [nationalization]."[26]

[22] Memorandum to Assistant Attorney General Baldridge, unsigned, n.d., Truman Papers, David D. Lloyd File, HSTL.

[23] Harry S. Truman, Executive Order 10340, April 8, 1952, Truman Papers, OF 272, HSTL.

[24] Statement to Congress, April 9, 1952, Truman Papers, OF 407-B, HSTL; *Congressional Record,* 82 Cong., 2 Sess., 1952, XCVIII, 3912.

[25] Harbison and Spencer, "The Politics of Collective Bargaining: The Postwar Record in Steel," p. 715.

[26] Clarence B. Randall, Radio and Television Address, April 9, 1952, Truman Papers, Charles S. Murphy File, HSTL.

Many outraged congressmen immediately demanded that Truman invoke the Taft-Hartley Act and some went even further. Senator Taft believed Truman's action to constitute "a valid case for impeachment."[27] George Bender introduced a resolution in the House to create a committee to investigate the possibility of impeaching Truman and on April 28 Paul Shafer, Michigan Republican, submitted an impeachment resolution.[28] Also Robert Hale, Republican from Maine, introduced a resolution to investigate the seizure and, if necessary, to recommend impeachment to the House.[29] The Senate debated cutting a supplemental appropriations bill to restrict funds necessary for government operation of the steel mills because of the conviction that the law should have been invoked.

Truman's response to this criticism was that the Taft-Hartley Act provided only for a fact-finding board investigation during the eighty-day injunction and could not prevent a shutdown. By acting as he did, Truman reminded Congress, a "delay—voluntarily—of 100 days in the work stoppage" was achieved. He acknowledged that some congressmen wanted him to invoke the law even at that late date, but any further delay would be "futile." Furthermore, it would be "unfair," he insisted, "to force the workers to continue at work another 80 days at their old wages." "To freeze the status quo by injunction would, of course, be welcomed by the companies, but it would be deeply and properly resented by the workers," he explained.[30]

Harold L. Enarson, a White House assistant, noted that the pro and con public opinion mail on the steel seizure ran "about half and half." He felt that the letters indicating "bewilderment and concern" were probably most representa-

27 New York *Times*, April 18, 1952.

28 *Congressional Record*, 82 Cong., 2 Sess., 1952, XCVIII, 4325, 4539.

29 *Ibid.*, p. 4222.

30 Harry S. Truman to Alben Barkley, April 21, 1952, Truman Papers, OF 272, HSTL.

tive of the public attitude on the issue and suggested selecting one of these letters for the President to answer personally.[31] The result was a letter from Truman to C. S. Jones, who had asked why the Taft-Hartley Act had not been used. Truman replied to this citizen that if he had invoked the law, "there inevitably would have been a work stoppage" because of the elaborate procedure required by the act. He then went through the steps of the procedure that were necessary before an injunction could be obtained and which, he explained, consumed time. Truman used this opportunity to elaborate on the administration theme that steel profits were high enough to justify refusing the requested price raise. He said the Iron and Steel Institute had reported that its members, who included some 90 percent of the industry, averaged $6.59 profit per ton "after taxes in the three years before Korea." For 1951 their profits came to $7.07 per ton "*after* taxes."[32]

The administration tried to publicize this letter to present its side of the controversy, but the press was not as cooperative as desired. When another citizen asked Truman if the newspapers were correct in stating that all steelworkers would be forced to join the CIO if union demands were fulfilled, he received a copy of the "Jones Letter." Truman added a note to this letter saying that only a few newspapers had printed it in full or even summarized it, but instead had been "busy printing the paid propaganda ads of the steel companies."[33]

The steel companies had filed suit in a federal court and on April 29 Federal District Judge David Pine ruled that the government seizure was illegal. The next day the Court

[31] Harold L. Enarson to John R. Steelman, April 15, 1952, Truman Papers, Charles S. Murphy File, HSTL.

[32] Harry S. Truman to C. S. Jones, April 27, 1952, Truman Papers, OF 407-B, HSTL.

[33] Harry S. Truman to Vic Householder, May 26, 1952, Truman Papers, OF 407-B, HSTL.

of Appeals stayed the effect of this order until the Supreme Court could rule on the case. The Supreme Court agreed to hear the case immediately and on June 2, by a 6-to-3 decision, held the seizure illegal and returned the mills to their owners.[34] The workers immediately began a strike which was to last for fifty-three days. On June 10 Truman made one final effort to prevent a work stoppage by requesting congressional authority to seize the strikebound plants. He told Congress that he would prefer their granting him this special power to his having to invoke the Taft-Hartley Act. Investigations, provided for by the law, already had been made, he said, and it would be unfair to require the workers to continue under their present wages when even the companies admitted they were entitled to more. Also, such an injunction would "take away management's incentive to bargain" as they would have nothing to lose by delay. Finally, he reminded Congress, invoking the Taft-Hartley Act "would not guarantee a restoration of full-scale production," whereas the special legislation he was requesting would accomplish that "primary objective."[35]

The congressional response to this application was a resolution requesting the President to use the Taft-Hartley Act and "the cat began the trip back to the White House." Harold Enarson then recommended invoking the law because failure to do so in the war emergency meant "only tragic loss in further delay." Then if the injunction failed to settle the dispute, this assistant said, "the cat . . . may claw the Congress not the President."[36] However, most of the

[34] *Youngstown Sheet and Tube Company v. Sawyer,* 343 U.S. 579 (1952). For a good brief presentation of the constitutional law aspects of the court decisions regarding seizure of the steel mills see Robert S. Rankin and Winfried R. Dallmayr, *Freedom and Emergency Powers in the Cold War* (New York: Appleton-Century-Crofts, 1964), pp. 150-64.

[35] Message to Congress, June 10, 1952, Truman Papers, OR, HSTL; *Congressional Record,* 82 Cong., 2 Sess., 1952, XCVIII, 6929-30.

[36] Harold L. Enarson to John R. Steelman, Memorandum, June 24, 1952, Truman Papers, OF 407-B, HSTL.

department heads and advisors advised against using the law,[37] so the bitter strike continued.

Because the Supreme Court invalidated the seizure and Congress refused to grant special seizure authority, the steel companies then "held all the advantages," according to Truman, and if the nation were to obtain steel it would be on their terms. By July 22 steel stock supplies were dangerously low, so President Truman called both sides to the White House for further negotiations and on July 24 a settlement was announced, thus ending the strike. The new contract provided for a 16-cent wage increase plus an estimated 5.4 cents per hour in fringe benefits. In return, the President "approved . . . with a reluctant heart" a price increase of $5.65 per ton on steel.[38]

The result of this strike could be called a victory for the steel industry. Although a wage increase was granted, it was less than the original union demand and the price increase was almost twice the $2.86 per ton the OPA would have allowed when the dispute began. In addition, the workers had worked five months under the old wages and conditions. But the President's actions in this controversy helped hold organized labor in the Democratic party in the approaching election. His actions convinced unions once again that he would use his power to assist them if he felt that there was justice in their cause. *Newsweek* commented that labor, "which had been drifting into a dangerous neutralism," was "lured back into the Democratic camp" by the President's continued refusal to invoke the Taft-Hartley Act in this strike.[39]

During the eight-month steel crisis, potential candidates for President were maneuvering for position and by the time the steel strike ended the two major parties had held their

37 Truman, *Memoirs*, II, 477.
38 *Ibid.*
39 *Newsweek*, XL (Aug. 4, 1952), 13.

conventions. General Dwight D. Eisenhower received the Republican nomination on the first ballot with 845 votes to 280 for Robert Taft. The vice-presidential candidate, Senator Nixon of California, was nominated by acclamation. *Newsweek* reported that Eisenhower had won "only after the most violent battle within the Republican party since 1912."[40] Taft went to Canada after the convention on an extended vacation, refusing to campaign for Eisenhower by pursuing an obvious inactivity that was imitated by many of his embittered supporters. The comment of the *New Republic* on the Republican choice was that it liked General Eisenhower as a man but wanted to know what he stood for "besides Youth, Motherhood and God." Not knowing Eisenhower's position on any issues, this magazine characterized the Republican candidates as "the Ulysses S. Grant–Dick Tracy ticket."[41]

The labor plank of the Republican platform advocated "retention of the Taft-Hartley Act," with changes necessary to insure "industrial peace."[42] The independent-minded Wayne Morse described this section of the platform as "verbose, platitudinous and evasive." He complained that the Republicans were making the same mistake as in 1948 by not telling labor and the American people "exactly what kind of legislation" they proposed.[43]

When the Democrats held their convention, Truman's choice, Governor Adlai Stevenson still refused to be a candidate. This left Estes Kefauver, Averell Harriman, Alben Barkley, and the Southern favorite Richard Russell of Georgia as the leading contenders. Since Stevenson refused to run, Truman endorsed Barkley. But Barkley

[40] *Ibid.* (July 21, 1952), p. 21.

[41] *New Republic*, CXXVII (July 21, 1952), 3.

[42] *Official Report*, 25th Republican National Convention Chicago, July 7-11, 1952, p. 318.

[43] Wayne Morse, "The GOP Platform," *New Republic*, CXXVII (Aug. 4, 1952), 12.

made the mistake, according to Truman, of meeting with all the labor leaders at the same time prior to the convention to request their support, and they refused.[44] Strangely enough, labor was backing Stevenson. Harriman and Kefauver were advocating repeal of the Taft-Hartley Act while Stevenson had merely recommended revision. But labor leaders were considering the total picture of picking the best candidate to win. They had learned in Ohio in 1950 that opposition to Taft-Hartley was not sufficient in itself to win an election.[45]

The Democratic platform again stated, "We strongly advocate repeal of the Taft-Hartley Act," because it had proven to be "inadequate, unworkable, and unfair." To replace the law, this plank proposed that "a new legislative approach toward the entire labor-management problem should be explored."[46] In comparing the labor planks of the two platforms, the New York *Times* observed that the Democrats were "trapped in the coils of a venerable political tradition" of not repudiating the policies of the party's titular head. This was the only reason, this newspaper declared, for the Democrats to again urge repeal of the law after the Eighty-first Congress had "repudiated the efforts of organized labor, with the all-out support of the White House, to turn the clock back to the Wagner Act." "By way of contrast," the *Times* intoned, the Republicans advocated "adopting such amendments . . . as time and experience show to be desirable."[47]

After acceptance of the platform, the convention began voting on candidates and Kefauver led on the first two ballots. But when Harriman withdrew and New York switched to Stevenson, the Stevenson bandwagon started.

[44] Truman, *Memoirs,* II, 495.
[45] *Newsweek,* XL (Aug. 4, 1952), 17.
[46] *Official Report,* Democratic National Convention, Chicago, July 21-26, 1952, p. 265.
[47] New York *Times,* July 25, 1952.

The Governor from Illinois won on the third ballot with 617½ votes against Kefauver's 275½ votes. Senator John Sparkman of Alabama was nominated as Stevenson's running mate. When Harry Truman addressed the convention following the selection of nominees he reminded the delegates that the Republicans were for only two things, the Taft-Hartley Act and the "discredited 80th Congress." He then pledged that the party would "fight for repeal of that good-for-nothing Taft-Hartley Act."[48]

The Democrats were as jubliant over the Republican disunity as Republicans had been over the 1948 Democratic split. *Newsweek* warned that Eisenhower faced greater obstacles than Dewey had in 1948 because the Democratic party was "united as it has not been since 1936." This magazine attributed much of the unity to the fact that labor was firmly back in the party. Labor support had been retrieved because Truman had refused to invoke the Taft-Hartley Act in the steel strike and because of the Democratic platform "promising repeal of the much denounced statute."[49]

In contrast to 1948, the Taft-Hartley Act did not become a major political issue in 1952. The major issues in this campaign were inflation, the Korean war, and communism and corruption in government, the latter two becoming most important and being expressed in chemical terms of K1C2. In August 1952 Elmo Roper asked people to indicate the two or three issues they thought were most important in this campaign. The response was 57 percent for halting rising prices, 51 percent for ending the Korean war quickly, 48 percent for keeping communists out of government jobs, and 35 percent for preventing corruption and dishonesty in government. Only 6 percent thought changing the Taft-Hartley Act was a leading question.[50] But to the NAM this

48 Address at Democratic National Convention, July 26, 1952, Truman Papers, OR, HSTL.

49 *Newsweek*, XL (Aug. 4, 1952), 13.

50 Roper, *You and Your Leaders*, p. 249.

law was an issue. This organization warned that "regardless of who wins, Taft-Hartley must be defended."[51]

At the beginning of the campaign the two leading candidates expressed similar views on the law. Eisenhower was quoted as saying that "we cannot make legislation that can compel people to work. That is regimentation. We have got to find a way, a means of respecting the advances labor has made . . . I believe that we should not give up these social gains."[52] Stevenson was caught in the dilemma of having advocated "modifications" before the convention and then having to run on the platform of repeal. In his first press conference after his nomination he tried to reconcile the contradiction. At this time he expressed the conviction that it was "more a question of form than of substance." He felt the area of agreement on labor policy objectives between employer and employee was increasing so possibly it would be "better to remove the political symbolism of the name 'Taft-Hartley' by repeal." But to him the result was more important than the method by which it was gained.[53] In a Labor Day speech at Detroit, one of the major areas of unionism, Stevenson boldly stated that he did not think the act was "a slave law," but added that "it was biased and politically inspired." He then proposed five basic principles as the basis for a new labor law: (1) the law must accept unions, like employer corporations, as the responsible representatives of their members' interests; (2) labor unions must conform to standards of fair conduct; (3) the law must outlaw unfair bargaining practices by both sides; (4) reject the use of the labor injunction; and (5) find new methods for handling national emergency disputes.[54]

Most labor leaders endorsed Stevenson for the presidency.

[51] National Association of Manufacturers, *The Washington Bulletin,* I, No. 3 (Oct. 7, 1952).

[52] *Newsweek,* XL (Aug. 4, 1952), 29.

[53] *Ibid.* (Aug. 11, 1952), pp. 19-20.

[54] *New Republic,* CXXVII (Oct. 20, 1952), 14-15.

The CIO early sanctioned his candidacy but Richard Gray of the building trades and William Hutcheson of the carpenters definitely favored Eisenhower, while John L. Lewis was reported "unpredictable."[55] The two major candidates took the unprecedented step of addressing the AFL annual convention in an attempt to win the support of this union. Eisenhower assured this convention that he knew the law "might be used to break unions" and "must be changed."[56] But, characteristic of much of his campaign, he spoke in generalities, making no specific recommendations. By contrast, when Stevenson spoke to the AFL delegates, he specifically advocated legalizing union security clauses, redefining secondary boycotts, and limiting, or ending, use of the injunction.[57] As a result, the AFL broke its tradition and for the only time in its history, with the exception of 1924, endorsed a presidential candidate, Adlai E. Stevenson.

The first Gallup Poll conducted after the conventions gave Eisenhower the lead with 47 percent, Stevenson 41 percent, and 12 percent undecided.[58] At the time of the AFL convention in September a Crossley Poll showed Eisenhower even further ahead with 52.8 percent and Stevenson 46.6 percent, with 0.6 percent other.[59] Then in this same month the character of Eisenhower's campaign underwent a drastic change and he received additional support.

Taft and his supporters, in disgust over the Chicago convention, had refused to campaign for Eisenhower. On September 12 Taft flew to Eisenhower's Morningside Heights home in New York. At this meeting apparently Eisenhower received instructions as to what he, as a Republican, stood for and Taft began to work for his election. Five days

55 *Newsweek*, XL (Sept. 15, 1952), 21.
56 *Ibid.* (Sept. 29, 1952), p. 32.
57 Gus Tyler, "The AFL Joins the Democrats," *New Republic*, CXXVII (Oct. 6, 1952), 8.
58 *Newsweek*, XL (Aug. 18, 1952), 17.
59 *Ibid.* (Sept. 22, 1952), p. 26.

previously, when asked his views on the use of the labor injunction, Eisenhower had replied that he did not know enough about the subject to discuss it. Taft now proceeded to explain the law's provisions and exacted the promise that Eisenhower would not accept an amendment authorizing plant seizure in a national emergency without special legislation.[60] This meeting seemed to be, to many Republicans as well as Democrats, a "sell-out" to the Taft wing of the party. And significantly, from this point on Eisenhower espoused many more traditional Republican policies than previously so that Stevenson, by comparison, seemed much more liberal. But the Republicans were now reunited and the Taft forces began to campaign for Eisenhower.

In the meantime President Truman was conducting a whistlestop campaign that gave, according to one observer, "an extraordinary lift to the Democrats" and dispersed "the gloom that had enveloped the Stevenson camp"[61] following the Eisenhower-Taft reconciliation. By the time of the election he had traveled over 15,000 miles in twenty-seven states and made more than 200 speeches on behalf of Stevenson.[62] In his tour Truman repeated his campaign tactics of 1948 by hitting specific issues, and again one of the most important of these was the Taft-Hartley Act. He told a group of miners in West Virginia that unions were not always "in the right," but the Republicans had produced a labor law that "bears down on people who belong to unions, whether the unions are right or wrong."[63] In May 1952 the *Wall Street Journal* had published an article entitled "Mr. Taft Has Some Ideas." This story reported that Republicans and Southern Democrats were "mulling over such schemes as putting labor under anti-trust laws, or simply breaking

[60] Edwin A. Lahey, "Eisenhower Moves Right," *New Republic*, CXXVII (Sept. 22, 1952), 8.

[61] *Newsweek*, XL (Oct. 20, 1952), 26.

[62] *Ibid.* (Nov. 3, 1952), p. 28.

[63] Remarks at Keyser, W. Va., Sept. 2, 1952, Truman Papers, OR, HSTL.

up nation-wide unions."[64] Truman quoted this to an audience, warning them that if the Republicans won the election they would "crack down on everybody except the special interests that put them into power."[65]

Truman admonished New Englanders for not "leading the fight to get rid" of the act. He said it was not "an academic question in New England" since the law was "hurting" them.[66] He explained to coal miners of Pennsylvania that the object of the Taft-Hartley Act "was to drive the laboring men back into slavery" and if the Republicans got "control of this country," that is what would happen. He pointed out that the Republican party represented "Wall Street and the National Association of Manufacturers in Congress" while the Democratic party supported "the plain people . . . against the lobbies." He had tried to get the Taft-Hartley Act repealed, he said, but the Republicans, "with Dixiecrats and Shivercrats," blocked it.[67] He suggested to coal miners in West Virginia the possibility that this "terrible, vindictive, anti-labor act" could "wreck the American labor movement." He cited as proof the *Business Week* article of December 18, 1948, which drew up a blueprint for using the law to destroy unions in a time of unemployment. He cautioned his listeners to "look out" if the Republicans won the election, because Senator Taft and his party had plans that would "pulverize the labor unions." He quoted the article in the *Wall Street Journal* of May 26, 1952, as an example of Republican intentions.[68]

Truman admitted that the Republican presidential candidate did not have a record on labor questions but said that

64 *Wall Street Journal*, May 26, 1952.

65 Remarks at Gerber, Cal., Oct. 3, 1952, Truman Papers, OR, HSTL.

66 Manchester, N. H., Oct. 16, 1952, *ibid.*

67 Wilkes-Barre, Pa., Oct. 22, 1952, *ibid.* Allan Shivers, Democratic governor of Texas, 1949-1957, was considered by Truman and other liberal Democrats at this time as being more of a Republican than a Democrat because of his policies.

68 Wheeling, W. Va., Oct. 23, 1952, *ibid.*

Eisenhower had "picked one of the most anti-labor men in Congress to be his running mate."[69] Truman reminded a gathering at Gary, Indiana, that Nixon had "worked for the passage of union-busting legislation even more punitive than the Taft-Hartley law."[70] At Terre Haute, Truman explained that the reason for Nixon's being "a favorite of the National Association of Manufacturers" was he had worked hard for the Hartley bill "which was even more violently anti-labor than the final product."[71]

But in spite of Truman's activities, the climax of the 1952 campaign came over the issue of the Korean war. Eisenhower had been criticizing the administration on its conduct in Korea and President Truman defied him to produce his "panacea to cure the situation." Truman felt that if Eisenhower had a solution it was his "duty" to explain it to him "and save lives now."[72] On October 24 Eisenhower accepted this challenge with the blunt sentence, "I shall go to Korea,"[73] and this undoubtedly affected last-minute voting decisions. One writer stated that the instant popularity of Eisenhower's Korean statement "demonstrated that Korea had been the dominant issue ever since the nominating conventions."[74] The final Gallup Poll before the election showed Eisenhower with 47 percent and Stevenson trailing with 40 percent. But 12 percent were still undecided,[75] and Eisenhower won most of the undecided vote.

The presidential race of 1952 inspired the largest vote in American history up to that time, with 61,637,951 casting ballots. Eisenhower received 33,938,285 popular votes against Stevenson's 27,312,217. Eisenhower received the greatest

69 *Ibid.*
70 Gary, Ind., Oct. 27, 1952, *ibid.*
71 Terre Haute, Ind., Oct. 27, 1952, *ibid.*
72 *Newsweek,* XL (Oct. 27, 1952), 27.
73 *Ibid.* (Nov. 3, 1952), p. 26.
74 Richard L. Neuberger, "The West—Eyes on Korea," *New Republic,* CXXVII (Nov. 17, 1952), 7.
75 *Newsweek,* XL (Nov. 10, 1952), 26.

number of votes any presidential candidate had yet received, although Franklin D. Roosevelt's 60 percent in 1936 was greater than Eisenhower's 55 percent of the total vote. Stevenson received the largest number any defeated candidate had been given. Eisenhower was elected with 442 electoral votes, being the first Republican to split the Solid South since Hoover in 1928. Stevenson received a total of 89 electoral votes, carrying only the nine states of West Virginia, Kentucky, Arkansas, Louisiana, Mississippi, Alabama, Georgia, South Carolina, and North Carolina. In addition, the Democrats lost control of Congress. The Eighty-third Congress was composed of 221 Republicans, 212 Democrats, and 1 Independent in the House and 48 Republicans, 47 Democrats, and 1 Independent in the Senate. Senator Wayne Morse, the Independent, had changed his politics as a result of the Eisenhower campaign, particularly over what he considered to be a surrender to the Taft-Jenner-McCarthy faction of the party, and now held the balance in the Senate.

Despite all that Harry S. Truman could do, there is little or no evidence that the Taft-Hartley Act played any significant part in the outcome of the presidential election of 1952. After refraining from use of the word "repeal" for over a year, Truman returned to the fray with a vengeance. Recalling perhaps the successful tactics he had employed in 1948, he again flayed the Eightieth Congress for enacting the Taft-Hartley Act and cast the blame for inflation upon the Republicans. But his efforts were in vain. The American people were more interested in other problems such as communism and the Korean war, and in spite of his flaming indictment he was unable to make the "Slave Labor Law" a major issue. Voters turned out in record numbers and elected their hero as President.

Eisenhower's extreme popularity, even among the nation's workers and in the Solid South, permitted his appeal to cut across party lines and draw from the Democratic and independent vote. The failure of congressional elections to follow the Eisenhower landslide and give the Republicans an overwhelming majority testified that the people were voting for a personality rather than for Republican principles. Although Stevenson received official labor endorsement, unions were unable to force labor legislation into the predominant position it had occupied in previous elections. Eisenhower was held in such high esteem that his stand on labor issues was immaterial. This election again proved that laborers vote their own inclinations regardless of the official union position. The Taft-Hartley Act was not a critical issue to workers in 1952, so the political tide continued to flow against unions and the Democratic party.

One study indicates that Eisenhower's victory could be attributed to the fact that 25 percent of his votes came from "1948 Democrats."[76] Based on the sample technique, this same investigation also concluded that 56 percent of union members voted Democratic in 1948 but that this percentage dropped to 42 in the 1952 election.[77] One of Eisenhower's speechwriters, who conceived the Korea pledge concept, feels that crediting this idea with the victory is a "vast exaggeration." He believes, and it seems far more logical, that the 1952 results were "a victory for the *man*," rather than any single issue such as frustration over Korea.[78] The overwhelming desire of the voters, after twenty years of Democratic leadership, was for a change, and this national hero seemed to embody qualities they were searching for in a President.

[76] Angus Campbell, Gerald Gurin, and Warren E. Miller, "Political Issues and the Vote: November, 1952," *American Political Science Review*, XLVII (June 1953), 369.

[77] *Ibid.*, p. 380.

[78] Emmet John Hughes, *The Ordeal of Power* (New York: Atheneum, 1963), pp. 32-47.

10

THE SIGNIFICANCE OF THE TAFT-HARTLEY ACT

SEVERAL important conclusions regarding the American labor movement and national politics can be drawn from a study of the early political history of the Taft-Hartley Act. When the act was passed, labor's immediate reaction was to call it a "Slave Labor Law" and to demand its repeal. But what appeared to be an unreasonable and groundless aversion to the law by organized labor was actually a deep-seated apprehension about the future. Although the slave-labor aspects of the statute failed to materialize, union officials were anxious lest, in a future period of possible mass unemployment, the act's more injurious provisions might be employed to destroy unionism and free collective bargaining, as was the alleged intent of some of the policy's sponsors. When repeal proved impossible, unions gradually began to accept the inevitable by insisting instead on removal of some of the statute's more objectionable features.

This new labor policy had the desirable effect of helping to cleanse organized labor of some of its more questionable methods and procedures. However, much of this was achieved by labor itself when it began purging communists from seats of union power and curtailing practices that had helped bring about the law. The American labor movement was forced to accept the restrictions imposed by public opinion on national labor policy, and union leaders realized the fallacy of their previous dependence upon the federal government for protection. Labor finally began to realize that it could no longer disregard the welfare and opinion of the public or rely too heavily upon the national government for defense against an irate public when labor abuses were committed. With the passage of time came the further realization that the so-called slave-labor features had not ruined unions.

The Taft-Hartley Act had the very important effect in national politics of stimulating union political activity to a greater degree than ever before. In this sense the intent of the law's sponsors was frustrated, as one of the act's purposes was to reduce the political activity and influence of organized labor. The enactment of this statute brought home to labor more clearly than any previous event the realization that the economic gains achieved could very easily be lost on the political field. Although unions had been active in politics prior to 1947, they were stimulated to a much greater degree of political endeavor after the passage of this law. Evading the political restrictions imposed by this policy, organized labor began spending more money and campaigning in national elections with much greater intensity. And with gradual acceptance of the fact that destruction of the statute was impossible, unions began to concentrate their political energy more realistically along the lines of preserving former gains rather than achieving new ones.

The Taft-Hartley Act also contributed heavily to labor unity. The great schism of labor into the AFL and the CIO, stemming from the opposing philosophies of whether to ignore or to organize the mass-production workers, had resulted in such ruinous practices as jurisdictional strikes, membership raids between unions, and rivalry between the two organizations who many times were working at cross-purposes, weakening the entire labor movement. The Taft-Hartley law, an attack from the outside, helped organized labor to comprehend its vulnerability and its common interests, with the result that the AFL and the CIO began to work more closely together, along with other organizations like the railroad brotherhoods, to achieve common ends. This cooperation was first apparent in the political sphere when both of the major international organizations accelerated their political activities. The passage of the Taft-Hartley Act impressed labor more deeply than ever before with the importance the political field held for the continued existence of unionism.

This increased political activity and cooperation did much to obliterate old grievances and lessen tensions between the AFL and the CIO. Both began to realize that labor unity was more important than the specific objectives of each union and was a necessity if organized labor were to withstand this and future onslaughts against the principles of free collective bargaining. Political cooperation in turn led to concerted action for other common labor goals and culminated in the merger of the AFL and the CIO in 1955. After several years of meetings and discussions organized labor was now united, at least on paper, as it had been prior to the CIO separation from the AFL in the thirties.[1]

In national politics the Taft-Hartley Act was but one

[1] It should be noted at this point that Arthur Goldberg described the activities of the CIO in expelling communist-dominated affiliates in 1948-1950 as a "major" development, since these unions were the most critical voices against merger. See Goldberg, *AFL-CIO: Labor United,* pp, 65-66.

aspect, albeit a most important one, of the postwar conservative reaction. Truman's veto of this law was one of the most important domestic decisions he had to make as President. His administration had been pursuing a moderate channel but at this point he had to decide between two courses. He could either align his administration with the popular wave of reaction and antiunion feeling and accept the bill, thus moving to the right, or he could take the progressive course of moving to the left, veto the bill, and strengthen the faltering Democratic-labor coalition begun by Roosevelt. Choosing the latter alternative, he assumed the New Deal progressive tradition which was to come to full flower in his Fair Deal program in 1949. And in doing so, Truman won the continued support of most of the country's labor leaders.

Truman created the Taft-Hartley issue with his veto and used it to the fullest political advantage. He was convinced that the Taft-Hartley issue was the main reason for his upset victory in 1948. While it is difficult to ascribe the results of a national election to any single factor, the Taft-Hartley Act undoubtedly served as one of the major components in his surprising triumph. This was a dispute upon which he could become personally agitated and he seemed to enjoy communicating his aversion to the law to the electorate. He made this one of the principal issues in his campaign and it was so widely and intensely discussed at this time that, following his election, it was generally assumed that the national labor policy would be changed. His failure to keep this campaign promise was not due to lack of endeavor on his part but to congressional reluctance in conceding that his mandate was valid.

After winning the election, Truman presented the new Democratic Congress with his Fair Deal program. This agenda consisted of the major issues he had raised in the previous campaign and which he believed were the basis for his election, the outstanding one being repeal of the Taft-

Hartley Act. But again the Southern Democrats joined the Republicans in Congress and defeated repeal of the law in 1949. This issue illustrates the operation of the double constituency in American national politics more clearly than any other episode in the postwar era. When the Republicans gained control of Congress in 1946, they claimed that the election was a command from the people to enact the statute since Republicans had made union abuse of power the principal issue in these elections. As Congress' constituencies are basically rooted in the agricultural, middle-class, and business groups which are fundamentally antiunion, and as there was a great outcry from these segments over union activities in the reconversion period, the Republicans could justifiably claim such a mandate. And the large majorities given the act in Congress, especially in the House which is supposedly close to the will of the people, seemed to verify this assertion.

But Harry S. Truman, having been elected President by all the people, could justify an edict from the country in 1948. However, when he attempted with all the forces at his disposal to execute his mandate, the conservative coalition in Congress, denying the validity of his claim, was able to block repeal of the law. Although a sufficient number of Democrats were elected in 1948 to enable the party to recapture control of Congress, a majority of congressmen returned who favored the law. Organized labor could influence the election of the President but in the postwar conservative reaction the middle-class, agrarian, and business constituencies could still control the legislative branch from which repeal of the hated act had to come. True to the interests of its constituencies, Congress refused to alter the curbs on union activities and power.

This indicated that the act would be repealed only when an overwhelming liberal victory would unseat a sufficient number of conservative congressmen and give the moderate and liberal elements a large congressional majority. But in the meantime the slave-labor features of the statute did not materialize and labor leaders and politicians found it increasingly difficult to stimulate public opinion against it. This was borne out when the Democratic presidential candidate in 1952 did not even attempt to make the law a major political issue as his predecessor had successfully done four years previously. By 1952 it was obvious that the Taft-Hartley Act was a permanent policy and that a grave mistake had been made in not accepting the modifications that could have been achieved in 1949.

After several years of protection by the federal government the conservative postwar reaction put organized labor on the defensive, both on the national and state levels. From 1947 on, unions were pressed, politically, to maintain their hard-earned gains, much less attain new conquests. The increased political activity of unions since 1947 accomplished much in political education of workers in preparation for elections and increased the importance and the effect of organized labor in national elections. Though rank-and-file members vote according to their own proclivities and union officials cannot always deliver the vote in a campaign, the political potential is present. "Political education" by the unions is successful in a limited way, increasing union prestige and prominence, especially in Democratic circles. The double constituency phenomenon in American politics became more pronounced in the immediate years after 1947. As unions suffered further setbacks, they increasingly placed their trust in a Democratic President for protection and assistance. Correspondingly, Democratic presidential aspirants found their greatest support in the large urban centers whose social and economic philosophy were antagonistic to that of the conservative coalition in Congress.

A major change in the double constituency phenomenon was begun in the early 1960's when the United States

Supreme Court handed down revolutionary decisions in regard to reapportionment of state congressional districts. This reapportionment issue originated primarily in the Negro civil rights movement of the post-World War II period. As Negroes achieved victories on the economic and social levels, they in turn placed greater emphasis on acquiring more participation on the political level, through action in federal courts to acquire their rights as citizens.

The first successful court case in this area came in 1960 when the Supreme Court declared unconstitutional an Alabama law that had drawn the boundary lines of the city of Tuskegee so as to exclude most of the Negro residents and thus deprive them of voting rights.[2] This decision was based upon the Fifteenth Amendment but also served as a modification of previous court interpretations that had determined reapportionment to be a political question and hence not justiciable.[3] The Alabama decision in turn provided exponents of reapportionment with the necessary lever they sought for judicial action and a suit was soon brought in federal courts to force the Tennessee legislature to reapportion itself agreeably to the requirements of the state constitution, a step that many rural-dominated legislatures had successfully avoided taking. This litigation was decided in 1962 when the Supreme Court determined that this issue was a justiciable question and remanded the case to District Court where it was to be heard and decided on its merits.[4]

This decision blasted the way open for urban forces, long denied their rightful share of political power on the state level, to force these rural-dominated state legislatures to reapportion on the basis of the massive shifts of population from rural to urban that had taken place in the preceding half-century. Litigation and legislative action was immedi-

[2] *Gomillion v. Lightfoot,* 364 U.S. 339 (1960).
[3] *Colgrove v. Green,* 328 U.S. 549 (1946).
[4] *Baker v. Carr,* 369 U.S. 186 (1962).

ately commenced in many such states by urban forces to compel a more equitable apportionment of legislatures. The climax of this effort through federal court action came in 1964 when the Supreme Court decided the case of *Reynolds v. Sims.*[5] In this precedent-shattering opinion, the high court ordered the state legislature of Alabama to reapportion its federal congressional districts. The reasoning behind this interpretation was that "legislatures represent people, not trees or acres. Legislators are elected by voters, not farms or cities or economic interests,"[6] and therefore, the principle of "one man, one vote" must be adhered to as closely as possible when establishing federal congressional districts. The sweeping reform, initiated by this decision, affected in some manner or degree over forty states.

In terms of future reapportionment, it would appear that these decisions might revolutionize our political process and will eventually make obsolete the dichotomy in our national political life. This reapportionment movement could ultimately break the rural-business domination of the House of Representatives. When the urban populations achieve their proper power in Congress, the national legislature may then be expected to legislate in the interests of urban laborers. This probability raises the question of possible future repeal of the Taft-Hartley Act. This query can be answered, however, in the light of recent developments since the *Reynolds v. Sims* decision, by placing it in the realm of improbability. Such a conclusion can be drawn from recent attempts to repeal one section of the Taft-Hartley Act, Section 14(b), which allows states to enact so-called right-to-work laws if they desire.

One of the major setbacks suffered by organized labor since 1947 came with the passage of right-to-work laws in some nineteen states after Section 14(b) permitted states

[5] *Reynolds v. Sims,* 377 U.S. 533 (1964).
[6] *Ibid.,* at p. 562.

to outlaw the union shop. When unions failed to secure outright repeal of the Taft-Hartley Act, they then focused their attention on repeal of Section 14(b) and persuaded the Democratic party to include such a plank in its 1964 platform. With the landslide victory of President Lyndon B. Johnson that year, and after the Democrats won a two-thirds control of both houses of Congress, organized labor felt certain that repeal of 14(b) would materialize. However, when the Eighty-ninth Congress produced a record amount of Great Society legislation, repeal of Section 14(b) became bogged down in the rash of legislative activity and late in the 1965 session it died from a Senate filibuster. The foes of repeal, led by Republican Senator Everett Dirksen of Illinois, renewed their filibustering activity when repeal of 14(b) was again introduced in the 1966 session. Following a three-week filibuster in the Senate, two attempts at voting cloture to end the debate failed and, although the measure remained on the Senate calendar, it was described as having "R.I.P." written beside it.[7] If this congressional fight is any indication of possible repeal of the Taft-Hartley Act, then one must conclude that, even if future reapportionment provides the sufficient number of urban-oriented votes for a majority in Congress, the rural minority, just like the South's fighting against Civil Rights legislation for decades, will be able to thwart repeal through a Senate filibuster. Although it is too early to tell, organized labor undoubtedly will find it necessary to live for quite some time with the Taft-Hartley Act.

[7] *Newsweek*, LXVII (Feb. 21, 1966), 31a.

BIBLIOGRAPHICAL NOTE

THE MOST important manuscripts used in this study are located at the Harry S. Truman Library, Independence, Missouri. The sub-divisions that are cited are the Harry S. Truman Papers, Official File (OF), Official Reporter (OR), President's Personal File (PPF), Press Conferences, White House Central File, John D. Clark Papers, Kenneth Hechler File, David D. Lloyd File, Charles S. Murphy File, Samuel L. Rosenman File, and Stephen J. Spingarn Papers. The Lewis Schwellenbach Papers are located in the Library of Congress. The manuscript papers of the Department of Labor are in the Labor and Transportation Branch of the Social and Economic Records Division of the National Archives; the papers cited in this group are Secretary Lewis Schwellenbach File, Secretary Maurice J. Tobin File, Secretary John W. Gibson File, John T. Metz File, and Lloyd A. Mashburn File. In addition, after the preliminary research, President Truman very graciously consented to an interview so that I could attempt to find answers to some of the decision-making problems covered by this investigation. However, it is difficult for anyone, including former Presidents, to recall the minute details of decisions over a decade later without prompting the memory with written records. So while this interview was not exceedingly profitable, it certainly presented a pleasurable experience to discuss these issues with the man who helped determine them, particularly when that person can still become agitated when the Taft-Hartley Act is mentioned. Several letters were sent to some of the principals involved in the Taft-Hartley Act asking for additional information, but unfortunately most of these queries went unanswered. The exception was James J. Reynolds, who very kindly responded to questions concerning the appointment of Robert L. Denham as NLRB general counsel.

The following list of secondary works is by no means exhaustive but includes many of the published works that I found most helpful in this study. Heading the list would be President Truman's *Memoirs* (Garden City, N. Y., 1955) which I found to be highly reliable in relation to the material found in the Truman Library. Eric Goldman's *The Crucial Decade—And After* (New York, 1961) is a well-written and interesting account of the postwar years. Wilfred E. Binkley's *President and Congress* (New York, 1962) is a good brief survey of the history of President-Congress relationships from the Constitutional Convention through the Eisenhower presidency. One can also find a great deal of interesting material on the presidency in Walter Johnson, *1600 Pennsylvania Avenue* (Boston, 1963), which covers this topic from Hoover through Eisenhower. The best Truman biographies are Josephus Daniels' *The Man of Independence* (New York, 1950) and Alfred Steinberg's *The Man From Missouri* (New York, 1962), although the former was written before the end of Truman's presidency and neither book made use of the Truman Papers.

Stephen K. Bailey's and Howard D. Samuel's *Congress at Work* (New York, 1952) was particularly helpful on the double constituency phenomenon and Lewis A. Froman, Jr., *Congressmen and their Constituencies* (Chicago, 1963), is a good brief account of political factors that affect congressional elections and subsequent influences on congressional voting. Dayton David McKean's *Party and Pressure Politics* (Boston, 1949) is the classic study of this topic. The best study of the Eighty-first Congress and its activities can be found in David B. Truman, *The Congressional Party* (New York, 1959).

Robert A. Goldwin (ed.), *Political Parties, U.S.A.* (Chicago, 1962), is a superior collection of essays analyzing the American political system. Samuel Lubell's *The Future of American Politics* (New York, 1952) is the classic account and analysis of American political life and behavior from the New Deal through the Fair Deal. Public opinion polls can be found in the *Public Opinion Quarterly* but also Elmo Roper, *You and Your Leaders* (New York, 1957), contains an interesting presentation and analysis of polls taken during the Truman years by one of the most famous pollsters of the period. Richard Rovere, *The American Establishment* (New York, 1962), is a good collection of some of the essays written by this penetrating political columnist; particularly interesting are his descriptions of experiences while following the campaign trails of presidential candidates. Many insights into the workings of the Democratic party can be found in Jack Redding's *Inside the Democratic Party* (New York, 1958), written by one of the main figures in the party during the Truman years. Louis Gerson's *The Hyphenate in Recent American Politics and Diplomacy* (Lawrence, Kans., 1964) is quite good on the political part played by hyphenated Americans but unfortunately it deals largely with the Polish-Americans. The best coverage of the 1948 presidential campaign and election is Jules Abels' *Out of the Jaws of Victory* (New York, 1959) and Karl A. Schmidt's *Henry A. Wallace: Quixotic Crusade 1948* (Syracuse, N. Y., 1960) is the best treatment of the Progressive campaign although rather sympathetic to Wallace. Fay Caulkins' *The CIO and the Democratic Party* (Chicago, 1952) presents a fine account of the important Taft election in 1950.

Joseph G. Rayback's *A History of American Labor* (New York, 1959), and Foster Rhea Dulles' *Labor in America* (New York, 1960) are perhaps the best one-volume surveys of the history of labor while Philip Taft's *The A. F. of L. from the Death of Gompers to the Merger* (New York, 1959) is the best single history of this union during the postwar years. Arthur Goldberg's *The AFL-CIO: Labor United* (New York, 1964) is the best account of the merger of these two unions, written by one of the major participants. Robert A. Brady's *Business as a System of Power* (New York, 1943) is valuable on the role of business in combating unionism through political power. The history of the activities of the federal government in dealing with organized labor is very well treated in John H. Leek's *Government and Labor in the United States* (New York, 1952). Irving Bernstein's *The Lean Years* (Boston, 1960) and *The New Deal Collective Bargaining Policy* (Berkeley, Cal., 1950) discuss the problems of labor in the 1920's and 1930's, and Milton Derber and Edwin Young (eds.), *Labor and the New Deal* (Madison, Wis., 1957), is an excellent collection of essays on this topic. Harry A. Millis and Emily Clark Brown, *From the Wagner Act to Taft-Hartley* (Chicago, 1950) is the best history of the administration of the Wagner Act, with one of the authors having served as an NLRB member during much of the period. The best history of organized labor during and immediately after World War II is Joel Seidman's *American Labor From Defense to Reconversion* (Chicago, 1953). Fred A. Hartley, Jr., *Our New National Labor Policy* (New York, 1948) is an account of the passage and the features of the Taft-Hartley Act by one of the authors of the law and contains an appendix that reprints the law.

INDEX